THE ARROWS COOKBOOK

*Cooking and Gardening from Maine's
Most Beautiful Farmhouse Restaurant*

Clark Frasier and Mark Gaier
with Max Alexander

FOREWORD BY Jeremiah Tower
PHOTOGRAPHS BY John Kernick

SCRIBNER

NEW YORK LONDON TORONTO SYDNEY SINGAPORE

SCRIBNER
1230 Avenue of the Americas
New York, NY 10020

For information about special discounts for bulk purchases,
please contact Simon & Schuster Special Sales:
1-800-456-6798 or business@simonandschuster.com

Illustrations by Robert Dohar, except those on pages 13, 106, 205, and 293 by David Evans

DESIGNED BY ERICH HOBBING

Set in Adobe Caslon

Manufactured in the United States of America

10 9 8 7 6 5 4 3 2 1

Library of Congress Cataloging-in-Publication Data

Frasier, Clark.
    The Arrows cookbook : cooking and gardening from Maine's most beautiful farmhouse restaurant / Clark Frasier
and Mark Gaier with Max Alexander ; foreword by Jeremiah Tower ; photographs by John Kernick.
    p.   cm.
    Includes index.
    1. Cookery, American—New England style. 2. Cookery—Maine. 3. Arrows (Restaurant) I. Gaier, Mark.
II. Alexander, Max (Max W.) III. Title.
TX715.2.N48F72 2003
641.5974—dc21   2003042460

ISBN 0-7432-3673-4

This book is dedicated to Dolores Gaier,
who gave us her love of cooking and home;

to Ruth Frasier,
who liked nothing more than having family and friends in her kitchen;

to Robert Gaier,
who instilled the value of hard work;

and to Vance Frasier,
who taught us that goals are what make life worth living.

CONTENTS

Spring
RETURN TO MAINE

APPETIZERS

SALADS

MAIN COURSES

SAUCES

SIDE DISHES

Summer
HIGH SEASON

SALADS

MAIN COURSES

SAUCES

SIDE DISHES

DESSERTS

Fall
LATE HARVEST

APPETIZERS

SALADS

MAIN COURSES

Winter
FAREWELL AGAIN

FOREWORD

Much ado is often made about the need for a sense of place and the life-fulfilling pleasure we feel when we find one. The restaurant Arrows is one of those places, and *The Arrows Cookbook* gives us just that pleasure.

Much has also been made during the last thirty-year revolution about the way America dines, and of its engine of "local," "fresh," and "organic." This cookbook is the substance of that movement that drove America to have the world's best "tables," and Arrows is one of them. Clark Frasier and Mark Gaier rightly claim that the process of preparing a wonderful meal starts with perfect ingredients and, at Arrows and in this book, the slogans of America's culinary revolution are actually lived, not just explained. Their flower, fruit, and vegetable garden is not just a showpiece or a public relations mantle, but is as much a part of the restaurant as the building itself and the cooking going on within it.

Some years ago, Clark and Mark stood at the cooking line in my restaurant in front of me and dreamed. Years later I stood with them at Arrows on one of its birthdays, on a warm American summer night, chilled Champagne in hand, and looked around at what had also been a dream of mine: a country restaurant supplied with what is grown on the land around it. I have never brought my dream to life, but these two men have, elegantly, simply, and with an honesty that will always be fresh and inspiring.

When I walked into Arrows's dining room for the first time, my heart stood still for a moment when I saw the enormous bouquet of wild and cultivated flowers at the entrance. The six-foot-long briar runners and whole branches of flowering fruit trees hanging at the entrance were a bit of each corner of the wild and cultivated garden brought inside. The arrangement surpassed any of my efforts in my restaurants, and I knew I was home.

The Arrows Cookbook takes us all there as well.

Jeremiah Tower

THE ARROWS
COOKBOOK

INTRODUCTION

All cooking is a process. Measure, mix, bake for an hour. Yet it is obvious that the process of preparing a meal begins long before the oven is heated. Name an ingredient, from anglerfish to zucchini, and it probably begins with a seed. The evolution of food from seed to supper has been the chief preoccupation of man throughout history.

The life of a restaurant is also a process. When Arrows opened in 1988, we had in mind a casual brasserie, not the elegant country destination it grew to become. And it was several years before we began growing our own food from seed.

Our journey to a two-hundred-year-old farm in northern New England began a continent (and several climate zones) away. After many years working for the talented San Francisco chef Jeremiah Tower of Stars, we decided to open our own restaurant. We had watched the gourmet craze that swept America during the 1980s from both sides of the kitchen door, and we had mixed feelings about America's new obsession with fine cooking. On one hand, any trend that pulled Americans away from the frozen-food aisle and back into the fresh produce section of the grocery store was a good thing. On the other hand, the new cuisine seemed driven more by status than sustenance. While striving for trendy cuisine based on the latest exotic flavor, Americans forgot their own good cooking.

But we remembered. Mark grew up in Ohio where his mother cooked every meal with fresh ingredients from the surrounding Amish countryside. On special occasions her dinners could rise to the level of elegance, but mostly she made solid, heartland suppers like Mark's favorite, pork roast. As a child Mark always looked forward to strawberry season, when he and his brothers and sisters would pick berries at a nearby farm all day, stop at the dairy for vanilla ice cream, and then go home—to wait impatiently as Mom baked pie.

Clark also grew up picking summer berries, near Loon Lake in Washington State, where he spent glorious vacations with his grandparents. There he would rise early to go trout fishing, cooking his catch over a sizzling charcoal grill at the end of the day. Such memories, tied tightly to family and home, constitute a culinary tradition in any society.

Of course, we did not intend to relive our boyhood memories in a restaurant. Nor could we deny our passion for cooking traditions from other cultures, especially the flavors that Clark grew to love during a year studying Chinese at the Beijing Language Institute. Asian cooks strive for balance and contrast—the philosophical notion of yin and yang as applied to cuisine, if you will. Sweet is contrasted with sour, hot with cool, crunchy with smooth, fried with steamed. Asian cooks pay great attention to individual ingredients, yet the combination transcends the specific.

It's easy to see the difference between Asian and Western cooking, but what struck Clark were the similarities. Watching Chinese peasants cure cabbages for the winter, he thought of sauerkraut, the Central European mainstay that evolved from the need (before refrigeration) to preserve summer's bounty. Curing pork into hams is a fall ritual in rural China, as it is on many farms in Maine. (Pigs are expensive to feed and shelter through the winter, so fall is the traditional time of slaughter around the world.) We wanted a restaurant that celebrated these universal culinary traditions, which are rooted in the march of the seasons.

Whether those seasons gallop or crawl depends on where you live, of course. In California, where the growing season stretches from February to November, we naturally turned to our abundant local crops for inspiration; Poached Garlic Soup with Thyme and Red Pepper Creams (page 214) was an early hit. Using fresh greens and herbs to lighten sauces became one of our trademarks. Here we were building on Southeast Asian cuisine, in which fresh herbs brighten the taste of hearty noodle soups like the Vietnamese national dish, *pho*.

Our plan was to open a restaurant where we lived in the California coastal town of Carmel. But jaw-dropping real-estate prices there turned our passion for food into a discouraging scramble for cash. We wanted to greet customers, not huddle with lawyers and bankers.

One evening in 1988 when we had really begun to despair, friends of Mark's called to say they were selling a restaurant in Ogunquit, Maine, an artists' colony and seaside playground for proper Bostonians since the nineteenth century. Mark had lived in Maine years earlier; he loved the state's rugged natural beauty, the fishing boats laden with lobsters and clams, and the deep-rooted locals who used humor and ingenuity to carve lives from the rocky terrain. A voice seemed to be saying, "Go east, young men." (Yes, we were young then.)

Off we flew to have a look, arriving in Maine during one of the harshest winters in memory. The restaurant, in a colonial-era farmhouse, was named Arrows—a whimsical reference to the home's authentic "Indian shutters," which were meant to protect settlers against attack. It was closed for the season; snow had drifted halfway up the first-floor windows, and the heat was shut down. Looking back that was probably a good thing. Had it not been so bone-chilling cold, we might have lingered long enough to notice all the work needed.

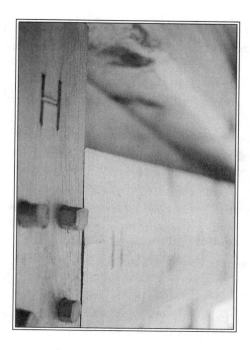

Instead we saw a home—and an old one at that. Built in 1765, it was constructed out of materials from the surrounding woods, like all houses of that time. The framework was made of massive spruce trees, cut with hand saws, then dragged, or "twitched," out of the forest by teams of oxen. Carpenters shaped the logs into square beams using a hand tool called a broadax. Highly skilled craftsmen called joiners cut the ends of the beams into mortises and tenons, perfectly matched joints that locked together the framework. (Metal fasteners, which had to be hand-wrought at great expense, were reserved for hinges and other essential moving parts.) This carpentry was so exacting that every joint was labeled and matched; today you can often see those Roman numerals or letters chiseled into the beams of New England farmhouses.

The house was speaking to us, and not just figuratively. Every time the biting northeast wind whistled through the gables, the old place creaked and moaned. We signed a lease with an option to buy, flew home to California, and packed our bags.

The phrase "What have we done?" could have been invented for that car trip east across the United States. The luxurious world of Bay Area restaurants quickly receded behind the interstate monotony of motels and McDonald's, and we arrived in Ogunquit on a cold, dreary day in March. Clark's parents, who lived in California, had come along on the drive to help us move and open the restaurant. In Maine we were joined by Mark's brother and his wife, who lived in Hampden, Maine, three hours north of Ogunquit.

From dawn to dusk we cleaned ovens, painted walls, and scoured floors. Clark's mother made grocery runs, and every night we collapsed, starving, around a table in the chilly bar to devour rib-sticking meals like black bean soup and cornbread, washed down with samples from the wine salesmen.

The pressure was enormous, but so was the sense of accomplishment and the love of our families working together. The gods of the hearth must have been smiling on us because we made our opening date just as our credit cards were maxing out.

The first menu was simple, in part because good ingredients were so hard to come by, but it was unlike anything the area had ever seen. Compared to California, with its long growing season and dedicated network of artisanal food purveyors, Maine was a culinary backwater. Thankfully that has changed. Ogunquit now boasts a grocery store with entire aisles devoted to organic foods, not to mention pristine heads of Belgian endive and radicchio. But in 1988 locally baked bread was unheard of, and the choice of cooking oil was corn, corn, or corn. We'll never forget our first Maine Thanksgiving. We had 120 reservations for a sumptuous New England feast of salmon, oysters, and roast turkey, and we spent Wednesday night in a frantic drive around the region looking for extra-virgin olive oil and fresh nuts. (We finally found both in nearby New Hampshire, which seemed to be the last stop for specialty food trucks.)

At least we had seafood. Lobsters, clams, scallops, and cod are literally sold on street corners in Maine, right off the back of fishermen's trucks. Impeccably fresh, these elemental New England ingredients formed the basis of our early cuisine, and we still cook with them daily. But we wanted more. We knew that the finest fish in the world were being hauled in every day, right off the coast of Ogunquit, and promptly flown to restaurants in New York and Tokyo. Local stores almost never carried halibut or bluefish, to say nothing of more exotic fare like sea urchins. Distributors with larger selections often didn't handle the fish properly. Now, thanks to conscientious purveyors, we get our pick of the freshest local mussels, striped bass, oysters, and tuna—not to mention *loup de mer* from France and crayfish from New Zealand that are still kicking when we open the case.

We weren't alone, of course, and as more Mainers began to demand better food, the local growers and fishermen responded. But in the meantime, the only way we could get good bread was to bake our own. And it didn't take long to realize that if we wanted produce like that in San Francisco, we'd have to grow our own.

Thus was the garden born of necessity, from a ragged field of witch grass at a time when iceberg was about the only lettuce we could order. Now, thanks to the tireless work of a succession of dedicated gardeners, our growing beds stretch over almost an acre of land, providing the restaurant with 270 varieties of vegetables, herbs, and edible flowers. It has, in fact, become the first destination for diners, who arrive early to stroll the grounds. Quite unintentionally, the garden conceived to fill the restaurant's needs is now a primary attraction.

We wish more American chefs would grow their own food. The main obstacle is that in America innovative cuisine chiefly emanates from big cities where gardens aren't practical. Yet in many countries the best chefs work close to the countryside—where the food is. Some of the greatest restaurants in France and Italy are off the beaten path, where the chefs tend primeval plots of asparagus and gooseberries.

Those chefs know what we have learned: Food from your own garden not only tastes better but also makes you a better cook. It's common knowledge that fresh-picked vegetables have more taste and a crisper texture than anything trucked into a grocery store; how else to explain the renaissance of local greenmarkets in towns and cities across America? But cooking homegrown food goes beyond a passion for freshness. On an even more elemental level, the process connects the cook to a cycle of nature that our ancestors understood intuitively but that, for most of us, has been lost in the modern world. Participating in that cycle—which begins with a seed, progresses to the dinner table, and concludes in the compost bin, where it begins again—is more satisfying than the pleasures of any single meal. When you cook homegrown food, you're not the "end user" of the food chain, you're in the middle of it.

This connection to nature is not just an intellectual conceit. The French have a word, *terroir,* that literally means soil but connotes something deeper and more personal—the unique soil of one's own land. They understand that on some cosmic level, man is rewarded in health and happiness when he consumes the vital goodness of his own land. It's why that carafe of rough local wine in a little French country *auberge* tastes so exquisitely perfect—and why it doesn't taste the same in Paris or Pennsylvania. If all that sounds vaguely spiritual, so be it. Gardens are heavenly places, and the world could use more of them.

You don't have to believe in the cosmic wisdom of cooking from the garden; it's enough to realize that your garden will make you smarter about food. When you stroll the produce section of the supermarket, what you notice about peppers, eggplants, and tomatoes are their differences. But in the garden you notice instead how similar they are. (All three are fruits because we eat the seed pod, but they are also all members of the *Solanaceae* family.) You notice their stalks, thick and woody but often in need of staking as the fruit ripens and swells; their long, drooping leaves; their five-pointed flowers with five separate stamen. You might also notice they attract the same insects. (Yes, even those pesky bugs can teach us.) By understanding this kinship in the garden, one begins to see how these vegetables can work together in the kitchen. That's how we came up with Polenta Lasagna (page 235), which marries these vegetables in a new way, but in a way that makes sense according to nature. Cooking from the garden has kept our culinary experiments firmly rooted (no pun intended) in a larger reality, and it will do the same for you.

We hadn't planned on being pioneers in a culinary wilderness, much less garden-club tour guides. Yet the harder we worked at creating our own food supply, the deeper kinship we felt with the colonial homesteaders who had built our farmhouse and cleared the land. As is so often the case, what began as a problem turned into a blessing. Self-sufficiency became our link to the past and began to inform every aspect of Arrows.

While we had always made abundant use of fresh herbs in our cooking, once we started gardening, herbs took center stage—in part because they were there. The truth is you're not going to run to the supermarket for a sprig of rosemary. But when you have rosemary—and mint, chervil, oregano, parsley, thyme, cilantro, basil, and sage—growing outside your kitchen door, you will find ways to use them every day.

Consider our love affair with root vegetables. In sunny California we almost never roasted turnips, beets, parsnips, and such; it's just not something you think of eating under a palm tree. But in Maine we came to realize why New Englanders cherish these hearty vegetables on cold nights, for the long, slow baking process fills the house with warmth and aroma. Now we plant whole sections of our garden in root vegetables.

For the first seven years, we lived above the restaurant and put all of our money into renovations. Like many people who buy an old country home, our life became a replay of that classic Cary Grant–Myrna Loy film, *Mr. Blandings Builds His Dream House*. There is a law of old farmhouses that says that as soon as you solve one major problem—say, the need for a new septic system—something else goes, like the well. One year brought new wiring, which allowed us to properly light the dining room. In another year we commissioned a local craftsman to make 125 black walnut and cherry chairs. In 1995 we bit the bullet and ripped out the claustrophobic kitchen, trashing the old equipment and building a brand-new space with high ceilings and dramatic casement windows overlooking the restaurant's entranceway. Clark's dad, an accomplished woodworker, made the beautiful hutch and wine stands in the dining room. Countless other refinements and improvements came every year.

Our wine list had been growing steadily to the point where our dirt-floor basement cellar was overflowing. When the *Boston Globe*'s wine critic, Robert Levy, gave us a great review in 1989, we knew it was time for a real cellar. A vacant space above the restaurant became a state-of-the-art temperature-controlled wine room.

Such was the process that took Arrows from simple bistro to dining destination. Our greatest satisfaction has been the loyalty of our customers, many of whom have been coming every week for fifteen years. Some are year-round locals, including folks from nearby Portland, a thriving small city with a vibrant waterfront district. Others are "summer people" who spend most of the year in cities far from Ogunquit. Still others make the hour-and-fifteen-minute drive north from Boston just to dine at Arrows. They all come for the food, the garden, and the friendship.

And they have far more choices in Maine today. In recent years the Maine dining scene has exploded, and we are gratified to see many other talented chefs opening restaurants in the Pine Tree State.

The newcomers remind us that the process never ends. Our next project is building an outdoor brick oven. The idea came from our young sous-chef Justin Walker, who loves grilling, smoking, and just about anything prepared outdoors. We liked his oven concept—and promptly put him in charge of it. Meanwhile there's always a new pepper or tomato to grow and a rare wine to find. At this writing, we're searching for a 1985 Taylor's Fladgate port. No distributor carries it, but we keep looking. Maybe next year.

SPRING

RETURN TO MAINE

 As do many businesses in Maine, Arrows goes into hibernation for part of the winter. The break is a fact of life for Maine's seasonal economy and provides an opportunity for reflection and rejuvenation that year-round restaurants don't have.

Our off-season is not just a time to kick back. Most years we travel across North America and often to Europe or Asia, where we seek out local recipes and wines, tour markets, and meet chefs—getting new inspiration for the coming season at Arrows. During a recent winter, we traveled to Tuscany for white truffles and Hawaii for outdoor barbecues. But we don't just hang around in the sun all winter. We also spent a week in icy Beijing, where the hearty food and dark Xiao Xing wine warmed us nightly.

When we returned to Maine in late March, we felt renewed and ready for another season as we opened up the house. Our garden wasn't so sure, however. It had disappeared under three feet of snow, and the greenhouse was so buried under drifts that it was actually dark inside. With the restaurant scheduled to open in mid-April, we had our work cut out for us. We just started shoveling. Once we got our raised garden beds cleared of snow, we were able to put Plexiglas over them and thaw the soil quickly. (Raised beds are elevated piles of earth surrounded by a wood frame. Covered with glass, they become miniature greenhouses called cold frames. For instructions on how to make your own, see page 80.) In three days, with snow still all around the beds, we were ready to plant. To meet our goal of putting greens on the table the first night we're open, we've been known to garden in snowshoes.

By late winter our master gardener is starting thousands of seedlings in her nearby nursery: 28 types of lettuce, dozens of tomato varieties, 15 eggplant species, 29 specialty greens, and on, and on. After the seedlings sprout, they go under banks of shop lights. With this system, Arrows can start as many as three thousand seedlings at once. You can do the same thing at home with a simple shop light (see page 61) or even a sunny windowsill.

Deciding what to grow is based on discussions we have every winter with our gardener, who keeps careful records of which varieties performed well over the previous summer. (Just about every vegetable comes in dozens of varieties, called cultivars, that are adapted to specific climates; thus King of the North bell pepper would be a poor choice in Florida.) Some cultivars like Brandywine tomatoes and Cippoline onions are stalwarts that we grow year in and year out. But last year we reintroduced some heirloom lettuce varieties that Arrows hadn't grown in years: the unusual sharp-lobed Hussard and a multi-colored heirloom variety called Freckles. Three new perennial strawberry beds should be yielding by next year; the challenge will be getting berries into the kitchen before our staff devours them.

Inside the house, winter's stillness is slow to leave, and we always feel we're interrupting. The doors squeak in complaint, and the dust seems deeded in place. Stripped of linens, silver, and flowers, the dining room is as barren as the snow-covered garden, except for the dozens of prosciutto hams hanging from the ancient beams. In late fall we begin the process of curing our own hams (see page 306), which are left to air-dry over the winter in the restaurant.

After we take down the hams, the hard work of spring cleaning begins. Every year we refinish the wood floors, paint every wall inside and out, and polish the chairs with beeswax. All the china, silver, and glassware is meticulously cleaned and polished. New uniforms and equipment are ordered. Everything has to look absolutely fresh, as if the restaurant were brand-new. In fact, every year it seems like we are opening a new restaurant.

Spring is also the time to reconnect with the local folks who provide us with fish and meat and to take stock of our cellars. Clark spends several weeks making an inventory of our wine; bottles from France must be ordered months in advance. One of our veteran waitresses, who also helps in the wine cellar, took an interest in fine ports last year; over the winter she researched the subject and came back with a wonderful list. Now we have a selection of seventeen ports, including a distinctive Ramos Pinto from 1983.

Mark and our sous-chefs conduct the annual ritual of friendly haggling with suppliers, negotiating everything from the availability of specialty cheeses to the price of ducks. Once the restaurant opens, there is little time to fret over food costs; on a Saturday night with a full reservation book, we consider ourselves lucky just to get the ducks through the door! Meanwhile our pastry chef is busy planning her lineup of spring breads and desserts.

Another important spring task is preparing floral arrangements. Arrows is famous for its massive displays of cut flowers, which Clark supervises. The tour de force is a floor-to-ceiling explosion of color called Big Bertha, which is the first thing guests see as they enter the dining room. The arrangement begins with massive cuttings of tree branches, which change throughout the season. In the spring we start with flowering trees. This year we went over to a friend's place that has massive old-growth lilacs and just started sawing. We literally hauled a truckload of lilacs. It's hard to believe these amazing trees are so carefree, gilding rural Maine in purple beauty and sweet fragrance every spring and asking for nothing in return. So much of the season's color has that spirit of determination. Brilliant yellow forsythia bushes deliver the first bloom of spring no matter how cold it is, and crab apple trees endure January's ice storms to burst into pink and white blossoms in spring. It's as if they, like us, can't wait any longer.

Around town the first real signs of spring come in late April when local farmers' markets reopen. Growers who've carefully tended their raised beds are selling the first spring greens. The gray landscape of winter recedes as crocuses unfurl in our flower beds. That's when we begin the most exciting spring task—planning the opening-night dinner, which has to dazzle. What's new in the garden is always the first inspiration—the first crops of spring include baby bok choy, arugula, Japanese mustard greens, and lettuce—but we draw upon our winter travels as well. We're always taking notes and filing away flavors in our "taste memory."

We also pay attention to what's in season around the country, and so should you. In early spring we cook fresh ramps and morel mushrooms from Michigan, and fava beans and peas from California. (Good grocery stores and specialty markets often carry these items in season.) Within a few weeks we are serving fiddlehead ferns, which grow along mossy stream banks throughout Maine. The arrival of local fiddleheads tells us that spring has finally arrived in New England. The garden is growing, the phone is ringing, and Arrows is again in full bloom.

# APPETIZERS

Asparagus Soup with Lobster, Morels, and Chervil

This is the ultimate spring soup. Few dishes could make a more elegant start to a celebratory dinner. It is not that hard to make, but be careful not to overcook the asparagus or it will lose its bright green color and turn mushy. We enjoy the delicate look of chervil, and its aniselike flavor brightens this rich soup. Chervil takes about six weeks to grow from seed, but you can plant it quite early (a month before the last frost) or grow it indoors in pots on a sunny windowsill.

Makes 6 servings

Kosher salt
2 bunches (36 spears) large asparagus, tough ends trimmed
3 cups Chicken or Vegetable Stock (page 23 or 24)
2 lobsters, 1¼ pounds each, steamed and shelled (pages 18 and 19)
2 cups heavy cream
1 tablespoon freshly squeezed lemon juice
8 tablespoons (1 stick) unsalted butter
4 ounces morel mushrooms, cleaned and trimmed
1 cup chervil sprigs, washed and dried

1. In a large pot bring 2 quarts water and 1 tablespoon salt to a boil. Prepare an ice bath by filling a medium bowl halfway with ice water. Put the asparagus in the pot, return to a boil, and cook for 1 minute. Drain the asparagus and submerge immediately in the ice

water. As soon as the asparagus are completely chilled, remove from the ice water and wrap in a clean kitchen towel to dry.

2. Cut off the tips (about 1 inch) of 18 of the asparagus spears and set aside. Cut the rest of the asparagus in half and set aside.

3. In the jar of a blender, combine half of the asparagus (but not the reserved tips) and half of the stock and purée until smooth, about 1 minute. Push the asparagus purée through a sieve to remove excess pulp. Repeat this process with the second half of the asparagus and stock. The asparagus purée can be made a day in advance and kept covered in the refrigerator.

4. Cut the lobster tails crosswise into ¼-inch medallions. Split each claw into 2 pieces by cutting across the flat side.

5. In a heavy saucepan whisk together the asparagus purée, cream, lemon juice, and 1 teaspoon salt. Warm over medium-low heat, stirring occasionally to avoid scorching the soup. When the soup is hot, reduce the heat to the lowest setting.

6. While the soup is heating, melt 4 tablespoons of the butter in a large sauté pan over medium heat. Add the morels and sauté, adding 1 teaspoon salt. Cook, stirring, until all the liquid is evaporated and the mushrooms are tender, 10 to 12 minutes.

7. Add the lobster, reserved asparagus tips, and remaining 4 tablespoons butter to the morels, then stir for a minute or so to warm everything through.

8. Ladle the soup into 6 warm bowls or soup plates. Using tongs or a slotted spoon, divide the lobster, morels, and asparagus among the 6 bowls. Garnish with the chervil sprigs and serve at once.

A Fresh Look at Lobster

Maine is rightly famous for its lobster. Most of the American catch comes from our state, which is one of the few places on earth virtually synonymous with a food item. (Idaho is famous for potatoes, but then so is Maine.) As chefs we think that's pretty impressive, and we find ways to cook lobster just about every night at Arrows. We don't have to go far to find them. A short walk down the road is our neighbor's barn, surrounded by his lobster traps and a tangle of brightly painted buoys. A few houses away lives another lobsterman; once a year his massive diesel-powered boat is hauled into the driveway for cleaning and repairs. Sometimes he spreads his cod-fishing nets (many lobstermen also bring in finfish) out on the lawn for mending.

Lobsters are a way of life along the rocky coast of Maine, and not just for the thousands of hardy men and women who trap them in frigid waters in all kinds of weather. The bright red crustacean is a major Maine tourist attraction, providing income for everyone from T-shirt makers to informal dockside restaurants, where the traditional "shore dinner" includes lobster, steamed clams, and corn-on-the-cob.

Most of those lobsters are plunged into cauldrons of boiling water, then served with melted butter, plastic bibs, and nutcrackers. It's simple and straightforward, and we've never met anyone who didn't like it. But at Arrows we like to experiment with our state's culinary specialty.

One of our favorite ways to cook lobster was inspired by our travels in Asia, where seafood is often steamed in bamboo racks over herbs and ginger. Back home in Maine, we discovered that fresh herbs and vegetables from our garden add a wonderful dimension to the delicate but rich flavor of steamed lobster. We recommend using Asian aromatics like ginger (which provides a sudden and searing "zip" of flavor), lemongrass (which lends a subtle green-citrus taste), and Vietnamese coriander (which has a licorice-like scent; if you can't find any, substitute Thai basil or mint). For a Western flavor, try garlic, shallots, thyme, marjoram, or other herbs.

Steaming works great for recipes in this book calling for cooked and shelled lobster meat. Just chill the steamed lobsters over ice in the refrigerator, then pick out the meat from the tail and claws (see page 19). To reheat lobster meat, warm it in a saucepan with a little butter over medium heat for about 5 minutes.

A few words about buying lobster. Thanks to advances in shipping technology, live Maine lobsters can now be bought at grocery stores across America. Just remember that *live* doesn't necessarily mean *fresh;* a lobster plucked from the briny deep weeks ago will not taste as good as one caught yesterday. A really fresh lobster is full of fight; if it doesn't flap its tail vigorously when plucked from the tank, choose another. Or you could move to Maine and get them from your neighbor. ☜

STEAMING LOBSTER, SOUTHEAST ASIAN STYLE

2 stalks lemongrass
2 cups water
1 cup white wine
$\frac{1}{2}$ cup rice vinegar
2 tablespoons thinly sliced gingerroot
2 sprigs basil
2 sprigs mint
2 sprigs Vietnamese coriander, Thai basil, or additional mint
2 sprigs cilantro
4 live lobsters, $1\frac{1}{4}$ pounds each

1. Cut the lemongrass into 2-inch pieces and smash with the side of a heavy knife.

2. Put the lemongrass and all the other ingredients except the lobster in the bottom of a large heavy pot. A standard clam steamer pot, which is inexpensive and sold in housewares stores, works best, but any large pot will do. Add about 1 inch salted water, then put a steamer basket, rack, or upside-down colander in the pot. Set the pot on the stove over high heat and bring to a boil.

3. Put the lobsters into the pot and cover tightly. Steam the lobsters for 14 minutes over a rapid boil. Remove the pot from the heat, and carefully remove the lobsters. Serve at once, or let cool and refrigerate in a covered container for up to 2 days.

NOTES

1. If you're more comfortable killing the lobsters before cooking, simply plunge a chef's knife straight down into the crosshatch on the thorax (it's about an inch behind the eyes). The lobster will be killed instantly; any flapping is the result of muscle contractions.

2. You can also cook the lobsters in a Chinese bamboo steamer, which is what we do at home. Each stackable basket of the bamboo steamer will hold 2 lobsters. Cooking time is the same as above. ⌒

SHELLING COOKED LOBSTERS

Removing, or picking, the meat from a cooked lobster is similar to the process for eating a whole lobster at the table. The difference is you'll be wearing an apron instead of a plastic bib, you'll have your serious kitchen utensils at your disposal, and the lobster won't be piping hot.

1. Twist the tail off the body, then break off the tail fins (at the very end) by bending them upward, revealing a hole in the tail cavity. Insert a fork into the hole and gently push the tail meat out through the other side. Using a chef's knife, make a small incision lengthwise along the back (or top) of the tail meat, just deep enough to reveal the dark, thin intestine. Remove and discard. Cut the tail into several medallions or leave whole, as the recipe requires.

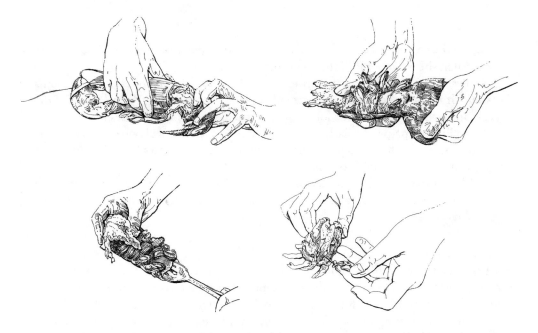

2. Twist the claws off the knuckles, then twist the knuckles off the body. Grasp the small pincer of each claw and bend it backward until it breaks off. Hopefully the meat inside the pincer will stay with the rest of the claw; if not, remove it from the piece you just broke off by tapping it on the counter or by inserting a toothpick. Using the back of a cleaver or chef's knife, crack the claws just enough so the shells can be pried open and the meat removed; you don't want to smash the meat. Alternatively, cut the claw open with sturdy kitchen shears. Remove the inedible translucent cartilage running through the middle of the claw.

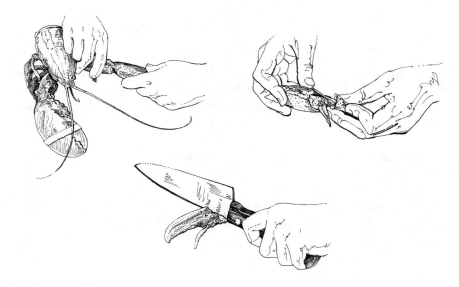

3. Use the back of a cleaver or chef's knife to crack open the knuckles. (You can also use kitchen shears here.) Pull the meat from the knuckles.

4. If you don't like to waste any lobster morsels, you can also remove the tiny amounts of meat from the walking claws, commonly referred to as the legs. Pull them off of the body, break them in half at the joint, and line them up on a counter or cutting board. Run a rolling pin perpendicularly over the claws, and the meat will pop out. Many people don't bother with this step and instead add the walking claws (and the rest of the lobster carcass) to vegetable or chicken stock.

5. It's best to use the lobster meat on the same day it is cooked, but if necessary you can put all the lobster pieces in a sealable plastic bag and store in the refrigerator for up to 2 days.

TOMALLEY

New Englanders have endless arguments about which tastes better—the lobster meat itself or the tomalley, that soft green liver. The arguments usually end when a tomalley partisan is challenged to trade his tail for someone else's tomalley—a transaction that has never occurred in lobster-eating history. But tomalley is undeniably tasty, both sweet and briny at the same time. We like to eat it right out of the shell, but it's also good spread on bread.

ROE

If you're lucky, you may find a female lobster filled with eggs, which are black as caviar when raw but turn bright red when cooked. (It is illegal for fishermen to keep lobsters with eggs showing on the outside, but when the eggs are still inside the body, there is no way to tell until the lobster is killed.) Eat the deliciously tangy eggs, also called coral, right out of the shell. You could also add them to an omelet the next morning. ∽

English Pea Soup with Condiments

Fresh peas are a treat for the eyes; nothing else in the spring garden looks quite so vibrantly green. Serve the condiments for this easy soup in small bowls on a platter to be passed by your guests.

Makes 6 servings

FOR THE SOUP
Kosher salt
'4 cups shelled English peas (about 3 pounds in the pod)
2½ cups Chicken or Vegetable Stock (page 23 or 24)
1½ cups heavy cream

1. In a large pot bring 2 quarts water and 1 tablespoon salt to a boil. Fill a medium bowl halfway with ice water.

2. Add the peas to the pot and cook for 2 minutes. Drain and transfer immediately to the ice water. As soon as the peas are completely cool, drain them in a colander.

3. Combine the peas with the stock and purée in the jar of a blender until very smooth, about 1 minute. Pour into a bowl and whisk in the cream and 1 teaspoon salt. The soup can be covered and refrigerated overnight.

TO SERVE
Small croutons
Bacon bits
Crème fraîche
Fresh herbs, such as chopped chives, tarragon, parsley, or thyme

Arrange the condiments in small bowls on a serving tray. Pour the pea soup into a medium saucepan. Warm over medium heat but do not let the soup get too hot as it will discolor. Ladle into 6 warm soup bowls and serve with the condiment tray.

NOTE: For a luxurious Maine twist on this soup, add the meat from 3 lobsters, steamed and shelled according to the directions on pages 18 and 19. Cut each tail crosswise into 5 medallions; leave the claws and knuckle meat whole. Melt 2 tablespoons butter in a large sauté pan over medium heat. Add the lobster and gently heat until coated in butter and warm. Do not overheat the lobster as it will get tough. Season with salt and pepper and arrange over the soup just before serving.

CHICKEN AND VEGETABLE STOCKS

Making stock is one of the most rewarding kitchen tasks because it is so elemental. Once you have some stock in your freezer, you can make sauces and soups quickly, even on a weeknight. Homemade stock makes food transcendent.

And yet, simple as it is, stock isn't foolproof. If you don't follow some basic rules, it can end up murky, with a muddled taste. What makes stock cloudy is prolonged boiling, so make sure you keep the heat at a low simmer after initially bringing the liquid just to a boil. The foam, which comes from impurities released by the bones under heat, should be skimmed off just when the stock comes to a boil; otherwise it adds a bitter taste. It's also a good idea to skim off fat early in the process, so it doesn't break down in the stock and confuse the flavor. You can also minimize fat by removing poultry skin and other loose fat before tossing the pieces into the pot.

Speaking of tossing things into the pot, resist the urge to dump lots of herbs into stock. We like our stock to be simple and direct, so we rarely use anything more than parsley, thyme, and bay leaf. (Tarragon, however, adds depth to vegetable stock.) Any other herbs should come later, in whatever dish the stock is being used.

When straining the completed stock through a sieve, don't drain to the very bottom because that's where the tiny particles have settled. You don't need every last ounce of liquid, and your stock will be clearer as a result. At Arrows we don't brown our chicken bones because we like chicken stock to be light in color and flavor.

Canned stock doesn't have the rich flavor of homemade, but it can be useful at times, and we usually keep some around at home. We would never use it to make sauces or gravy, but it's okay in risotto, for braising meat (which will then fortify the stock with its own flavors), and in some Asian stir-fries. You can also use canned stock in a simple last-minute pasta sauce with a little butter to give it some richness. Most canned stocks are fairly salty, so be sure to season accordingly, or stick with low-sodium versions.

We like Swanson's chicken and vegetable stocks, in either a can or a box. Specialty markets often carry nice organic stocks; the store-brand organic chicken stock sold at Trader Joe's is quite good. We don't use bouillon cubes, which have lots of unpronounceable additives.

Chicken Stock

Makes about 2 quarts

2 tablespoons olive oil
1 large yellow onion, peeled and chopped
1 large carrot, peeled and chopped
4 stalks celery, chopped
5 pounds chicken parts (necks, backs, and wings), skinned
5 quarts water
6 sprigs flat-leaf parsley
4 sprigs thyme
2 bay leaves

1. Warm the olive oil in a large pot over medium heat. Add the onion, carrot, and celery and sauté them until they start to soften, about 10 minutes.

2. Add all the remaining ingredients to the pot and bring just to a boil. Immediately reduce the heat so that the liquid simmers. Skim the foam and fat that rise to the surface.

3. Simmer uncovered for about 5 hours, skimming occasionally, until the liquid is reduced by half.

4. Strain the stock through a sieve into a nonreactive container and refrigerate uncovered overnight or until cool. The next day, remove and discard any congealed fat from the surface. Cover and refrigerate for up to 3 days or keep frozen for up to 2 months.

Vegetable Stock

Makes about 2 quarts

2 tablespoons olive oil
2 medium yellow onions, peeled and chopped
3 large carrots, peeled and chopped
6 stalks celery, chopped
4 ounces shiitake mushrooms, cleaned and halved
4 ounces white mushrooms, cleaned and halved
2 sprigs thyme
2 sprigs tarragon
2 sprigs flat-leaf parsley
2 bay leaves
12 whole black peppercorns
4 quarts water

1. Warm the olive oil in a large pot over medium heat. Add the onions, carrots, and celery and sauté, stirring occasionally, until lightly browned, about 15 minutes.

2. Add the mushrooms, thyme, tarragon, parsley, bay leaves, and peppercorns and cook, stirring, until the mushrooms are softened, about 5 minutes. Add the water and bring just to a boil. Immediately reduce the heat so that the liquid simmers.

3. Simmer uncovered for about 3 hours, skimming occasionally, until the liquid is light golden brown.

4. Strain the stock through a sieve into a nonreactive container and refrigerate uncovered until cool. Cover and refrigerate for up to 3 days or keep frozen for up to 2 months.

Asparagus with Mizuna, Blood Orange Vinaigrette, and Prosciutto

Raising asparagus takes time. At Arrows our asparagus patch is seven years old, and we are just starting to get a good crop. This dish uses the first of the season's asparagus, which arrives right at the end of the blood orange season in supermarkets. If you don't want the prosciutto, just leave it out; the asparagus and mizuna are great on their own.

Makes 6 servings

5 blood oranges
Kosher salt
$\frac{1}{2}$ teaspoon freshly ground black pepper
$\frac{1}{4}$ cup red wine vinegar
$\frac{1}{4}$ cup olive oil
$\frac{1}{4}$ cup extra-virgin olive oil
2 bunches (36 spears) large asparagus, tough ends trimmed
12 very thin slices prosciutto, preferably Parma or homemade (page 306)
4 ounces mizuna or other field green (about 4 handfuls), washed and dried

1. Squeeze the juice of 3 of the blood oranges through a fine sieve into a medium stainless-steel saucepan. Use a peeler to remove the zest of 1 blood orange, avoiding the bitter white pith, then finely chop the zest with a sharp knife. Add the zest to the juice and bring to a boil over medium heat. Cook until the liquid is reduced by half. Set aside to cool.

2. Section the remaining 2 oranges according to the instructions on page 310.

3. Combine 2 teaspoons salt and the pepper in a medium bowl. Add the reduced juice and the vinegar. Whisk in both olive oils and set the vinaigrette aside. The vinaigrette will keep covered in the refrigerator for up to 2 days.

4. In a large pot bring 2 quarts water and 1 tablespoon salt to a boil. Fill a medium bowl halfway with ice water. Add the asparagus to the pot and cook for 30 seconds. Drain the asparagus in a colander, then immediately plunge it into the ice water. Allow the asparagus to chill completely, then remove from the water and wrap in a clean kitchen towel to dry.

5. Toss the asparagus in a bowl with half of the vinaigrette. Arrange 2 slices of prosciutto on each of 6 chilled plates and place 6 asparagus spears on each plate. Toss the mizuna with the remaining vinaigrette and divide among the plates. Sprinkle the plates with the orange sections. Serve at once.

BROWN BUTTER

Brown butter is easy to make and adds a rich nutty flavor when sautéing tiny spring vegetables like baby leeks or greens (but not more delicate-tasting vegetables like peas). We love its rustic taste with fiddlehead ferns and asparagus—two vegetables that come from the forest. (Cultivated asparagus is no different from that growing in the wild.) And we love it with greens. For a simple side dish, toast a handful of pine nuts in a little brown butter, toss in some greens and parsley, and cook until the greens wilt.

To make brown butter, cook 8 tablespoons (1 stick) unsalted butter in a heavy saucepan over medium heat until golden brown. Transfer the butter to a heatproof container (otherwise it will continue to brown and possibly burn) and set aside to cool. You will have about 6 tablespoons brown butter. It will keep covered in the refrigerator for a week.

Fiddlehead Ferns with Brown Butter and Bundnerfleisch

One of the special treats of a New England spring are fiddlehead ferns, which grow wild along mossy stream banks. They are simply the immature leaf fronds of ostrich fern plants that have not yet opened. Fern leaves are poisonous once they open and can only be enjoyed in this early stage, when they taste like a cross between artichokes and asparagus. Not everyone enjoys this "forest food," but we find that the sweet, nutty taste of brown butter adds smooth richness to the woodsy flavor of ferns.

After a fiddlehead is removed from the stalk, the cut end starts to turn brown. Be sure to trim back the stem (about ¼ inch) to the healthy green section before cooking.

Bundnerfleisch is a German cured beef, similar to Italian bresaola, found in specialty food stores or delis. You could substitute bresaola, prosciutto, or even smoked salmon for a totally different take on this dish.

Makes 6 servings

Kosher salt
2 pounds fiddlehead ferns, trimmed and washed
24 paper-thin slices bundnerfleisch
6 tablespoons brown butter (page 26)
½ teaspoon freshly ground black pepper

1. In a large pot bring 2 quarts water and 1 tablespoon salt to a boil. Fill a medium bowl halfway with ice water. Drop the fiddleheads into the pot and cook for 1 minute. Drain the fiddleheads in a colander, then submerge in the ice water until completely cool. Let the fiddleheads drain well in a colander and wrap them in a clean kitchen towel to dry.

2. Arrange 2 slices of bundnerfleisch on each of 6 room-temperature plates.

3. Put the brown butter in a large sauté pan over medium heat. Add the fiddleheads and toss gently, adding ½ teaspoon salt and the pepper. Heat for a minute or two until they are warm, then divide the fiddleheads among the 6 plates. Serve at once.

Deep-Fried Squid with Parsley and Almond Sauce

This dish is inspired by the aromatic Catalan cuisine of Barcelona, where ground nuts are often used to thicken and flavor dishes. It makes a delightful first course, but if you add a salad and some roasted potatoes, it could be a great light dinner. The sauce also goes well with white fish like turbot or halibut and even with steamed clams.

It's easiest to buy fresh squid already cleaned from your fishmonger, but you can do it yourself. First pull the tentacles and head from the body. Cut off and discard the head and "beak" (that's the hard ball about the size of a pearl). Reserve the tentacles for the dish. Remove and discard the long, thin, transparent "quill" from inside the body. Peel off the skin with your fingers under cold running water and rinse out the inside of the body. Unless you're stuffing the squid, slice the body crosswise into rings and add to the tentacles. You're ready to cook.

Makes 6 servings

FOR THE SAUCE
1/4 cup olive oil
1 small yellow onion, peeled and finely chopped
1/4 cup toasted blanched almonds (page 272), finely chopped
4 cloves garlic, peeled and finely chopped
1/2 cup dry sherry
2 tablespoons finely chopped flat-leaf parsley
8 tablespoons (1 stick) unsalted butter, at room temperature
Kosher salt
Freshly ground black pepper

1. Warm the olive oil in a medium stainless-steel saucepan over medium heat. Add the onion, almonds, and garlic and sauté until the onions are translucent, about 5 minutes. Add the sherry and parsley and cook, stirring occasionally, until the liquid is reduced by half.

2. Reduce the heat to low and whisk in the butter, a tablespoon at a time, working

quickly. Do not let the mixture boil. Add salt and pepper to taste. Keep covered in a warm place for up to 1 hour.

FOR THE SQUID

¼ cup toasted blanched almonds (page 272)
1 cup all-purpose flour
1 teaspoon kosher salt
¼ teaspoon freshly ground black pepper
Vegetable oil for frying
1 pound cleaned fresh baby squid, sliced (about 1½ pounds
    before cleaning)

1. Grind the almonds in a food processor fitted with the metal blade for about 30 seconds, or finely chop by hand. Be careful not to grind too long or the almonds will turn into a paste. Mix the almonds, flour, salt, and pepper in a large bowl. Line a large plate or platter with several layers of paper towels.

2. To a heavy pot add enough vegetable oil to come about 3 inches up the side. Heat the oil to 350 degrees F, as measured on a kitchen thermometer, or until a drop of the flour mixture placed in the oil immediately starts to sizzle.

3. Using your hands, coat the squid pieces in the flour mixture and shake off the excess. Carefully drop the squid into the hot oil. Do not crowd the pot; if necessary, fry in 2 batches. Fry the squid until light brown, about 1 minute. Remove with a slotted spoon and transfer to the paper towels to drain.

TO SERVE

Ladle some of the sauce onto each of 6 warm plates. Distribute the squid evenly among the plates and serve at once.

Maine Peekytoe Crab Cakes
with Spicy Chive Mayonnaise

For years, Maine crabs, which locals had long called "Peekytoes" for their oddly bent legs, were considered a nuisance by fishermen and thrown back because the meat was too hard to pick out. But the meat was too tasty to ignore for long. Around 1997 fish purveyors started hiring Down East ladies to cook and pick the crabmeat, and a seafood delicacy was born and its chic status sealed when *The New York Times* ran a feature on it. At Arrows we have been cooking this crab for well over a decade, prizing it for its delicate flavor. If you follow this recipe, you will never have a better crab cake.

Makes 6 servings

FOR THE CHIVE MAYONNAISE
1 cup Aïoli (page 158)
½ cup finely chopped chives
2 teaspoons Tabasco sauce
1 teaspoon paprika

Combine all the ingredients and set aside. The mayonnaise can be kept covered in the refrigerator for up to 1 day.

FOR THE CRAB CAKES
4 tablespoons (½ stick) unsalted butter
1½ cups fine bread crumbs
1 tablespoon kosher salt
1 teaspoon freshly ground black pepper
1 pound Maine crabmeat; if unavailable, substitute any fresh crabmeat
¼ cup freshly squeezed lemon juice
¾ cup sour cream
About ½ cup all-purpose flour, plus additional for coating
3 tablespoons vegetable oil

1. Melt the butter in a large sauté pan over medium heat. Add the bread crumbs, salt, and pepper and stir with a large spoon until the butter is fully incorporated. Remove from the heat and let cool.

2. Place the crabmeat in a large bowl and pick through it, removing any bits of shell. Add the lemon juice to the crabmeat and toss. Mix in the sour cream, ½ cup flour, and the bread crumbs. Form the crab mixture into 6 hamburger-size patties, each about ½ inch thick. (If the mixture seems too wet, add a little more flour.) Coat each crab cake with flour.

3. Warm the vegetable oil in a large sauté pan over medium-high heat until hot. Add the crab cakes and cook until very brown, about 2 minutes on each side.

4. Place 1 crab cake onto each of 6 warm plates. Garnish each one with a dollop of the chive mayonnaise.

NOTE: Chive flowers make a nice garnish for this dish.

Grilled Lamb Brochettes on Basil Skewers with Spicy Basil–Cilantro Marinade

When Clark lived in Beijing as a student, one of his favorite things to do was to get a group of friends together and ride bikes to the legendary Roast Meat Restaurant, situated in an ancient part of Beijing overlooking a small pond where old men fished. The first floor of the restaurant was crowded and noisy with drop-in business. The upstairs dining room overlooked the pond and had a huge inverted wok upon which tender morsels of meat would sizzle. In the center of the spacious room sat an old pot-bellied stove, and over the fire was a double boiler with a ceramic bottle of Xiao Xing wine, China's dark and heady version of the more familiar sake.

The marinade in this recipe evokes the style of the food at Roast Meat Restaurant. The skewers used for this brochette are basil stems left to dry over the winter. When the meat is grilled, they give off great flavor.

Although there are many ingredients in the marinade, it's easy to make. Be sure to start a day ahead or the marinade won't be nearly as good. For a dipping sauce, put out rice vinegar, soy sauce, and chile paste; tell your guests to mix them together according to their tastes, as the Chinese do.

Makes 6 servings

4 oranges
1 cup basil leaves, washed and finely chopped
1 cup cilantro leaves, washed
½ cup Xiao Xing wine (available at Asian markets) or dry sherry
2 tablespoons sesame oil
2 tablespoons soy sauce
2 tablespoons vegetable oil
2 tablespoons Chinese chile paste (available at Asian and specialty markets)
2 tablespoons finely chopped garlic
2 tablespoons finely chopped fresh gingerroot
2 tablespoons Sichuan or pink peppercorns
1 pound lamb loin, cut into 1-inch cubes

20 to 24 dried basil stems (page 240), cut into 4-inch lengths,
    or bamboo skewers

1. Use a vegetable peeler to remove the zest from the oranges, avoiding the bitter white pith, and put the zest in a large bowl. Squeeze the juice from the oranges, measure 1 cup, and pour it into the bowl.

2. Add all the remaining ingredients except for the lamb and basil stems to the bowl and mix well. Add the lamb cubes and toss to coat. Cover the bowl and refrigerate for 24 hours or at least overnight.

3. Start a charcoal or gas grill or preheat the broiler.

4. Because the basil skewers are delicate, first poke a hole in the center of each cube of meat with a metal skewer or the point of a small knife, then thread 2 cubes of meat onto each basil stem.

5. Grill the skewers over a medium-hot fire, turning as needed until pink inside, about 4 minutes. Be careful not to place the exposed part of the skewers directly over the fire. Serve at once.

NOTES

1. Garnish with orange slices, basil, and cilantro leaves if desired.

2. Serve with ice-cold Chinese beer like Tsing Tao or warm Xiao Xing wine.

SALADS

SALUTE TO SALADS

Almost every time a food magazine writes a story on Arrows, our salads get top billing. We're thrilled because we love salads. Neither of us can remember a dinner without salad when we were growing up, and as adults we live on salads, every day. We like them best when they're not fussed over but left clean, simple, and, above all, fresh. Few dishes are as enticing.

It just so happens that in the restaurant world we're in a minority, because salads are an afterthought for most chefs. Traditionally chefs are trained for the main course—the fish item, the grilling, the saucing, all the more complicated aspects of cooking. Salads get pushed to the side, literally and otherwise. Even in fairly nice restaurants, the salad course is often a sad afterthought that the waiter tosses together with a bottled dressing. (Don't even go there. Nothing is easier than making your own vinaigrette; see page 40.)

Salads are a part of the main course at Arrows, where we serve Maine Sweet Clams with Risotto and Arugula (page 141) and Grilled Maine Bluefin Tuna with Tomatoes and Gremolata Aïoli (page 150). But you don't have to get that elaborate; you don't even have to try very hard. Just about any grocery store in the United States now has the makings of a great salad.

By the way, we're not talking about those bagged mesclun mixes, which are never very fresh. You'll do much better to buy a couple different heads of lettuce, along with some arugula or watercress, and use them over a few days. Once you get into the homemade salad habit, those heads will go fast. (For more salad ideas, see page 121.)

Even iceberg lettuce (which is very hard to grow at home in case you were wondering) has great potential. Add some grapefruit or orange sections along with thinly sliced red onion, and you've got a first-course salad.

For a dinner party, assemble a trio of salads (page 127), as we do at Arrows. Plan for contrasts like crunchy (nuts and croutons) and soft (Boston lettuce), or hot (warm goat cheese toast) and cold (iceberg again!). The first salad could be a creamy Waldorf cole slaw; the second, a sharp vinaigrette over red and golden beets; and the third, a watercress salad with blue-cheese dressing. Each alone would make a great family dinner salad; together they make a stunning party course.

Whatever you do, don't make it too complicated. Salads should be simple. Our favorite? It would be hard to top a plate of butterhead lettuce with slices of garden-fresh heirloom tomatoes, good wine vinegar, extra-virgin olive oil, and cracked pepper. Okay, you could top it with shavings of Reggiano Parmesan. ∾

GROWING LETTUCE

Lettuce is one of the things that Arrows is best known for, and we take it seriously in our garden. In fact we grow about 28 types of lettuce. Some, like the crispy tooth-edged Reine de Glace, are longtime favorites that our customers ask for by name. But every year we try something new as well. Variety is the name of the lettuce game, and even a small home garden can feature several different types.

Lettuce is easy to start from seed indoors. It actually prefers cool temperatures (some varieties won't germinate above 68 degrees F) and comes up quickly. You can also direct seed—sow the seeds right into the garden soil—as long as you water the bed daily until the sprouts emerge; that's your sign that the roots are developing and the plant is capable of reaching down into the ground for water. Lettuce takes from four to six weeks to mature from seed to harvest stage.

When choosing lettuce varieties to grow, think about color and texture in your salad. Grow at least one red lettuce; we like Red Merlot, a small and incredibly flavorful looseleaf heirloom from the Netherlands. (Looseleaf varieties, rather than iceberg, are the easiest to grow and harvest because you can pull off individual leaves without sacrificing the whole plant.)

You'll also want a butterhead or Bibb variety, such as Sucrine. We love to serve butterhead lettuce with a selection of artisanal Vermont cheeses as an after-dinner course. (Pick three or four cheeses you like from a specialty shop that lets you sample before you buy; aim for a mix of aged sheep's, goat's, and cow's milk cheeses, preferably made from raw milk. Serve with slices of Black Walnut Bread, page 270.)

Then there are the romaine lettuces, which have strong central ribs and are the classic choice for Caesar salads. One popular romaine that you'll never see in a grocery store is Forellenschluss, an Austrian heirloom that is speckled green and red. (The name means "speckled trout" in German.) Consider growing a frilly lettuce like Lollo Rossa, a red-and-green variety that looks great in a mesclun mix.

Another important consideration when choosing lettuce is seasonal hardiness. Some varieties, like the popular looseleaf Black Seeded Simpson, do very well in the spring and fall "shoulder" seasons, but when it gets hot, they bolt, sending up a tall, central shoot that carries the flowers. Bolting is an important part of many plants' reproductive cycle; the tall stem is more visible to bees, which pollinate the flowers and hasten the development of seeds. However, from a culinary standpoint, bolting is bad, for it makes the leaves taste bitter. So in high summer, grow bolt-resistant types like Summer Crisp. ❧

GREENS IN YOUR GARDEN

Greens are one of our favorite things to grow at Arrows, yet many home gardeners haven't tried them. That's a shame because they can be used in the kitchen in so many ways, from stir-fries to salads. Some, like mizuna, are what our gardener calls "cut-and-come-agains": cut them down to the ground and they'll come back for another harvest. In fact, a 20-foot row of greens should last a home gardener all summer.

Greens come in two basic categories: Asian and Western. Asian greens, like the frilly Japanese mizuna or the more common bok choy, cook up quickly in stir-fries but are mild enough for fresh salads. Western greens include the classic American mustard greens like Red Giant and Osaka Purple (both of which are fairly spicy) and the European-style salad greens like endive and chicory (harvest by picking the outer leaves) and frisée and chard (cut them right to the ground and they'll come back up). Other specialty greens we grow for salads include arugula, chrysanthemum (the flowers are also edible, see page 191), dandelion, and mâche, which is also known as corn salad or lamb's lettuce. The spinachlike green called amaranth is delicious in salads and looks beautiful in the garden with its wide, maroon-tinged leaves. Orach is another green similar to spinach but red in color. We love to serve broadleaf and crinkled cress (relatives of watercress), so we always keep some on hand.

Sow seeds for greens directly in the soil in June or start them indoors or in cold frames earlier. Around here they have a real nemesis in flea beetles, but row covers keep them away. (See Beating the Bugs, page 132.) ♒

First-of-the-Season Lettuce Salad
with Herb Vinaigrette and Goat Cheese Toasts

It is always exciting to see the first lettuces of spring poking their heads out of the ground. Our gardeners usually have a fit because we want to pick them so young, but who can stand to wait? You can also use field greens such as arugula, mizuna, and tatsoi, and herbs such as tarragon or parsley for more texture and flavor.

Makes 6 servings

FOR THE VINAIGRETTE
½ cup coarsely chopped chives
½ cup flat-leaf parsley
¼ cup extra-virgin olive oil
¼ cup olive oil
¼ cup champagne vinegar
1 shallot, peeled
1 tablespoon whole-grain mustard
2 teaspoons kosher salt
10 whole black peppercorns

Combine all the vinaigrette ingredients in the jar of a blender and process until smooth. The vinaigrette will keep covered in the refrigerator for up to 2 days.

TO SERVE
6 ounces first-of-the-season lettuce (about 1 medium head),
    washed and dried
12 Creamy Goat Cheese Toasts (page 82)

Using your hands, gently toss the lettuce with enough vinaigrette to nicely coat the greens, but do not drown them. Arrange the lettuce on 6 chilled plates. Garnish with the goat cheese toasts and serve at once.

Tossing Greens

Tongs and other salad-tossing implements make great serving utensils, but for salads they are a waste of time. The main reason is that lettuce is delicate, especially homegrown lettuce, which is not hybridized for toughness to withstand shipping in cardboard boxes. Utensils bruise and tear tender lettuces. Another reason is that in a good salad every green leaf is evenly coated with dressing. Utensils cannot do that.

So what should you use instead? Your spotlessly clean hands, of course. They are gentle on the lettuce and able to spread the dressing around much better. It's easiest to pour the dressing into the bowl first, then add the lettuce, then pull the dressing up through the salad.

Vinaigrette Made (Even More) Simple

One of the first techniques every cook should learn is how to make a simple vinaigrette. The proportions are not written in stone; we use twice as much oil as vinegar, but you may prefer a different ratio. Start with a bowl large enough to hold the salad. Sprinkle some kosher or sea salt into the bowl and grind in fresh black pepper to taste. Add any good white wine vinegar; we like champagne vinegar, which is not bubbly at all but made from the same chardonnay grapes that go into Champagne. Use a wire whisk to blend the seasonings into the vinegar until the salt dissolves. Then drizzle in olive oil, whisking vigorously until the oil and vinegar bind into an emulsion. Add lettuce, toss, and serve. Simple vinaigrettes will keep covered in the refrigerator for up to 3 days.

A word on olive oil: In general, we like to use a mix of extra-virgin olive oil and regular olive oil in our vinaigrettes. We like the flavor of fruity, high-quality, cold-pressed extra-virgin olive oil but often find it too assertive; the two types combine for a milder, more pleasant taste that doesn't overpower foods, especially tender homegrown lettuce. If you absolutely love the stronger flavor of extra-virgin olive oil, you can certainly use only it in these recipes.

Rocket with Lemon–Hazelnut Vinaigrette

Our heated greenhouse is our refuge in the early spring. Often snow is piled up several feet deep around it, but inside we can still pick baby field greens such as rocket, which is small, tender arugula. (You can often find rocket at farmers' markets.) The peppery flavor of rocket works well with the buttery taste of hazelnut oil and the tartness of fresh lemon.

Makes 6 servings

¼ cup freshly squeezed lemon juice
1 teaspoon kosher salt
½ teaspoon freshly ground black pepper
¼ cup olive oil
¼ cup hazelnut oil
6 ounces rocket (about 6 handfuls), washed and dried
½ cup toasted blanched hazelnuts (page 272)

1. Combine the lemon juice, salt, and pepper in a large bowl. Gradually whisk in the olive and hazelnut oils. The vinaigrette will keep covered in the refrigerator for up to 3 days.

2. Using your hands, gently toss the rocket with the vinaigrette. Divide the rocket evenly among 6 chilled plates. Transfer the toasted nuts to the salad bowl and toss just to coat them. Sprinkle the nuts on top of the greens and serve.

HOW TO MAKE NUT-FLAVORED OILS

We make vinaigrettes (page 40) with nut-flavored oils like hazelnut, walnut, and pistachio. (Genuine nut oils, which are extracted from the nuts themselves, are expensive and don't keep well; try them in small quantities.) To make nut-flavored oils at home, cook a handful of nuts in a cup or so of vegetable oil over medium heat until nicely toasted, 5 to 10 minutes. Transfer the oil and nuts to a bowl or glass jar and let them steep covered for a day or two at room temperature to infuse the flavor. Drain the nuts (use them on salads) and store the oil in the refrigerator for up to 3 months.

Warm Dandelion Greens with Bacon Vinaigrette

When it is still a bit chilly in the New England spring, nothing tastes better than a salad of wilted dandelion greens. Besides being a warm comfort on a cool night, the fresh greens tantalize with hints of the unfolding season. If you do not have dandelion greens, you can substitute just about any other hearty green such as Napa cabbage, Swiss chard, or spinach. This salad is great served with warm crusty sourdough bread.

Makes 6 servings

8 ounces thickly sliced bacon (about 6 slices), cut into 1-inch pieces
6 ounces dandelion greens (about 6 handfuls), washed and dried
2 tablespoons champagne or white wine vinegar
1 teaspoon kosher salt
½ teaspoon freshly ground black pepper
½ cup olive oil

1. In a large stainless-steel sauté pan over medium heat, cook the bacon until crisp, about 5 minutes. Remove the pan from the heat and use a slotted spoon to transfer the bacon pieces to a paper-towel-lined plate. Reserve the bacon fat in the pan.

2. Toss the greens in a large bowl with the vinegar, salt, and pepper so they are evenly coated and the salt and pepper is evenly distributed. (A trick for getting just the right amount of vinegar is to tip the bowl on its side, holding back the lettuce with your hand, and pour off any extra vinegar.)

3. Add the olive oil to the bacon fat in the sauté pan and warm over medium heat until hot but not smoking. Add the greens and bacon and stir constantly for about 1 minute until the greens are just wilted.

4. Divide the salad among 6 warm plates and serve at once.

NOTE: You can substitute 6 ounces chicory (about 1 medium head) for the dandelion greens and toss in 4 ounces Cheddar cheese, cut into 1-inch matchsticks.

✦MAIN COURSES

Sautéed Maine Cod with Caramelized Endive

Many New Englanders consider cod a pedestrian fish, possibly because it was once so plentiful. Indeed the cod market was a major part of the region's economy in the nineteenth century, when lobster was considered "trash food." Today, because of overfishing, cod has become increasingly rare and more expensive. Yet when it is fresh and cooked properly, few fish are as meltingly sweet—almost like freshwater bass. In this recipe, caramelized Belgian endive adds a nutty, slightly bitter flavor that contrasts nicely with the sweetness of the fish.

Makes 6 servings

6 large Belgian endives
2 tablespoons balsamic vinegar
Kosher salt
Freshly ground black pepper
2 tablespoons unsalted butter
3 tablespoons clarified butter (page 44) or olive oil
6 skinless cod fillets, 6 ounces each

1. Preheat the oven to 450 degrees F.
2. Pull the endives apart into individual leaves, discarding the tough inner cores. In a bowl combine the endive leaves with the vinegar. Sprinkle with 1 teaspoon salt and ¹/₂ teaspoon pepper. Toss to coat the leaves evenly.
3. Melt the butter in a large stainless-steel sauté pan over medium heat and continue to heat until it starts to turn light brown. Add the endive and cook, tossing gently, until the leaves start to caramelize. Set aside in a warm place.

4. Heat the clarified butter in a large ovenproof sauté pan over medium-high heat until it is very hot. Sprinkle the cod fillets lightly with salt and pepper on each side. When the clarified butter is very hot but not smoking, gently place the cod fillets in the pan. Cook for 1 minute and turn the fish with a spatula. (Depending on the size of your pan, you may have to sauté the cod in 2 batches.) Transfer the pan to the oven. (If you sautéed the cod in 2 batches, arrange them on a baking sheet large enough to hold them all.) Cook the cod in the oven for 3 minutes until just firm.

5. Arrange the endive on 6 warm plates and top with the cod fillets.

NOTE: For a more elegant dinner, serve this dish with Spring Leek Cream Sauce (page 64).

CLARIFIED BUTTER

Clarifying removes all the water and milk solids from butter. The result lasts longer and doesn't burn at high heat, so we use it for pan-browning and sautéing. It's really easy to make: Put the butter in the top of a double boiler or in a small pan over very low heat. After it melts, keep it at a very low simmer for 10 minutes or so. During this time, the water will sink to the bottom and the milk solids will float to the top. Skim off the solids with a spoon, then "decant" the butter by pouring it slowly through a sieve, leaving the water in the bottom of the pan. One stick of butter will yield about 6 tablespoons clarified butter. Store covered in the refrigerator for up to 2 months. ✎

Sautéed Dover Sole with Peas, Tarragon, and Button Mushrooms

Dover sole is one of nature's special gifts. Caught off the coast of England, it is the most buttery and delicate of the flatfish family, yet it won't fall apart in cooking. It has such a reputation that lesser types of sole are sometimes falsely labeled Dover. A reputable fishmonger is your best protection. If you are celebrating a special occasion and your local fish market has Dover sole, splurge and try this recipe. Have your fishmonger skin and fillet the fish for you.

Makes 6 servings

> Kosher salt
> 2 cups shelled English peas, about 1½ pounds in the pod
> 8 tablespoons (1 stick) unsalted butter
> 2 cups small button mushrooms (about 8 ounces), cleaned and trimmed
> Freshly ground black pepper
> 6 skinless Dover sole fillets, 4 to 6 ounces each
> 2 tablespoons clarified butter (page 44)
> 1½ cups Chicken or Vegetable Stock (page 23 or 24)
> ¼ cup tarragon leaves

1. In a large pot bring 2 quarts water and 1 tablespoon salt to a boil. Fill a medium bowl halfway with ice water. Add the peas to the pot and cook for 1 minute. Drain the peas in a colander and submerge them immediately in the ice water. When the peas are completely cold, remove them from the water and drain well.

2. Melt 2 tablespoons of the butter in a medium sauté pan over medium-high heat. Add the mushrooms and season with 1 teaspoon salt and ¼ teaspoon pepper. Cook the mushrooms for several minutes until the liquid starts to exude. Continue to cook for several more minutes until all the liquid is gone from the pan. Remove the mushrooms from the heat and transfer to a plate.

3. Preheat the oven to 400 degrees F.

4. Sprinkle the sole fillets lightly with salt and pepper on both sides. Melt the clarified butter in a large ovenproof sauté pan, preferably nonstick, over medium-high heat

until very hot but not smoking. Add the sole fillets to the pan. Brown for 30 seconds, then gently flip the fish. (Depending on the size of your pan, you may have to sauté the sole in 2 batches.) Transfer the pan to the oven and continue to cook for 2 minutes until the flesh is just firm. (If you sautéed the sole in 2 batches, arrange them on a baking sheet large enough to hold them all.)

5. While the fish is cooking, combine the stock, peas, and mushrooms in a medium saucepan. Bring to a boil and add the tarragon leaves. Cook for 30 seconds, then turn the heat to low. Add the remaining 6 tablespoons butter, a tablespoon at a time, swirling the pan. Do not boil. Season with salt and pepper to taste.

6. Spoon the pea and mushroom mixture onto 6 warm plates. Place a sole fillet on each plate and serve at once.

COOKING FISH FILLETS

A combination of stovetop searing and oven baking is the best way to get fish fillets well browned and crisp on the outside and perfectly cooked and moist on the inside. The oven provides uniform heat from all sides so it penetrates to cook the center of the fillets without burning them. If the weather is too hot to turn on the oven, you can cook fish all the way through on the stovetop: Start with medium-low heat and, once the fillets brown, turn it to low. You'll need to extend the cooking time a bit past the oven-time recommendations because the heat is lower and coming only from the bottom. ✑

Crispy Trout with Ginger and Lemongrass

In Thailand, fresh herbs are used abundantly and nowhere more so than in the preparation of seafood. Thai-style herbs go particularly well with trout, a mild-tasting, farm-raised fish that benefits from bold flavor combinations. (Wild trout has a much more intense taste than farm-raised, but it is nearly impossible to find unless you catch it yourself.) In this dish the flavor of the herbs and lemongrass will permeate the trout. It is great served with Scallion Pancakes (page 83) and Vietnamese Clear Dipping Sauce (page 161).

When selecting trout, as with all fish, trust your sense of smell and feel and look carefully before buying. The eyes should be clear, the skin uniform and glossy, the flesh firm.

Makes 6 servings

6 stalks lemongrass, yellow part only
1 piece gingerroot about 3 inches long, peeled and cut lengthwise
    into thin slices
12 sprigs cilantro
12 sprigs mint
12 sprigs basil
6 whole boneless trout, 6 to 8 ounces each
½ cup all-purpose flour
2 teaspoons kosher salt
1 teaspoon freshly ground black pepper
3 tablespoons vegetable oil

1. Preheat the oven to 400 degrees F.

2. With the blunt side of a heavy cleaver or knife, pound the lemongrass stalks to flatten them slightly. Cut each stalk in half. Stuff 1 stalk, one-sixth of the ginger, and 1 sprig of each herb in the cavity of each trout.

3. Mix the flour, salt, and pepper in a large shallow pan. Coat each trout with the seasoned flour and set aside.

4. Heat the oil in a large ovenproof (preferably nonstick) sauté pan over medium-high heat until nearly smoking. Add the trout and cook until the underside is browned, about

1 minute. Flip the trout and brown the other side. (Depending on the size of your pan, you may have to brown the trout in 2 batches.) Transfer the pan to the oven. (If you browned the trout in 2 batches, arrange them on a baking sheet large enough to hold them all.) Bake until the flesh is opaque and flaky, about 4 minutes.

5. Place 1 trout on each of 6 warm plates. Garnish with the remaining basil, mint, and cilantro sprigs and serve at once.

PLANNING A KITCHEN GARDEN

"The older I get, the smaller my garden," a wise man we know once said. Even better is to start small. If you're a beginning gardener, don't race out and do too much. It's better to have a small, beautifully tended garden than an oversized, overgrown plot that you don't have time to weed. Think about how much time you can reasonably spend in the garden, and be realistic. Ten minutes a day? (Try two tomato plants, lettuce, and some herbs.) An hour a day? (Grow a few more tomatoes, a zucchini vine, a couple of peppers, and more herbs.) One morning on the weekend plus time after work every day? (Add greens, spinach, chard, carrots, beets, onions.) If you have lots of space (and even more time), try moving into peas, beans, corn, and winter squash.

Whatever your ambitions, pick a site that gets full sun as close as possible to the kitchen. Plan on a couple of beds, three feet wide and twice as long, separated by paths lined with bark mulch, which slows down the weeds and looks tidy. (You'll still need to weed the beds themselves, although a layer of compost or salt marsh hay (a coastal grass that, unlike normal hay, is free of weed seeds) will keep weeds to a minimum.

When ordering seeds, ignore the catalog photos of happy gardeners hefting bushels of blue-ribbon corn and pumpkins. Start instead with herbs, which are the basis of so many dishes. Make them the building blocks of your garden as well. Thyme, for example, is a must for seasoning soups and meats. Parsley and chives (which come up every year) are easy to grow and incredibly versatile in the kitchen. Dill is simply not optional; we must have it, for salmon as well as pickling. At Arrows we grow many types of basil: Genovese and Nufar (both Italian pesto staples), cinnamon, lemon, and Thai, which has a slight hint of anise. Basil is great in Asian stir-fries and noodle soups. If you are more adventurous, grow chervil, lemongrass, cilantro, and Vietnamese coriander.

We know you want to grow tomatoes, so go ahead. Experiment with a few, but keep it simple. One cherry tomato vine will deliver zillions of tomatoes all summer, and you can even grow it in a patio pot. Add two reliable slicing heirlooms—Red Brandywine and Green Zebra make a nice contrast—and a heavy-producing sauce tomato like Amish Paste, and you're set for summer. Lettuce is easy and rewarding, because you can pick your own salad every night. Grow Simpson, Red Oakleaf, Grand Rapids, and other looseleaf varieties that allow you to harvest continuously.

Finally consider some of the perennial vegetables such as rhubarb (the earliest spring crop in Maine) and lemony sorrel, which the French use in soups and as an accompaniment to seafood. Plant either of them once, and you'll rarely think about them again—except when you're hungry. ✑

Roasted Poussin with Lemon Thyme and Sourdough Stuffing

Poussins are baby chickens that weigh about a pound. They have a delicate taste that goes well with the flavors of spring—and they make a beautiful and dramatic presentation. Poussins can be obtained at specialty food markets. You can substitute Rock Cornish game hens, which are not "game" at all but simply young chickens (a cross between the Plymouth Rock and Cornish strains), weighing from 1½ to 1¾ pounds. (You'll need to increase the roasting time to 1 hour.) They are generally found in the freezer section and, therefore, not as tender or moist as fresh poussins. (You can also simply use a 3½-pound chicken, which will take about 1½ hours to roast.) Lemon thyme, which has a nice zing, is no longer considered very exotic. You can find seedlings in most garden centers.

Makes 6 servings

2 cups cubed sourdough bread
8 tablespoons (1 stick) unsalted butter
2 leeks, light parts only, cut crosswise into ¼-inch-thick rings,
    well washed and dried
Kosher salt
Freshly ground black pepper
1 cup morel mushrooms, cleaned and trimmed
1 cup Chicken Stock (page 23)
6 poussins, about 1 pound each, or other fowl (see above)
2 tablespoons olive oil
2 teaspoons lemon thyme leaves
2 teaspoons chopped tarragon

1. Spread the bread cubes on a baking sheet and allow to dry overnight.

2. Melt the butter in a large sauté pan over medium heat. Add the leeks, 1 teaspoon salt, and ½ teaspoon pepper and sauté for 3 minutes. Add the morels and cook for another 3 minutes. Add the chicken stock, bring to a boil, and cook for 30 seconds.

3. Transfer the leek mixture to a large bowl and stir in the bread cubes. Let the stuffing cool in the refrigerator.

4. Preheat the oven to 450 degrees F.

5. Brush the poussins with the olive oil, sprinkle with the herbs, and season with salt and pepper.

6. When the stuffing is completely cool, fill the cavity of each poussin with some of the mixture. Tie each poussin's legs together with kitchen twine. Put the birds in a roasting pan, then in the oven. Immediately reduce the heat to 350 degrees and roast for about 40 minutes until the legs move easily when wiggled and the juices run clear when the meat is pricked with a knife.

7. Remove from the oven, untie the legs, and serve at once. If you like, strain the pan juices through a fine sieve into a small saucepan; using a spoon or ladle, skim off and discard the fat. Gently reheat and pour some of the remaining pan juices over each bird.

Grilled Quail with Rhubarb Compote

Rhubarb is one of the first crops of spring, when it usually appears in dessert pies, often with strawberries. This recipe features it in a savory dish. You can substitute 3 small ducks or chickens for the quail, in which case you should split the birds and allow a half for each person. Cooking time should then increase to about 15 minutes per side. This dish goes well with Chive Mashed Potatoes (page 175).

Makes 6 servings

FOR THE QUAIL
12 quail, about 4 ounces each; have your butcher remove the breastbones
$^{1}/_{4}$ cup extra-virgin olive oil
$^{1}/_{4}$ cup tarragon leaves
1 tablespoon coarsely cracked black peppercorns

In a bowl toss the quail with the olive oil, tarragon, and peppercorns. Cover the bowl with plastic wrap and refrigerate for at least 4 hours, turning the birds twice during this time if possible.

FOR THE RHUBARB
1 small red onion, peeled and finely chopped (about $^{1}/_{2}$ cup)
1 tablespoon olive oil
2 tablespoons finely chopped gingerroot
3 medium stalks rhubarb, cut into 1-inch pieces
$^{1}/_{4}$ cup brown sugar
$^{1}/_{4}$ cup red wine vinegar

In a large heavy-bottomed saucepan set over medium heat, sauté the onion in the olive oil until translucent, about 5 minutes. Add the ginger and cook for another minute. Add the rhubarb, sugar, and vinegar and reduce the heat to low. Cook for about 5 minutes until the rhubarb begins to get soft and the other ingredients are melded together. Remove from the heat. The compote can be made 2 days in advance and refrigerated in a sealed nonreactive container. Bring to room temperature before serving.

TO GRILL THE QUAIL AND TO SERVE

1 tablespoon plus 2 teaspoons kosher salt
$\frac{1}{4}$ cup champagne vinegar
$\frac{1}{2}$ teaspoon freshly ground black pepper
$\frac{1}{4}$ cup olive oil
$\frac{1}{4}$ cup extra-virgin olive oil
4 ounces frisée (about 1 small head), leaves separated, washed and dried

1. Start a charcoal or gas grill.

2. Sprinkle the quail with 1 tablespoon of the salt. Grill the quail over a medium-hot fire for 12 to 15 minutes, turning as needed onto all sides, until the juices run clear when the meat is pricked with a knife.

3. While the quail is grilling, combine the vinegar, the remaining 2 teaspoons salt, and the pepper in a large bowl. Gradually whisk in both olive oils. (The vinaigrette will keep covered in the refrigerator for up to 3 days.) Add the frisée and toss to coat with the vinaigrette. Divide the salad evenly among 6 room-temperature plates.

4. Place 2 quail on each plate and spoon some of the compote on top of each one. Serve at once.

Smoked Duck Breast with Swiss Chard and Pearl Onions

Smoking, one of the oldest methods of preserving food, is practiced around the world. It almost certainly began with people drying meat or fish over a fire, then noticing the smoke imparted a pleasant, robust flavor. (Although wood smoke does contain substances that kill bacteria, the effect is minimal, so smoking is usually combined with other preservation techniques like salting or drying.) In Maine you can still find fishermen who run roadside smokehouses, where they sell their own smoked haddock or alewives.

For this recipe, we first cure the duck breasts with garden herbs and salt overnight, then smoke them slowly over apple or hickory wood. The process transforms the flavor of the meat, imparting a sweetness that is similar to the taste of really good ham.

Makes 6 servings

FOR SMOKING THE DUCK
1/4 cup kosher salt
1 tablespoon whole black peppercorns
6 cloves garlic, peeled and thinly sliced
6 large boneless duck breasts, skin on, about 6 ounces each
16 sprigs rosemary
12 sprigs thyme
12 bay leaves
2 cups wood chips for the grill (such as hickory, mesquite, cherry, or apple), soaked in water for at least 1 hour

1. One day ahead of time, toss the salt, peppercorns, and garlic in a bowl. Coat each duck breast with the salt mixture and shake off the excess salt. Combine the rosemary, thyme, and bay leaves in a large shallow pan. Arrange the duck breasts, skin side up, on top of the herbs. Place another pan on top of the duck breasts and a heavy weight, such as a can of olive oil, several cans of tomatoes, or even a couple of bricks, in the top pan. Refrigerate overnight.

2. Start a moderate fire in your grill. Drain and toss a handful of the soaked wood chips either on top of the coals when they are hot or in the smoker box of a gas grill. Position

the duck breasts skin side down, away from the heat on the grill and allow to smoke for at least 1 hour, adding another handful of wood chips about every 20 minutes. Remove the duck breasts when the meat is still red in the center and refrigerate.

FOR THE VEGETABLES AND TO COOK THE DUCK

2 cups pearl onions, peeled
18 baby white turnips, peeled
3 tablespoons olive oil
Kosher salt
Freshly ground black pepper
3 tablespoons butter
½ cup Chicken Stock (page 23)
8 ounces small Swiss chard leaves or large spinach leaves
2 teaspoons thyme leaves, chopped

1. Preheat the oven to 375 degrees F.

2. Toss the pearl onions and turnips with the olive oil and some salt and pepper in a shallow ovenproof casserole. Cover with foil and roast, shaking the pan every 10 minutes or so, until the vegetables are soft and just slightly brown, about 45 minutes. Remove from the oven and set aside to cool.

3. Raise the oven temperature to 450 degrees F.

4. Warm a large sauté pan over medium-high heat until very hot. Arrange the duck breasts, skin side down, in the pan and reduce the heat to medium. Cook for 4 minutes, then pour off the excess fat. (Depending on the size of your pan, you may have to sauté the duck breasts in 2 batches.) Transfer the pan to the oven and cook for 2 minutes. Flip the breasts and cook for another 2 minutes until the duck feels firm when pressed with your finger. (If you sautéed the duck breasts in 2 batches, arrange them on a baking sheet large enough to hold them all.)

5. While the duck breasts are in the oven, combine the butter and stock in a large sauté pan and warm over medium heat. Add the chard and cook, stirring occasionally, for 1 minute until the leaves are wilted. Add the pearl onions and turnips and heat through, about 1 minute. Add the thyme and season with salt and pepper.

6. Divide the vegetables evenly among 6 warm plates. Remove the duck breasts from the oven, place them on a cutting board, and cut each breast crosswise into 6 slices. Arrange the sliced duck breasts on top of the vegetables. Serve at once.

BABY VEGETABLES

We grow lots of baby vegetables at Arrows because they have a delicate flavor and look great on the plate. They also make sense if you don't have much gardening space; you can plant them close or grow them in containers. Not all vegetable varieties are suitable for immature harvest (some need more time to develop flavor or color), but over the years we've discovered some real winners in the baby vegetable category.

For baby beets we plant Chioggia (an Italian heirloom distinctive for its alternating red and white rings), Pronto, and Golden (a mild-tasting, orangish yellow beet). Good carrots include Babette, Minicor (sweet and fast growing), and our favorite, Thumbelina—a round Parisian-type carrot that has an incredibly creamy texture. Thumbelina is also good if you have clay soil, which tends to distort conventional finger-shaped carrots. For baby turnips, try Hakurei. Not all young leeks have much flavor, but we like King Richard, which we pull when about $1/4$ inch in diameter. We also harvest all varieties of bok choy when small.

Baby corn is a favorite accompaniment to grilled meats and fish. It's also a way to enjoy growing corn if you don't have a lot of room. To get baby corn, simply plant regular corn 2 to 4 inches apart (rather than 12 inches for a full-size yield). Harvest when the ears are a few inches long. The best part is that you can eat the cob too.

Not many people think of harvesting baby green beans, but we love the tender flavor of Tavera (a small bush variety with beans that have long, slender white seeds) and Nichols (a pole version with 6-inch pods and striking purple flowers). To enjoy the baby beans, pick the pods when they are $1^1/2$ to 2 inches long.

When cooking baby vegetables, we like to keep it simple so as not to overpower their tender flavor with other ingredients. The best technique is to simply blanch them, then reheat them briefly in a little butter (see page 67).

Spring Lamb Loin with Rosemary

The strong, piney taste of rosemary goes well with lamb. It's also one of those herbs, like oregano and marjoram, that you can dig up in the fall and move indoors for the winter. Then you'll have it fresh in the spring, when lamb is at its best. To grow rosemary indoors, pick a plant that's not too big, say a foot or so high. Water it well, then dig out enough of the roots and soil to fill a 10- or 12-inch round pot; they like to be a little root bound, so better to have a pot that's slightly small rather than too large. Water it again after positioning it snugly in the pot (you may need to add a little potting soil) and transfer it to a sunny spot in the house. Don't let it get too dry and be sure to bring it outdoors again in spring, because rosemary can't really survive indoors year-round. (You can replant it in the ground or keep it going in a large pot.)

Makes 6 servings

1 boneless lamb loin, about 2 pounds
¼ cup rosemary leaves
2 teaspoons thyme leaves
1 teaspoon whole black peppercorns
2 tablespoons olive oil
Kosher salt
Freshly ground black pepper
6 sprigs rosemary, for garnish

1. One day ahead of time, fit the lamb loin in a shallow dish. Add the rosemary leaves, 1 teaspoon of the thyme, the peppercorns, and olive oil and turn the loin several times to evenly coat it with the herbs and pepper. Cover with plastic wrap and marinate in the refrigerator overnight.

2. Preheat the oven to 450 degrees F.

3. Remove the lamb from the refrigerator. Brush off and discard the marinade. Place the lamb loin on a roasting rack in a roasting pan and sprinkle all over with salt and pepper and the remaining thyme. Roast for 20 minutes until it feels slightly firm when pressed with your finger or when it registers 140 degrees F on a kitchen thermometer. (The lamb will be medium rare.)

4. Remove the lamb from the oven and let sit for a minute. Slice the lamb loin cross-

wise against the grain and divide evenly among 6 warm dinner plates. Garnish with the rosemary sprigs and serve at once.

NOTE: This lamb is great served with Chive Mashed Potatoes (page 175) and Spring Leek Cream Sauce (page 64).

SAUCES

Citrus and Parsley Gremolata Vinaigrette

This is a colorful vinaigrette and a light way to dress up scallops, white fish, and shrimp without masking the flavor of the seafood. It's also a tangy summer barbecue marinade: Just toss it with chicken, salmon, halibut, or even rib-eye steak for about 1 hour, then use the sauce to baste the meat while grilling.

Makes about 2 cups

1 teaspoon kosher salt
½ teaspoon freshly ground black pepper
¼ cup finely chopped flat-leaf parsley
2 tablespoons grated lemon zest
2 tablespoons grated orange zest
1 tablespoon grated lime zest
2 tablespoons freshly squeezed lemon juice
2 tablespoons freshly squeezed orange juice
1 tablespoon freshly squeezed lime juice
1 lemon, peeled and sectioned (page 310), then coarsely chopped
1 orange, peeled and sectioned, then coarsely chopped
1 lime, peeled and sectioned, then coarsely chopped
2 teaspoons garlic, peeled and finely chopped
1 teaspoon anchovy paste, optional
½ cup olive oil
½ cup extra-virgin olive oil

1. Put the salt and pepper in a bowl. Add the parsley, citrus zest, juice, and sections, the garlic, and anchovy paste if using.

2. Gradually whisk in both olive oils. The vinaigrette will keep covered in the refrigerator for up to 1 day.

Starting Seedlings

Starting your own seedlings lets you grow more unusual and interesting plant varieties than you can find at garden centers, which generally cater to folks who just want a "tomato." Serious enthusiasts spend their whole lives perfecting the science (and art) of botanic growth, but you can start many plants in your own home without too much effort or specialized equipment. The most important assets are patience and care, both of which will reward you with the miracle of a new plant. It's always hard to believe that those tiny seeds have within them the power to make tomatoes or eggplants, but then they sprout—and before you know it, the ratatouille is ready!

Start with the soil, which shouldn't be soil at all, in fact. Always use a sterile commercial mix high in peat and vermiculite. Don't use garden soil, which can contain bacteria that cause seedlings to wilt. Put the moistened commercial mix in a plastic seed flat or cell-type tray (available at home centers), scatter seeds on the surface, and barely cover them with a little of the mix. Most seeds need some light to germinate. It helps to cover the tray with a plastic dome lid, which keeps the soil moist and warm, like a miniature greenhouse. Place the trays in a sunny window (turning them daily) or, even better, under a fluorescent shop light. (Special "grow lights" are not necessary.) You're trying to duplicate the brightness of the sun, so position the light as close to the plants as possible without touching them. Our gardener has entire rooms in her house filled with these lights, where she starts thousands of seedlings for the restaurant.

Most seeds will germinate at around room temperature, but pepper and eggplant seeds need to be at 80 degrees F or higher. If your house has radiant floor heat, you're all set—just put the tray on the floor in front of a window. Otherwise the best way to germinate heat-loving seeds is to place an electric heat mat (sold in catalogs and at garden centers) under the tray.

Check the trays every day and make sure the planting mix stays moist. (Use a misting bottle to spray the soil mix.) After the sprouts emerge and are large enough to handle, gently

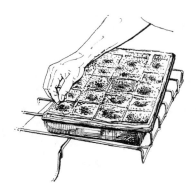

transfer them to individual 3-inch pots or the larger cell trays that hold twenty-five or so plants. The tiny stems are quite fragile, so try to hold new seedlings by the leaves. Water carefully so as not to upset the seedlings; the safest way is to "bottom water": Put the pots in a tray of lukewarm water and let it soak into the soil. Then return the pots under the lights or to the sunny window.

Plants grown indoors tend to get leggy (too tall and spindly) and weak, so they need to be "hardened off" before they're set in the ground. About a week before transplant time, take them to a shady area that's protected from wind, and let them experience the outdoors in a low-impact way. Be sure to bring them in before dark. Each day gradually introduce them to more full sun but keep them out of the wind. After a week they should be ready for the great outdoors. ᕦ

14 Easy Seeds

These are crops you grow from seeds (or seed equivalents like bulbs) put directly in the ground without starting indoors. Some, like corn and squash, take a lot of space; others, like spinach and carrots, can be grown in small beds.

Beans Wait until all danger of frost has passed before planting beans. Sow pretty close together, about 2 inches apart.

Beets Sow the seeds in spring and enjoy beets mid-summer. There's generally no need to thin (pulling smaller plants to give larger ones room to mature) as the beets spread out around each other while growing.

Carrots Plant the tiny seeds in deeply tilled soil, then thin ruthlessly to about 2 inches apart after growth appears.

Chard This relative of the beet is incredibly easy to grow from seed.

Corn Sow kernels in warm soil (at least 65 degrees F) after the last frost date in your region. Corn will not germinate in cold soil!

Garlic Plant individual bulbs in late fall, and they'll be ready by late summer.

Kale This hardy green often overwinters, even in Maine. Sow the seeds just about any time during the growing season.

Lettuce Most lettuces prefer cool weather, but none can handle frost; sow in mid-spring.

Parsnips Like its relative parsley, the seeds take a long time to germinate, but once they sprout, not much can stop them.

Peas A cool-weather crop, peas should be sown as soon as the ground can be worked but not during a cold rainy spell, which can rot them. If you have acidic soil (as we do in Maine), add lime or wood ash to the planting bed, preferably in the previous fall.

Potatoes You can grow these from seeds, which form in tiny flowers on the above-ground plant, but nobody does that. The best way to grow potatoes is from potatoes—actually the eyes. Plant large chunks of potato (each piece should have at least two eyes, and it's fine if they're sprouting) in spring. Much folklore surrounds the planting of potatoes. By tradition they are planted when the dandelions bloom, and old-timers swear they come up better if you plant on the new moon.

Radishes Radishes are fun to grow because they come up so fast. Sow in mid-spring and every three weeks thereafter for a continuous supply.

Spinach Sow spinach in early spring as soon as the ground is workable. It doesn't like acidic soil, so plan to add lime in the fall for next year's planting.

Squash Like corn, squash loves heat; don't push the season by starting too early.

Spring Leek Cream Sauce

This is a versatile, simple sauce. Use it with white fish, roast pork and chicken, or lamb.

Makes about 2 cups

2 cups heavy cream
Kosher salt
2 medium leeks, light parts only, cut crosswise into ¼-inch rings,
    well washed
½ cup Chicken or Vegetable Stock (page 23 or 24)
Freshly ground black pepper

1. In a heavy saucepan set over medium heat, bring the cream to a boil and cook until it is reduced by half.

2. In a large pot bring 2 quarts water and 1 tablespoon salt to a boil. Fill a medium bowl halfway with ice water. Add the leeks to the pot and cook for 1 minute. Remove the leeks from the water and submerge them immediately in the ice water. When the leeks are cold, drain them in a colander, then wrap them in a clean kitchen towel to dry.

3. Combine the leeks with the stock in the jar of a blender and process until smooth.

4. Add the leek purée to the reduced cream and season with salt and pepper. Warm the sauce gently over medium heat. Serve immediately or keep warm in a covered container for up to 1 hour.

# SIDE DISHES

Spring Leeks in Vinaigrette

Leeks, standing like rows of soldiers, always look wonderfully odd in the garden. Usually they are harvested in the late summer or fall, when they attain gargantuan size. But we like them in the late spring, when they are the size of scallions, extremely tender, and full of flavor. Serve these leeks in vinaigrette with prosciutto and Potato-Chive Bread (page 84) for a first course or a light lunch, or as a side dish with roasted chicken or grilled meats or fish.

Makes 6 servings

Kosher salt
6 small, tender leeks, light parts only, cut crosswise into ¼-inch rings,
    well washed
½ cup finely chopped flat-leaf parsley
¼ cup finely chopped tarragon leaves
¼ cup champagne vinegar
1 tablespoon Dijon mustard
½ teaspoon freshly ground black pepper
¼ cup olive oil
¼ cup extra-virgin olive oil

1. In a large pot bring 2 quarts water and 1 tablespoon salt to a boil. Fill a medium bowl halfway with ice water. Add the leeks to the pot and cook for 1 minute, then drain and plunge into the ice water. When the leeks are completely chilled, remove them from the ice water, drain thoroughly, and set aside.

2. Combine the herbs, vinegar, mustard, salt to taste, and the pepper in a medium

bowl and whisk in both olive oils. The vinaigrette will keep covered in the refrigerator for up to 2 days.

3. Add the leeks to the vinaigrette and marinate at room temperature for 1 hour. Toss all the ingredients again just before serving.

BLANCHING VEGETABLES

Blanching is an easy technique we use every day in our kitchen. The process involves quickly boiling vegetables in salted water until they are almost cooked, then plunging them into a bath of ice water for a minute or two to stop the cooking and preserve the bright color of the vegetables. Just before serving, you can reheat them in a little stock and butter, or just some brown butter (page 26), which brings them to the perfectly cooked stage. You can also simply dress the vegetables with a vinaigrette (page 40) and serve them at room temperature.

Blanching in advance makes it easy to prepare vegetables quickly at serving time, which is useful when you're preparing a complicated dinner for guests. But the technique is about more than control and convenience. The ice water seems to "shock" the vegetables into a form of suspended animation; they taste fresher and cleaner than veggies cooked straight through, and they definitely stay greener. Blanching also preserves more nutrients because the vegetables don't cook as long.

To blanch vegetables, use a big pot with lots of boiling salted water. The more water, the quicker it will return to the boil after adding the vegetables. Salt adds flavor and also keeps bright green veggies from discoloring. Although it's not required, a large mesh basket with a handle makes the job much easier. Simply fill the basket with the vegetables, then lower it first into the boiling water, then later into the ice bath. That way you don't have to stand around picking ice out of the vegetables. And if you're blanching multiple batches, you can keep the water boiling away in between. (Alternatively, just drop the vegetables in the boiling water and drain in a colander before transferring them to the ice bath.)

Cooking time varies depending on the type of vegetable and how fresh it is. As a general rule, check after a couple of minutes in the boiling water; the vegetable should still have a bit of bite when you take it out.

Grilled Asparagus
with Shaved Reggiano Parmesan

You can never have too much asparagus in the spring, and you can never get your grill out too early. This is a classic Italian way of serving asparagus, and it's one of our favorites. Quickly browning asparagus on the grill gives it a rustic look and retains its fresh, crunchy texture. If you like, arrange the asparagus on top of thinly sliced Parma ham and serve with toasted bread on the side.

Makes 6 servings

1 (4-ounce) chunk Reggiano Parmesan
Kosher salt
36 spears asparagus, preferably pencil thin, tough ends trimmed
2 tablespoons extra-virgin olive oil
Freshly ground black pepper

1. Using a sharp vegetable peeler, shave the Parmesan into curls and set aside.

2. In a large pot bring 2 quarts water and 1 tablespoon salt to a boil. Fill a medium bowl halfway with ice water. Put the asparagus in the pot and cook for 30 seconds. Drain the asparagus in a colander and immediately plunge into the ice water. As soon as the asparagus is cold, remove it from the ice water and wrap it in a clean kitchen towel to dry.

3. Toss the asparagus and olive oil in a bowl and sprinkle with salt and pepper to taste.

4. Start a charcoal or gas grill.

5. Grill the asparagus over a medium-hot fire for about 30 seconds until distinct charred lines form on the spears; roll them over and cook for another 30 seconds. Make sure the spears stay perpendicular to the grill, so they don't fall through. Arrange the asparagus on a platter or individual plates, sprinkle the top with the Parmesan curls, and serve at once.

Baby Bok Choy with Chives and Smoked Ham

In the spring we grow row upon row of bok choy in our greenhouse. Outside one of the first herbs to appear is chives, so the two ingredients combined are a natural for us. Although a cold frame or greenhouse allows earlier harvest of greens and lettuce, bok choy are quite hardy and can be started outdoors as soon as the ground has thawed enough to be worked. Serve this side dish with Grilled Rib-Eye Steak (page 154) or Lemongrass and Lemon Roasted Chicken (page 152).

Makes 6 servings

2 tablespoons vegetable oil
6 cloves garlic, peeled and thinly sliced
6 heads baby bok choy, leaves pulled apart, washed, and dried
½ cup Chicken Stock (page 23)
2 teaspoons soy sauce
4 ounces Smithfield or other smoked ham, cut into 1 x ¼-inch matchsticks
1 bunch chives, cut into 1-inch lengths, about ½ cup

1. In a large sauté pan or wok warm the oil over medium-high heat until just smoking. Add the garlic and sauté, stirring frequently, until barely golden brown, about 2 minutes.

2. Add the bok choy and sauté, stirring constantly, until the leaves start to wilt. Add the chicken stock, soy sauce, and ham and cook until the liquid is reduced by half.

3. Transfer the bok choy to a serving dish. Sprinkle with the chives and serve at once.

NOTES
1. You can leave out the ham and substitute Vegetable Stock (page 24) for the chicken stock if you wish.

2. Bacon can be substituted for the ham; add it to the pan with the garlic.

Braised Egyptian Onions in Amarone Wine

Egyptian onions appear in late spring. The bulb looks like a shallot, but the plant is distinguished by a dramatic seed pod that hangs from a shoot two feet off the ground. They self-sow and, like most onions, are easy to grow. In the kitchen, Egyptian onions are versatile, lending themselves well to roasting and sautéing. We like this preparation because it can be used as a chunky sauce with beef, veal, or pork, but it is also good with meaty fish such as salmon or tuna. Shallots can be substituted for the Egyptian onions.

Amarone is a rich, velvety red wine from the Italian Veneto region that is made with grapes partially dried in the sun—raisin wine, if you will. The technique, which dates back to ancient Roman times, yields a flavor that is much more concentrated (almost like a liqueur) than wines made from fresh grapes. The closest substitute would be a rich Italian red wine like Brunello or Barolo.

Makes 6 servings

18 Egyptian onions or medium shallots
1 cup Amarone, Brunello, or Barolo
¼ cup raisins
¼ cup sugar
3 sprigs rosemary
12 whole black peppercorns

1. Preheat the oven to 300 degrees F.
2. Cut off the green part and the root end of the onions. Peel off the outer skin.
3. In a casserole combine all the other ingredients, then add the onions. Cover the casserole with foil or a lid and bake for 30 minutes until the onions are very tender. Uncover and cook for another 20 minutes until the liquid is reduced by half and is thick and syrupy. Remove the rosemary sprigs and serve.

NOTE: The onions can be roasted a day in advance and kept refrigerated in a covered nonreactive container. Reheat on the stove or in the oven before serving.

ONIONS

Onions are easy to grow, ignored by pests, and take up very little space. What more could you ask for? They also give you a choice in planting: Bulbing onions can be grown from seed (started indoors in late winter or sown directly in the ground in spring) or from tiny onion bulbs, which are called sets. We grow them both ways at Arrows. Our onion beds always include small Italian Cippoline types (great for shish kabobs and for braising), scallions, red onions (for slicing and late-summer salads), and Walla Walla—a big yellow onion that's almost as mild as the Georgia-grown Vidalia but more suited to the North.

Pay attention to climate recommendations when buying onion seeds or sets because they are day-length sensitive; to thrive, they need a certain number of daylight hours, which is determined by your latitude. Also note that some onions are suitable for long storage (put them in a basket in a cool dark place like the garage, and you'll have onions all winter), while others are better eaten right away (like Walla Wallas).

We also grow two types of shallots (always from bulbs) and loads of leeks from seed. We harvest our leeks small, but if you want them to get massive, start the seeds in February and transplant them when they are pencil size. Harvest soon after the first frost. If you wait until the ground freezes to pull them, they'll go nowhere.

One of our favorite onions to grow is the Egyptian, also called Walking Onion (right). In the spring it produces delicious green stalks, which can be used like scallions; by fall, the plants send up shoots topped by tiny brown bulbils. These so-called top sets can be cut off, stored wrapped in the refrigerator, and replanted in spring, when the process begins all over again. They make it incredibly easy to have scallions every year.

Gratin of Ramps and Morels

Spring comes late in Maine, and even with a greenhouse and cold frames, our garden is limited in the early season. So we augment our crops by paying homage to spring in other regions—with morels from the Northwest and ramps from the Midwest. Morels are distinctive mushrooms with netted caps and a meaty flavor. Ramps are wild scallion-type onions with broad leaves that look like lily-of-the-valley; their flavor is less spicy than cultivated scallions and more garlicky. Morels and ramps can be found in farmers' markets, specialty stores, and online. This gratin is extremely simple, and components of the dish can even be made a day ahead of time. Serve as a first course or accompaniment to roast lamb or grilled steaks.

Makes 6 servings

24 ramps
Kosher salt
4 tablespoons (½ stick) unsalted butter
4 ounces morel mushrooms, cleaned and trimmed
½ teaspoon freshly ground black pepper
¼ cup champagne vinegar
2 tablespoons finely chopped tarragon
½ cup olive oil
½ cup Tomato Concassé (page 179)
4 ounces Gruyère cheese, thinly sliced

1. Cut off the ends of the ramps, making sure to cut just the roots or the ramps will fall apart. Immerse the ramps in a large bowl of cold water. Gently wash to remove any sand or dirt and peel off the thin outermost layer.

2. In a large pot bring 2 quarts water and 1 tablespoon salt to a boil. Fill a medium bowl halfway with ice water. Add the ramps to the pot and boil for 30 seconds. Drain the ramps in a colander and submerge immediately in the ice water. When the ramps are thoroughly chilled, remove them from the water and wrap in a clean kitchen towel to dry.

3. Melt the butter in a large sauté pan over medium heat. Add the morels and season with 1 teaspoon salt. Cook, stirring, over medium-high heat until the morels are tender

and the liquid in the pan is evaporated, 10 to 12 minutes. Transfer the morels to a plate to cool.

4. Preheat the oven to 425 degrees F.

5. In a large bowl combine 1 teaspoon salt, the pepper, vinegar, and tarragon. Gradually whisk in the olive oil. Add the ramps, morels, and tomato concassé and toss to coat evenly.

6. Transfer the ramp mixture to a large shallow baking dish and cover with the cheese. Bake until the cheese is golden and bubbling, about 15 minutes. Serve at once.

NOTES

1. The ramps and morels can be cooked a day in advance. The vinaigrette also can be prepared a day ahead but do not add the ramps, mushrooms, or tomato concassé.

2. If you cannot find spring ramps, substitute scallions or the smallest leeks you can find.

DIGGING THE DIRT:
COMPOST AND SOIL STRUCTURE

Soil is quite literally the foundation of your garden, yet many people disregard it because digging dirt isn't as much fun as starting seedlings or planting flowers. But if your soil is poor, you'll be fighting an uphill battle all season. Much better to roll up your sleeves beforehand and get the soil in shape. Improving soil is not a matter of dumping in a bunch of fertilizer, which eventually leaves the soil burnt out and depleted. You need to change the structure of your dirt.

By far the most common garden problem is clay soil. Clay retains too much moisture for most plants; the roots get "cold feet," which slows growth and often kills them. At the other extreme, sandy soil drains too quickly, drawing nourishment away from the roots. Ideal soil is a mix of clay, sand, and compost, which is organic matter that provides both nutrients and structure. Good soil is "loamy"; it feels crumbly and moist but not slippery (a sign of too much clay) or granulated (excessive sand).

If your soil seems poor based on that description, take heart: almost no one has perfect soil naturally. The way to improve both clay and sandy soils is to add compost, lots of it. You can make your own from kitchen scraps, but you probably won't get nearly as much as you need. Plan on buying compost, every year, at a garden center. It comes in bags, and there are many different kinds ranging from rotted seaweed to peat moss to bat guano. (Avoid cottonseed meal and mushroom compost, both of which contain pesticide residues.) And make sure any compost you buy has no sewage sludge (check the label) because it might include dangerous chemicals that are the residue of industrial processes. If you have a big garden, find someone local who can deliver compost by the truckload; you'll save a lot of money in the long run. An entire dump truck of compost might seem excessive, but trust us—the pile won't look nearly so big when it's sitting next to your garden. Besides compost doesn't go bad; it only gets better with age.

At Arrows we use a lot of composted manure, mostly from cows. If buying manure from a local source, inspect it carefully beforehand and ask questions. It should be at least a year old; fresh manure can burn plant roots and actually suck nitrogen out of the soil as it decomposes. It can also be unsanitary. You want manure that has already begun to decompose, a process that generates considerable heat, killing pathogens and weed seeds. It should smell and look earthy. If it contains earthworms, all the better, but you don't want manure with big white grubs, which are often the larvae of plant- and lawn-devouring beetles. Horse manure tends to have a lot of weed seeds, which pass easily through the animal's digestive tract; if we had horses we would certainly use it, but we wouldn't go looking for it otherwise. Chicken and sheep manures are quite strong and need to be thoroughly decomposed—two years is ideal—before it can be spread on a garden.

Amending your soil doesn't have to be back-breaking labor. You can rent a rototiller from most garden centers. If you have a huge plot and live anywhere near the countryside, it's easy to find a farmer who will show up with his tractor and do the job in an hour. If you've got a pile of compost to spread, make sure the tractor has a front loader. (Tractor work costs about $40 an hour here in Maine, which covers labor and depreciation on these expensive machines.)

Another soil enhancer we use at Arrows is called greensand, which is a mineral additive that provides potassium (tomatoes and peppers are heavy potassium feeders) and improves drainage. It is mined from deposits that were once part of the ocean floor. We also use lime, which adds alkalinity to our acidic Maine soi!.

Many other mineral balancers are available, depending on your needs. You can buy inexpensive soil test kits at garden centers, but they only tell you what's wrong, not how to fix it. Much better is what we do: Send soil samples to the county extension office (check in your local phone book for your state's agricultural department) every year. For about $10, they'll give you a complete analysis of your soil and recommend solutions. Just this past year, we learned of several new deficiencies in our garden soil that we didn't have the year before. What a bargain! Consider it cheap health care for your garden. ᴓ

Asparagus and Dry Jack Cheese Custard

Monterey Jack cheese, which was first made in Carmel Valley, California, has become a supermarket staple. Fewer people are familiar with Dry Jack, its sophisticated cousin. According to legend, a delivery of Monterey Jack was left in a San Francisco store shortly before the big earthquake of 1906. After the quake, the cheese was forgotten in a cool back room for several weeks. When the grocer discovered the cheese, he assumed it was ruined. To his surprise, it tasted delicious. Thus began the practice of drying Jack cheese. Whether the legend is true or not, Dry Jack is a wonderful creamy hard cheese, a bit like fine Parmesan. And like Parmesan, it is perfect with asparagus. Look for Dry Jack at supermarkets or specialty cheese shops. Alternatively, you can substitute Reggiano Parmesan or Asiago cheese. These custards go well with roasted meat or fish, or could be served as a light lunch along with a salad.

Makes 6 servings

Kosher salt
1 bunch (18 spears) medium asparagus, tough ends trimmed
1 cup heavy cream
2 large eggs
1 large egg yolk
¼ cup grated Dry Jack cheese

1. In a large pot bring 2 quarts water and 1 tablespoon salt to a boil. Fill a medium bowl halfway with ice water. Put the asparagus in the pot, cook for 1 minute, and drain. Submerge the asparagus immediately in the ice water. As soon as the asparagus are completely chilled, remove from the ice water and wrap in a clean kitchen towel to dry.

2. Transfer the asparagus to a food processor fitted with the metal blade and process for about 30 seconds. (Alternatively, run the asparagus through a food mill.) Stop the machine and scrape down the bowl with a rubber spatula. Process for another 30 seconds until the purée is smooth.

3. In a bowl whisk together the cream, eggs, and egg yolk. Add the asparagus purée, cheese, and 1½ teaspoons salt and whisk together.

4. Preheat the oven to 350 degrees F.

5. Divide the custard evenly among six 4-ounce ramekins. Arrange the ramekins in a

roasting pan, spacing them evenly. Carefully pour ½ inch hot water into the bottom of the pan. Bake for 30 to 40 minutes until the custards seem firm when the ramekins are gently tapped. Serve at once or keep covered in a warm place for up to 1 hour.

NOTE: You can use foil ramekins instead of ceramic ones. Once the custards are baked, let them set for 5 minutes. With a paring knife, poke a tiny slit in the bottom of each foil cup, then invert onto serving plates. Lift the foil cups off the custards and serve.

Asparagus and Hollandaise Gratin

What takes this dish into another dimension is the final step of browning the hollandaise under the broiler, which adds a deeper, almost caramel flavor to the asparagus. Try it with the tender young spears of early spring, when it's still cold outside. We use whole butter (instead of clarified) to make our hollandaise because we feel it makes a lighter and tastier sauce.

Makes 6 servings

Kosher salt
36 thin spears asparagus, tough ends trimmed
$\frac{1}{4}$ cup heavy cream
4 large egg yolks
2 teaspoons freshly squeezed lemon juice
8 tablespoons (1 stick) unsalted butter, cold
$\frac{1}{4}$ teaspoon freshly ground black pepper

1. In a large pot bring 2 quarts water and 1 tablespoon salt to a boil. Fill a medium bowl halfway with ice water. Put the asparagus in the pot and cook for 1 minute. Drain the asparagus and submerge them immediately in the ice water. As soon as the asparagus are completely chilled, remove them from the ice water and wrap them in a clean kitchen towel to dry. Arrange the asparagus in two or three layers in a shallow baking dish.

2. Preheat the broiler.

3. Whisk the heavy cream in a bowl until thick but not too stiff. When you lift the whisk, the cream should fall in very soft ribbons.

4. Bring 1 inch water to a simmer in the bottom part of a double boiler. Combine the egg yolks and lemon juice in the top part of the double boiler, set over the bottom part, and whisk constantly until the egg mixture turns light in color and thickens, about 5 minutes. Be careful to keep the water at a gentle simmer to keep the eggs from scrambling. Gradually start adding the butter 1 tablespoon at a time. After all of the butter has been added, remove the bowl from the heat and whisk in the cream, $1\frac{1}{2}$ teaspoons salt, and the pepper.

5. Ladle the hollandaise over the asparagus and put the dish under the broiler. Broil

until the sauce starts to brown, less than a minute; watch it carefully so it does not burn. Remove from the broiler and serve at once.

BEDTIME STORY:
USING RAISED BEDS TO EXTEND THE SEASON

Harvesting lettuce and other greens from a Maine garden in mid-April is quite a challenge, for most northern gardeners have barely begun planting. Sometimes guests at Arrows in early spring have a hard time believing their salads come from our own garden—until we point them out the backdoor and let them see for themselves.

Our secret is raised beds, which give us a real jump on the season—especially when covered with clear Plexiglas, which turns them into miniature greenhouses called cold frames. At Arrows, where we harvest 120 heads of lettuce every week in the summer, we use 40 raised beds, each of them 6 x 4-feet and held in place by cedar planking. For home gardeners, one such bed is probably enough. It's simple to build—think of it as a sandbox for plants—and we promise it will transform the way you garden.

In cold climates what delays spring planting is soil temperature; you can't start seeds in ground that's frozen or even mucky from melting snow. Every spring becomes a waiting game—waiting for soil that's drained and warm.

But because the soil in a raised bed is above the ground, air and warmth circulate all around it, and it drains quickly. When the outside ground is still frozen, covered raised beds can be warm enough to plant lettuce and greens. We're talking greens in mid-March in Maine—an amazing concept!

For covers we use clear Plexiglas (check your Yellow Pages for dealers); it is lighter and stronger than glass and can be screwed into a simple wooden frame. Some people recycle old window panes; make sure they don't have loose or peeling paint, which could contain lead. Either way, you'll want to attach the cover with hinges on one long side of the bed, so it can be opened easily. A notched two-by-four, with one end stuck into the ground, holds the lid open on hot days.

In late spring we remove the plastic covers entirely and replace them with a wire-mesh frame. The mesh supports a breathable fabric row cover that lets in water and light but keeps out pests, especially flea beetles, tiny bugs with a big appetite for greens. These row covers, available by mail from Johnny's Seeds and at many garden centers, are a fantastic way to control bugs without spraying poisons. We use them religiously at Arrows, and for the sake of our environment, we hope you will too.

Once you build your cold frame, fill it two-thirds of the way with a good rich topsoil (available bagged at garden centers or delivered in bulk from a landscaper) that includes about 30 percent sand for good drainage. Then add about half of a 3.8-cubic-foot bale of peat moss and a 2-inch layer of compost. (We like a mixture of decayed manure, vegetable matter, and seaweed.) Mix it all together thoroughly along with a balanced organic fertilizer like Pro-Gro. Depending on your soil's pH level, you may also need to add dolomitic lime (to reduce acidity) and greensand (a mineral additive that builds potassium and strong root growth). We test the pH of every bed every spring, using kits available from seed suppliers. It's a good idea to do the same in your own garden.

By the way, your raised bed and cold frame also extends the growing season on the back end, keeping you in fresh lettuce through Thanksgiving. With all the money you'll save on grocery-store greens, you may decide to build a second raised bed next year. ❧

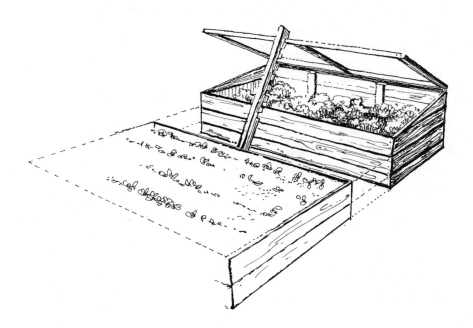

Creamy Goat Cheese Toasts

These cheese toasts go well with salads, as part of an antipasto platter, or just on their own as a canapé. If you like, add a tablespoon of chopped flat-leaf parsley or a teaspoon of chopped thyme leaves.

Makes 12 toasts

12 (¼-inch) slices sourdough baguette
2 tablespoons olive oil
2 ounces mild fresh goat cheese
1 teaspoon freshly squeezed lemon juice
1 teaspoon kosher salt
½ teaspoon freshly ground black pepper
¼ cup heavy cream

1. Preheat the oven to 325 degrees F.
2. Toss the bread slices in a bowl with the olive oil. Transfer to a baking sheet and bake until very light golden brown, about 8 minutes. Remove from the oven and set aside to cool.
3. Put the goat cheese in a bowl and break it up with a spoon. Stir in the lemon juice, salt, and pepper, then gradually work in the cream. The goat cheese mixture can be made a day ahead and kept well covered in the refrigerator.
4. Using a butter knife, spread the goat cheese on the toasts.

Scallion Pancakes

Scallion pancakes go great with lots of our Asian-inspired dishes, such as Lemongrass and Lemon Roasted Chicken (page 152), Crispy Trout with Ginger and Lemongrass (page 47), and Sautéed Halibut with Thai Red Curry (page 148). But these pancakes can take the place of bread at just about any meal.

Makes 20 pancakes

3½ cups all-purpose flour
12 tablespoons (1½ sticks) unsalted butter, cold, cut into cubes
1 tablespoon kosher salt
¾ to 1 cup water, at room temperature
2 tablespoons vegetable oil
12 scallions, green part only, washed, dried, and thinly sliced

1. In the bowl of a food processor fitted with the metal blade, combine the flour, butter, and salt, and pulse until the mixture resembles cornmeal. (Alternatively, combine the ingredients by hand or with a pastry cutter in a large bowl.) While pulsing, pour ¾ cup water through the machine's feed tube in a steady stream until the dough comes together. If the dough does not come together, add the remaining water 1 tablespoon at a time. Turn the mixture onto a worktable and knead together just once or twice to combine. Wrap in plastic wrap and let rest for 30 minutes to 1 hour. You can keep the dough covered in the refrigerator for up to 1 day; bring to room temperature before proceeding.

2. Divide the dough into 20 equal balls and keep covered with a clean kitchen towel so that the dough doesn't dry out. On a well-floured table roll 1 piece of dough into a round 7 to 8 inches in diameter. Brush with oil and sprinkle with scallions to cover the surface. Starting at one edge, roll up the dough jellyroll fashion, then coil the roll into a spiral, like a cinnamon roll. Set the spiral aside, cover, and roll and shape the remaining balls in the same manner.

3. Starting with the first one, roll each piece again into a 7- to 8-inch circle. While working on one piece, remember to keep the remaining bits of dough covered. Do not stack the finished pancakes.

4. Warm a heavy sauté pan over medium-high heat. Add a pancake to the pan and cook for about 1 minute until the underside is golden brown. Flip and cook the other

side for 1 minute. Transfer to a plate and cover with a clean kitchen towel to keep warm. Repeat with the remaining pancakes, adding each to the stack on the plate as it is finished. If not serving immediately, you can wrap the pancakes in foil and store at room temperature for up to 1 day. Just before serving, reheat the wrapped stack for 10 minutes in an oven that has been preheated to 350 degrees F.

10 Veggies That Let You Have a Life

In our years of gardening at a busy restaurant, we've learned to pay special respect to crops that are easy to grow and care for. Here's our top-ten list of low-maintenance veggies—perfect for a beginning gardener or a busy summer.

Beans You have two choices: bush-type or the longer vining pole-type. Bush beans are easier (you don't need to set up support poles), but they take up more room at ground level. Some beans are best when harvested young, as are green beans; others are meant to stay on the vine until they dry, when they are shucked for soup beans. Another variety is the shell bean, such as the French Flambeau or the classic lima. Wait until they've swelled in the pod, then harvest, shuck, and cook.

Beets Beets take so little care, the main danger is forgetting about them until they get huge and tough. Harvest when medium-size, about as big as a baseball, or smaller.

Carrots The only real work with carrots is tilling your soil well, so they grow straight and long.

Garlic Plant the bulbs in fall and harvest the garlic in August. (It keeps for months in a cool, dark place like the garage.) That's it. If you've only had supermarket garlic, prepare yourself for the real thing, which is as juicy as an apple and almost as sweet. Save some heads to plant for next year, and you'll never buy garlic again.

Lettuce All lettuce grows quickly as long as it isn't too hot. If there's any left by summer, it will bolt and start to taste bitter. Pull it up and sow new seeds for a fall crop.

Onions Pests in onions are virtually nonexistent. For the biggest onion crop, keep the bed weed free; mulching helps slow weeds.

Parsnips Parsnips will last through the winter if you leave them in the ground. In fact, frost tends to sweeten them.

Peas Peas need a trellis or some kind of support but little care beyond that. They don't like heat and will shrivel and fade by mid-July. You can plant another crop then for fall, although it won't do as well as the spring crop.

Radishes Keep radishes well watered, and in just under a month they'll be ready.

Spinach As long as your soil isn't too acidic, spinach is easy to grow in the spring and fall, when it doesn't bolt quickly.

Potato-Chive Bread

We love going outside and grabbing handfuls of fresh chives, which come up early in spring and stick around until late fall. They are a classic garnish for baked potatoes, which benefit from the green color and strong flavor accent. Here we are going for a similar taste but in a bread. This is a great way to use leftover mashed potatoes.

Makes two 8 by 5-inch loaves

1½ (¼-ounce) envelopes active dry yeast
1 cup lukewarm water
5 cups all-purpose flour
½ cup Chive Mashed Potatoes (page 175)
6 tablespoons unsalted butter, very soft
4 teaspoons sugar
2¼ teaspoons kosher salt
¾ cup whole milk, lukewarm

1. In a small bowl dissolve the yeast in ¼ cup of the warm water.

2. In the bowl of a standing mixer fitted with the dough hook, combine the flour, mashed potatoes, butter, sugar, and salt.

3. Pour the milk and the remaining ¾ cup water over the dissolved yeast and stir to combine. With the mixer running on low speed, start adding the liquid to moisten the dry ingredients. Once all of the liquid has been added, increase the speed to medium and mix until the dough pulls away from the sides of the bowl, about 3 minutes. If the dough is too wet, add a bit more flour, a teaspoonful at a time. If it is too dry and doesn't come together, add a bit more water, a teaspoonful at a time. Mix on medium speed for about 6 minutes until the dough is elastic. (Alternatively, combine the yeast mixture with the other dough ingredients in a large bowl, then turn it out onto a lightly floured board and knead by hand until it is smooth and elastic.)

4. Transfer the dough to an oiled bowl and cover with a large clean plastic bag, leaving room for the dough to rise. Let rise in a warm place (80 to 85 degrees F) until doubled in size and light to the touch, about 45 to 60 minutes.

5. Oil two 8 x 5-inch loaf pans and set aside.

6. Turn the dough onto a lightly floured work surface and divide it in half. Roll out

each piece into a 14 x 7-inch rectangle. Starting from one of the short sides, roll up each rectangle like a jellyroll, pinching the ends and seams to seal. Place the loaves, seam side down, in the prepared pans. Cover the loaves with a clean cloth and let rise again in a warm place until doubled in size, 30 to 45 minutes. The dough should rise about 1 inch above the top of the pans, and when the dough is lightly poked, an indentation should remain.

7. Preheat the oven to 350 degrees F.

8. Bake for 35 to 45 minutes until the loaves sound hollow when tapped. Remove immediately from the pans and cool on racks. The bread will keep, well wrapped, at room temperature for up to a day or frozen up to a week.

DESSERTS

GUESS WHO'S COMING TO DINNER?

Our former pastry chef Lucia's first night at Arrows was one for the record books. It was the summer of 1991, and she was a little anxious about starting her new job. It didn't help when the staff began joking that Julia Child was coming for dinner. Restaurant workers are always playing games on new employees—it's like an initiation, to see who measures up. Lucia shook her head and minded her own business.

But around eight o'clock, everybody started acting really nervous—as if it were *their* first night on the job. And then Lucia heard that unmistakable voice, coming through the kitchen door. Suddenly there she was—Julia Child—hovering over Lucia's standing mixer. "I just *love* to see women in the kitchen!" she bellowed. "How long have you worked here?" Well, of course, Lucia had to tell her it was her first night, and they both laughed.

Cooking for Julia Child was quite an honor for all of us, but especially for Lucia, who admires the way Julia brought her own style to the cuisine of a country that was not her own—in her case, France. Likewise, Lucia tries to reflect the cooking of her native Mexico in a setting that is about as far from Mexico as one can get in the United States. In her adopted home of Maine, she is always looking for ways to enliven desserts with vibrant colors, which—as she says—are in her Mexican blood. The garden is a good place to begin. Maine blueberries make the most amazing purple ice cream (page 198), and fragrant pink rose petals transform a rustic granita into a brilliant summer palette (page 287).

The garden also inspires with its herbs. We tend to think of herbs in savory dishes, like Onion and Rosemary Focaccia (page 180). But many herbs, like cinnamon basil and chocolate mint, add unexpected flavors to shortcakes (page 183) and other delicate sweets. At Arrows, we infuse caramel sauce with the flavor of lemongrass (page 348).

One technical note: Lucia learned how to cook from her mother, who had her way of doing things. One result is that she does not use the French technique of whisking sugar into egg yolks when she makes custard. (Sorry, Julia!) Instead she adds all the sugar to the milk or cream, which she believes gives superior results. In both cooking and gardening, there is often more than one right way. ✑

Strawberries with Cinnamon–Rhubarb Sauce

Here's a fresh twist on that New England church supper standby, strawberry rhubarb pie. In this dish the strawberries are fresh, which always appeals to us. The cinnamon rhubarb sauce also goes well with Cinnamon Basil Shortcakes (page 183). Try to find organic strawberries or grow your own in lots of compost; they like very rich soil.

Makes 6 servings

1 pound rhubarb stalks, washed and cut into 1-inch pieces
1 cup water
¾ cup sugar
1 teaspoon ground cinnamon
3 cups strawberries, hulled and quartered

1. Stir together the rhubarb, water, sugar, and cinnamon in a medium stainless-steel saucepan. Bring to a boil over medium heat, then reduce the heat to low. Simmer until the rhubarb is tender and falls apart, about 15 minutes.

2. Remove the rhubarb mixture from the heat, transfer to the jar of a blender, and purée until smooth. Strain the purée through a sieve set over a stainless-steel saucepan, pushing through as much of the pulp as possible.

3. Bring the strained purée to a boil over medium heat and reduce, stirring occasionally, until very thick. Remove from the heat. Once cool, the sauce will keep covered in the refrigerator for up to 2 days or in the freezer for up to 1 month. Before using, warm the sauce over low heat, stirring frequently.

4. Arrange the strawberries in 6 bowls and top with the warm sauce.

DEER DIARY

Deer have become serious pests for suburban gardeners, thanks to residential sprawl and a host of complicated ecological factors. Munching in gardens is not good for deer. They do best on a diet of forest food, not romaine lettuce. Garden feeding also encourages deer to congregate, hastening the spread of disease and causing them to abandon their forest trails. Thus when predators like coyotes arrive, the deer have no escape routes. And when deer head for gardens, they inevitably cross roads—a dangerous situation for both man and beast. The Maine Department of Fisheries and Wildlife advises never feeding or otherwise encouraging deer to hang around your house.

If you plan to fence out deer, think tall—a mature deer can jump a 5-foot fence from a stand. To protect our extensive tulip and other beds from foraging deer (they devour the flower bulbs just as they begin to sprout), we erected a 10-foot-high wire fence all around the restaurant and its yard—but not the vegetable garden, which doesn't seem to interest them much. The visible section of the fence in front of the house comes down before we open in mid-April. By then the deer have moved back into the woods.

Three-Cherry Clafouti with Mint

Clafouti is a cake and custard all in one. It's easy to make and delicious both warm and at room temperature, making it perfect for a spring picnic. We like to use a mix of cherries and types of mint, but this is also good with just one variety of each.

Makes 10 servings

½ cup plus 1 tablespoon sugar
1 cup all-purpose flour
1⅓ cups half-and-half
4 large eggs
1 tablespoon pure vanilla extract
3 cups cherries, preferably a mix of red, black Bing, and Rainier, washed and pitted
1 cup loosely packed mint leaves, preferably a mix of varieties such as pineapple, spearmint, and chocolate, washed and dried

1. Preheat the oven to 350 degrees F.

2. Butter a 10-inch round baking dish, such as a pie dish or a fluted ceramic tart mold, and sprinkle the 1 tablespoon sugar over the bottom of the dish.

3. Stir together the flour and ½ cup sugar. Whisk the half-and-half, eggs, and vanilla together in a bowl, then whisk in the flour mixture to make a smooth batter.

4. Arrange the cherries in the bottom of the dish and slowly pour the batter on top to cover them evenly. Bake for 30 minutes until the custard is puffy, golden brown, and seems set when the dish is tapped lightly. Remove from the oven and set aside to cool for at least 1 hour. The clafouti can be stored well wrapped at room temperature for up to 1 day.

5. When ready to serve, stack the mint leaves in piles of about 8 leaves each. Using a very sharp chef's knife, thinly slice the leaves crosswise.

6. Cut the clafouti into 10 wedges and transfer to individual plates with a metal spatula. Sprinkle with the strips of mint.

HOW TO BUILD HERB BOXES

Even if you live in an apartment, you can grow herbs in boxes indoors (on sunny windowsills) or outside on small terraces. You don't need much—a container of thyme and rosemary is a good way to start—and they add a great deal to your cooking. Boxes also allow harvesting long past the outdoor season if you bring them in to a sunny window before the frost. (How well your herbs do over the winter depends on how much sun they get; if they die, just start new ones in the spring.)

Cedar boxes can be purchased at garden centers, but they tend to be stapled together and rather flimsy. If you have basic woodworking skills and a circular saw, you can easily make your own much better and cheaper. Buy 1-inch stock of genuine red or white cedar, not pressure-treated lumber, which contains poisonous chemicals that can leach into the soil. For fasteners, stick with galvanized or stainless-steel ring-shank nails. If you plan to haul them indoors during winter, don't make the boxes larger than about 1 x 2 feet; otherwise they'll be too heavy to move when filled with soil and water. A foot of depth is plenty. Make sure you drill several drainage holes in the bottom, which should be lined with wire mesh or screening (available at hardware stores or home centers) to keep out rodents. Remember that indoor boxes will need trays underneath them; check garden centers for plastic trays and plan your boxes accordingly. For soil use a sterile peat-based medium like Pro-Mix, which drains well but holds water.

You can paint your boxes if you like (use exterior acrylic, not oil), but it's best to leave them raw. After a year or so, the cedar will turn a lovely silver gray. ◁

Pecan Pound Cake with Balsamic Sabayon and Strawberries

Sabayon is a foamy dessert sauce, the same as Italian zabaglione. Either the sabayon and strawberries or the pound cake makes a fine dessert on its own, but the tart sabayon sauce is a perfect contrast to the sweet, nutty cake.

Makes 6 servings

FOR THE POUND CAKE
16 tablespoons (2 sticks) unsalted butter, at room temperature
1 cup sugar
4 large eggs
$\frac{1}{2}$ cup sour cream
$1\frac{1}{2}$ teaspoons pure vanilla extract
$1\frac{1}{2}$ cups all-purpose flour
$1\frac{1}{4}$ cups toasted chopped pecans (page 272)

1. Preheat the oven to 325 degrees F. Butter and flour a 9 x 5 x 3-inch loaf pan.
2. With an electric mixer (or by hand using a wire whisk), beat the butter and sugar together until light in color, 3 to 5 minutes. Add the eggs one at a time, beating to blend each one. Stir in the sour cream and vanilla. Add the flour and stir until it is incorporated. Fold in the pecans.
3. Spread the batter in the prepared pan. Bake for 50 to 60 minutes until a toothpick inserted in the center comes out clean. Remove from the oven and cool for 5 minutes. Unmold and cool completely on a rack. The cake will keep well wrapped in plastic wrap at room temperature for up to 3 days.

FOR THE SABAYON
4 large egg yolks
5 tablespoons water
$\frac{1}{4}$ cup brown sugar
1 tablespoon balsamic vinegar
$\frac{1}{2}$ cup heavy cream

1. While the pound cake is baking, prepare the sabayon. Fill a large bowl halfway with ice water and set aside. Have ready a smaller stainless-steel bowl that just fits into the ice bath.

2. Bring 1 inch water to a simmer in the bottom part of a double boiler. In the top part of the double boiler, whisk together the egg yolks, water, brown sugar, and vinegar. Place the top part of the double boiler in the bottom pan and cook, whisking the mixture vigorously, until it is thick and tripled in volume. Immediately pour the sabayon into the smaller bowl and set in the ice bath. Continue whisking until the sabayon is cool.

3. Whip the cream with a wire whisk in a bowl until soft peaks form, then fold the cream into the sabayon. Cover and refrigerate until ready to use or up to 1 day.

TO SERVE
2 cups strawberries, hulled and quartered

Cut the cake into 18 slices each ½ inch thick. Fan 3 slices of pound cake on each of 6 plates and top with strawberries and a scoop of sabayon.

Rhubarb Gelato
with Mexican Wedding Cakes

These small, melt-in-your-mouth cookies go by many names around the world: tea cakes in Russia, snowballs in America, and wedding cakes in Mexico, where they are traditionally served at special occasions. You can make either the cakes or the gelato without the other if you wish.

Makes about 1 quart gelato and about 3 dozen (1-inch) cookies, or 6 servings

FOR THE GELATO
1½ pounds rhubarb stalks, washed and cut into 2-inch pieces
    (about 6 cups)
½ cup water
1½ cups sugar
1½ cups whole milk
½ cup heavy cream
6 tablespoons light corn syrup
⅓ cup powdered milk
½ teaspoon kosher salt

1. In a medium stainless-steel pot combine the rhubarb, water, and ½ cup of the sugar. Bring to a simmer over medium heat and cook until the rhubarb falls apart and all of the liquid is evaporated, about 20 minutes. Remove from the heat and set aside to cool.

2. Stir together the milk, cream, corn syrup, powdered milk, salt, and the remaining 1 cup sugar in a medium saucepan set over medium heat. Bring the mixture to a boil. Strain the hot liquid into a bowl and chill completely in the refrigerator.

3. Put the rhubarb in the jar of a blender and purée until smooth. Strain through a sieve, making sure as much rhubarb goes through as possible. Discard the remaining pulp.

4. When the milk base is cold, stir in the strained rhubarb. Freeze in an ice cream machine following the manufacturer's instructions. Serve at once or store in a sealed container in the freezer for up to 1 week.

16 tablespoons (2 sticks) unsalted butter, at room temperature

$\frac{1}{2}$ cup powdered sugar, sifted, plus additional for dusting

1 tablespoon pure vanilla extract

2 cups all-purpose flour

1 cup lightly toasted pecans (page 272)

1. Preheat the oven to 350 degrees F.

2. With an electric mixer (or by hand using a wire whisk), beat the butter, sugar, and vanilla on medium speed until light and fluffy, 3 to 5 minutes.

3. Combine the flour and pecans in the bowl of a food processor fitted with the metal blade and process for 1 to 2 minutes until the nuts are finely ground. Add the flour mixture to the butter and stir until the dough holds together.

4. Form the dough into 1-inch balls and arrange 1 inch apart on a parchment-lined cookie sheet. Bake for 10 to 15 minutes until light golden but not brown. The bottom will be darker than the top, so watch them carefully. Cool for about 5 minutes, then dust with or roll in powdered sugar. Dust again if the sugar is absorbed into the dough; the sugar should coat the outside of the cookies completely.

TO SERVE

Arrange 2 scoops gelato in each of 6 chilled bowls. Tuck a couple of cookies in each bowl or pass them separately on a plate.

Honey-Lavender Ice Cream

Every spring our pastry chef heads for the lavender; she really looks forward to its wonderful fragrance in the garden. When she goes out to gather garnishes for desserts, she always touches the lavender so that the fragrance lingers in her hands. Bees are also attracted to lavender, the nectar of which makes excellent honey. Any type of honey will do in this recipe, but we prefer a lighter honey, such as clover. Dark honey like buckwheat has a more intense flavor that can mask the aroma of the lavender.

Makes about 1½ pints, or 6 servings

2 cups whole milk
2 cups heavy cream
½ cup sugar
4 tablespoons fresh or 2 tablespoons dried lavender flowers,
    plus additional for serving
10 large egg yolks
½ cup honey

1. Fill a large bowl halfway with ice water. Have ready a smaller bowl that fits inside the ice bath, and a fine sieve.

2. Stir together the milk, cream, sugar, and lavender flowers in a large saucepan and bring to a boil. Take the saucepan off the heat, cover, and let the mixture steep for 20 minutes.

3. Whisk together the egg yolks and honey in a large bowl. Slowly pour the hot liquid into the yolk mixture, gently whisking to combine. Return the mixture to the saucepan and cook, stirring constantly with a wooden spoon, over medium heat until the mixture reaches a temperature of 180 degrees F or it thickens just enough to coat the back of a spoon. Immediately strain the mixture through the fine sieve into the smaller bowl, pressing on the lavender to extract the flavor, and place the bowl in the ice bath. Stir occasionally until completely chilled.

4. Freeze the mixture in an ice cream machine following the manufacturer's instructions. Serve at once or store the ice cream in a sealed container in the freezer for up to 1 week.

5. Scoop the ice cream into 6 chilled dessert bowls and sprinkle with lavender flowers.

FLOWER POWER

Every kitchen garden should include flowers, and not just for beauty. For one thing, many flowers are edible (see page 191), adding sublime flavor and perfume—not to mention color—to salads and desserts. Flowers also attract honeybees that pollinate many vegetables and fruits, increasing production. Finally, some flowers, including marigolds, deter bugs like aphids.

At Arrows we grow thousands of flowers—annuals, perennials, and bulbs—for food, for arrangements, and for the fun of it. We start most flowers, including perennials, from seed indoors. But we also buy plugs (potted perennials that have been growing for about a year) when we need to get them off to a quick start. We love wildflowers like Maine's legendary lupines and black-eyed Susans (*Rudbeckia*) and the flowering trees and bushes—lilacs, apples, and forsythia. In the springtime nothing is more beautiful and pure than tulips and daffodils.

To get the most cut flowers out of your garden, remove spent blossoms (gardeners call it deadheading) so the plant's energy goes to making new flowers, not seed pods. It's best to cut flowers in the morning, when the stems are full of water they've absorbed overnight. Put the cut stems directly into a bucket of water (bring it to the garden with you). Inside keep arrangements out of direct sunlight.

10 Flowers to Grow in Your Garden

Aster   Brought from the colder regions of China by a Jesuit missionary in the eighteenth century, asters come in a range of colors, with blossoms from 2 to 5 inches across on stalks from 2 to 3 feet, depending on the variety. It's best to start seeds indoors in late winter.

Bachelor's Button   Also called cornflower, these annuals make 1-inch flowers in shades of red, white, and blue on 2-foot stalks. They are easy to grow directly from seed after the last frost.

Delphinium   A perennial, and one of the few truly blue (as opposed to purplish) flowers, with petals borne on 2-foot-high spikes. They last forever in a vase; outdoors, they make the garden come alive.

Gladiola   People tend to think of them as funeral flowers, which is too bad. They're big and have a lot of color, and they look fantastic in the garden or in a vase.

Larkspur   The multicolored flowers grow on 4-foot spikes, which are best cut when about half the blooms have opened. Larkspur makes excellent dried arrangements; just hang bunches upside down until dry.

Lily   These majestic plants can tower 6 feet or higher, but most are in the 3-foot range. Orange day lilies are the classic wild version, and they line roadsides in Maine during July and August. Thanks to breeders who continue to develop new hybrids, the choice of color and style is literally endless; every year, new lilies come out. Buy quality bulbs and you'll get many more blossoms on the stalk.

Peony   Dramatic and sweet smelling, this fist-sized perennial doesn't last long as a cut flower. The plant lasts decades in the garden, however.

Phlox   We like the taller varieties, which grow to about 2 feet and attract hummingbirds. The red and white flowers grow in 3- to 4-inch clusters.

Sunflower   We grow twenty types, from the towering Moonwalker to the pot-sized Sonja. Unusual varieties include Moulin Rouge, which has burgundy to black petals, and Autumn Beauty, with flowers the color of autumn leaves. For earliest bloom, we start sunflowers in small pots in the greenhouse, but you can grow them directly from seed as well.

Zinnia   Easy to grow from seed, zinnias are one of the showiest annuals in the garden. Their orange, yellow, red, and even white flowers grow as large as 6 inches on stalks reaching 4 feet. They tend to flop with overhead watering, so keep the sprinkler away. ᴼ—

SUMMER

HIGH SEASON

Maine's license plate has boasted *Vacationland* since the 1930s, and with good reason. California may have a corner on the endless summer, but no place in the United States evokes summer vacation like Maine. The man who first defined the art of getting away, nineteenth-century naturalist Henry David Thoreau, celebrated the state's vast wilderness in his book *The Maine Woods*. Environmental pioneer Rachel Carson was inspired by Maine's island-studded coast to write *The Sea Around Us* in 1950. Thanks to Robert McCloskey's best-selling *Blueberries for Sal,* every child knows that Maine's most famous summer crop goes "kuplink, kuplank, kuplunk" when dropped in a little tin pail. And Hollywood figured out long ago that Maine's leisurely pace could inspire characters with a bit *too* much time on their hands. Searing dramas like *Peyton Place, A Summer Place,* and *In the Bedroom* were set or filmed in Maine, as was the perennially foggy Gothic soap opera *Dark Shadows*.

Happily enough, the Maine of fiction and fantasy largely exists. It's still the most forested state in the union, with the highest percentage of seasonal homes, according to the 2000 Census. City kids from Boston and New York still flock to the Pine Tree State for summer camp during July and August, when Maine's population triples. Rich folk with big homes on small islands still gas up their seaplanes at the public landing, where they address the harbormaster as "sir." Less formal folks kick back in cabins, in canoes, and over the fire pit. From the coast to the foothills of rugged Mount Katahdin (northern terminus of the Appalachian Trail), the Maine landscape is still largely rural, and carpeted in blueberries, lupine, and daylilies. It's a state of two-lane roads that wind past small farms with big barns, and general stores with wide porches, pickle barrels, and penny candy. It's a place where merchants leave the cash register open when they go out back, so customers can make their own change. If you go by the thermometer, summer is the shortest season in Maine. But by any other measure, it's the season when time stands still.

Of course, not everyone in Maine is lying around all summer. Among the hardest-working summer people are lobstermen, blueberry pickers—and restaurant owners. At Arrows summer is the defining season of the year, and not just because the restaurant is packed every night. For us summer is the culmination of all our plans, the season when we can get really creative with the bounty of our garden—bushels of tomatoes and peppers in every color, riots of roses and nasturtiums, dozens of herbs, and every kind of berry imaginable. The daily harvest in our summer garden takes five hours!

Using that harvest in new and different ways is always a challenge. It's enormously satisfying to do your grocery shopping at home, which is what happens when you have your own garden. But even a small home garden can become intimidating by August, when seedlings you could barely glimpse in May are now exploding over the fence and sagging under the weight of ripe vegetables. As anyone with children knows, the miracle of growth can also be a little scary! What do you do with all that stuff?

But if you concentrate on what's absolutely freshest, it's hard to go wrong. Even in the August garden, different crops reach their peaks of ripeness and flavor at different moments. Tomatoes can stay on the vine for a long time; if the eggplants are so big they're scraping the ground, leave the tomatoes for a few days and make Roasted Eggplant and Lentil Soup with Sage Butter (page 210). Or just make a purée (page 212) to serve as a dip with pita bread. If the cilantro looks good, chop some into the dip, and it will be even better. On the other hand, a vigorous row of parsley, tarragon, and chervil might inspire an herb salad to toss over grilled fish.

Sometimes you have to think fast. A whole row of spinach is almost ready to pick, and the weatherman is forecasting a 95-degree heat wave in two days. Spinach can't take the heat, so out it comes and possibly into a warm spinach salad (page 231). The secret is to stay flexible and work with what your garden delivers. If you stroll the garden as you would the farmers' market, selecting what's freshest, you'll quickly be able to put together a memorable meal.

You can even do it on a weeknight as long as you keep a little olive oil or butter on hand for roasting or sautéing, and a piece of Reggiano Parmesan for grating. Those basic ingredients will turn almost any vegetable into a main course, especially if you cook up a batch of rice on the side. (Combine 2 cups rinsed jasmine rice and 2 cups water in a medium saucepan; bring to a boil, lower the heat, cover, and simmer for 15 to 20 minutes.)

A challenge for home gardeners are those times when you have just a little bit of each vegetable: a few snap peas that matured late, some green beans that came early, a handful of small carrots that you thinned out, the single first zucchini of July, and a head of broccoli that somehow made it past June. When that happens to us at home, we think stir-fry because you can toss in each small portion of vegetables at just the right time, so everything is done at once. With all stir-fries, start by sautéing aromatics like onion, garlic, and ginger in oil. Then add meat, if any, and then vegetables that take longest to cook, like broccoli florets and sliced carrots. Gradually add the more tender vegetables, such as green beans, followed by snap peas and julienned zucchini. Finally, add herbs, greens, and scallions. It's a good idea to have some chicken stock and soy sauce on hand for moistening the stir-fry. (Even better would be Thai Red Curry, page 148.) Trust us—this impromptu stir-fry from your garden will taste better than any Chinese takeout you've ever had!

Freshness means more than "just picked." Some flavors like mint, cilantro, and the large Asian radish called daikon are so bright and clean that one bite makes you do a double take. Here the word *fresh* is more like a swim in the Gulf of Maine than fruit off the vine. And it screams summer. Mint is incredibly easy to grow (in fact, it's difficult to stop) and versatile because it can be used in both savory and sweet dishes. If you have nothing other than a pot of mint growing on your patio, you can have a taste of summer in every meal.

Summer food is also about color. We love making Spicy Corn Relish (page 169), Roasted Pepper Pesto (page 165), and Tomato Chutney (page 252) because they bring the wonderful colors of summer to the table. For main courses in summer, we love cooking outdoor food such as Grilled Maine Bluefin Tuna with Tomatoes and Gremolata Aïoli (page 150) and Grilled Rib-Eye Steak with Herbs and Caramelized Onions (page 154).

We also think fried food is great in the summer, when we whip up batches of Maine Peekytoe Crab Cakes (page 30) and Jeremiah's Crispy Okra (page 110). Every warm, crunchy bite evokes memories of summer roadside stands.

Most of all, we like to have fun with summer food. On the Fourth of July, we make ice cream cones with homemade red, white, and blue scoops of raspberry, vanilla, and blueberry ice cream (page 198). One of our favorite tricks is to take classic American summer barbecue food and add a new twist—like our Thai-Style Corn-on-the-Cob (page 171) or Seared Orange and Cabbage Salad (page 174). Cole slaws are great summer side dishes because they can be made ahead of time—a wonderful advantage when you've got better places to be than a hot kitchen.

Not everything comes from our garden, of course. We spend a lot of time with the local merchants who supply us with fish and meat, learning what's available. You don't have to own a restaurant to get first-class treatment from your local food suppliers. Most are quite passionate about their business, and once they realize you care as much as they do about good food, they will talk your ear off. Go down to the docks and off to the farmers' markets; talk, listen, and observe. One day you'll hear about an amazing catch of giant scallops that just came in. From your walk in the garden that morning, you know that the chile peppers are finally ripe. That's how we came up with Grilled Sea Scallops with Chile Pepper Sauce (page 144).

Inside the restaurant, things are really hopping in summer. The lilacs in the Big Bertha flower arrangement have long since been replaced by oak branches and surrounded by sprays of delphiniums, dahlias, and lilies, which are refreshed every day and changed completely once a week. Every afternoon we wander to the garden with an espresso to grab a moment of relaxation "backstage" before our nightly show begins. The sun is still hot and high in the sky, projecting rainbows across the mist from the lawn sprinklers. Soon they are turned off, leaving the trellised roses to glisten in the light. As the sun settles

below the treetops, guests for the early seating start to arrive—a typical assortment of Kennebunkport summer residents, local couples, and Boston artists—and they mingle in the garden, ogling tomatoes and chatting with the staff. You don't often see elegantly dressed people wandering through manicured gardens these days. It always reminds us of a scene from an earlier century, which seems appropriate given the age of our house. It's fun to imagine all the great summers this house has seen. Then again, when it's summer in Maine, nobody's counting.

APPETIZERS

Chilled Gazpacho with Lobster and Lime Crème Fraîche

Few dishes are as refreshing on a hot summer day as gazpacho. In Maine we embellish this classic Spanish "liquid salad" with lobster.

Makes 6 servings

2 yellow bell peppers, seeded and ribs removed
1 red bell pepper, seeded and ribs removed
8 large tomatoes, peeled and seeded (page 179)
1 red onion, peeled and cut into quarters
1 teaspoon finely chopped serrano chile
½ cup cilantro leaves
½ cup red wine vinegar
¼ cup red wine
1 tablespoon kosher salt
12 whole black peppercorns
3 lobsters, 1¼ pounds each, steamed and shelled (pages 18 and 19)
½ cup crème fraîche or sour cream
2 tablespoons freshly squeezed lime juice
6 scallions, halved lengthwise, then cut into 2-inch matchsticks

1. Cut 1 yellow pepper into small squares and set aside for garnish. Quarter the remaining yellow pepper and the red pepper.
2. Working in batches, purée the peppers, tomatoes, onion, chile, cilantro, vinegar, wine,

salt, and pepper in the jar of a blender until smooth. Transfer the purée to a bowl. Cover and refrigerate until cold and ready to serve, up to 1 day in advance.

3. Cut the lobster tails crosswise into ¼-inch medallions. Split each claw into 2 pieces by cutting across the flat side.

4. In a small bowl mix together the crème fraîche and lime juice.

5. Divide the gazpacho among 6 deep soup plates or shallow bowls. Top with the lobster, yellow pepper squares, crème fraîche, and scallions.

Asparagus with Mizuna, Blood Orange Vinaigrette, and Prosciutto (page 25)

Pumpkin Soup with Curried Pumpkin Seeds (page 207)

Winter Greens with Pink Grapefruit and Red Onion (page 309)

Grilled Maine Bluefin Tuna
with Tomatoes and Gremolata Aïoli (page 150)

Sugar Snap Pea and Rock Shrimp Salad (page 136)

New Zealand Cockles with Chinese Dark Wine and Ham Sauce (page 304)

*Plank-Roasted Salmon
with Rosemary-Mustard Vinaigrette (page 317)*

Cucumber and Cherry Tomato Salad (page 223)

Grilled Rib-Eye Steak
with Herbs and Caramelized Onions (page 154)

Lemongrass and Lemon Roasted Chicken (page 152)

*Smoked Duck Breast
with Swiss Chard and Pearl Onions (page 54)*

*Roast Turkey (page 323)
and Sauternes-Braised Apples
with Currants (page 264)*

Super-Moist Apple Cake (page 278)

Orange–Blackberry Tart (page 186)

Rose Petal Granita (page 287)

Red, white, and blue ice cream (Raspberry, Blueberry, and Vanilla, page 198) make the perfect patriotic dessert for Fourth of July.

Fennel Salad with Prosciutto

We've cooked fennel many ways, but this is one of our favorites. None of its powerful, aniselike flavor is lost, and it never has that mushy texture you sometimes get with other methods. Serve it as a first course or for lunch or with other salads.

Makes 6 servings

Finely grated zest and juice of 2 lemons
2 tablespoons extra-virgin olive oil
2 teaspoons finely chopped garlic
Kosher salt
Freshly ground black pepper
2 large bulbs fennel
12 thin slices prosciutto, preferably Parma or homemade (page 306)

1. In a medium bowl combine the lemon juice and zest, olive oil, and garlic; season with salt and pepper to taste. The vinaigrette will keep covered in the refrigerator for up to 2 days.

2. Halve the fennel bulbs lengthwise and cut out the cores. Slice crosswise as thin as possible. Toss the fennel with the lemon vinaigrette to coat.

3. Arrange 2 slices prosciutto flat on each of 6 plates. Mound the salad on top and serve.

NOTES

1. This dish can be garnished with lemon wedges and fennel tops if desired.

2. A mandoline works well for slicing fennel.

3. The prosciutto can be rolled into rosettes, if you prefer, and placed on top of the salad.

Jeremiah's Crispy Okra
with Tomatoes, Pesto, and Bacon

Cooking okra presents the daunting task of bringing out that wonderful flavor without the gummy texture most people dislike. When okra is picked directly from the garden, the first step to a delicious dish has already been taken. Fresh okra is firm, bright in color, and crisp. In the market avoid okra that is faded or soft.

Classic southern gumbo takes advantage of okra's gummy character to thicken the dish, perhaps the most clever use of a somewhat compromised vegetable. But our favorite way to cook okra, which we learned from Jeremiah Tower at Stars, is to dredge it in cornmeal and then sauté. The flavor is tremendous, and the gluey texture disappears into the batter. Many southerners brought up on okra—and leery that a couple of Yankees would attempt to cook it—have been wowed by this preparation.

Makes 6 servings

FOR THE PESTO
1 cup fresh basil leaves (save any nice tops for garnish)
¾ cup olive oil
¼ cup finely grated Reggiano Parmesan cheese
¼ cup pine nuts
Juice of 1 lemon
1 teaspoon chopped garlic
1 teaspoon kosher salt
½ teaspoon freshly ground black pepper

Combine all the ingredients in the jar of a blender and purée until smooth.

FOR THE OKRA
12 slices bacon
4 large tomatoes, preferably of different colors, sliced ¼ inch thick
Kosher salt
Freshly ground black pepper
1 pound fresh okra, cut into ¼-inch rounds

½ cup cornmeal
¼ cup olive oil
12 basil tops for garnish

1. Cook the bacon in a large sauté pan over medium heat until crisp, about 5 minutes. Transfer to a paper-towel-lined plate and keep warm on the back of the stove.

2. Arrange the tomatoes on 6 plates and sprinkle with salt and pepper.

3. Combine the okra with the cornmeal in a bowl and toss with your hands to coat. Transfer the okra to a sieve and shake off the excess cornmeal. Warm the olive oil in a large sauté pan over medium heat and add the okra. Sprinkle with salt and pepper and slowly sauté, stirring only occasionally, until the okra is golden brown, 4 to 6 minutes.

4. Divide the okra on top of the tomatoes and drizzle with the pesto. Arrange 2 strips of bacon on each plate, garnish with the basil tops, and serve at once.

NOTE: The pesto is best served the same day it is made.

Grilled Antipasto Platter

While working at Stars in San Francisco, we would often ask a bunch of friends down to Carmel for a weekend getaway. Clark's parents loved to have their house invaded by young people drinking champagne, dancing, and, above all, cooking. This antipasto platter was one of our weekend creations. Serve it as a first course or as a spectacular platter for a party buffet.

Makes 6 servings

12 spears asparagus, tough ends trimmed
1 bulb fennel, cut into 8 wedges
1 red bell pepper, stemmed, seeded, and cut lengthwise into 6 wedges
1 yellow bell pepper, stemmed, seeded, and cut lengthwise into 6 wedges
1 head radicchio, cut into 6 wedges
1 medium zucchini, cut lengthwise into about 6 slices
1 medium yellow summer squash, cut lengthwise into about 6 slices
6 scallions, tops trimmed by about 1 inch
½ cup plus 2 tablespoons olive oil
Kosher salt
Freshly ground black pepper
1 baguette
½ cup Aïoli (page 158)
24 thin slices prosciutto, preferably Parma or homemade (page 306), optional
1 pint mixed olives

1. Start a charcoal or gas grill.

2. Arrange the asparagus, fennel, peppers, radicchio, zucchini, summer squash, and scallions on a baking sheet. Drizzle with ¼ cup of the oil and sprinkle with salt and pepper. Flip the vegetables, drizzle with another ¼ cup oil, and sprinkle with salt and pepper. Split the baguette lengthwise in half and brush each side with 1 tablespoon oil. Put the aïoli in a small bowl in the center of a large serving platter.

3. Arrange the vegetables on a medium-hot grill and cook until lightly browned on the underside, about 3 minutes; the actual time will depend on the temperature of your grill.

Turn the pieces and brown the other side for about 3 minutes. As the vegetables are fin-ished, transfer them to the platter. Toast the baguette on the grill for less than a minute, watching it carefully to avoid burning it. Cut the toasted baguette into 6 pieces and arrange them on the platter.

4. Arrange the prosciutto if using on the platter with the grilled vegetables and bread, and sprinkle the vegetables with the olives.

> NOTE: The vegetables can be grilled up to 2 hours ahead of time and kept covered at room temperature. It is not necessary to serve the dish hot.

Lobster and Fresh Vegetable Spring Rolls

Soft, crunchy spring rolls with peanut sauce are a surefire hit at an outdoor cocktail party. They're also a great way to use some of that endless zucchini and summer squash from the garden. These are based on spring rolls we've had in Thailand, but we've added lobster for a Maine touch. Crab or shrimp, both of which are used extensively in Southeast Asia, work just as well. Serve these spring rolls with Seared Orange and Cabbage Salad (page 174) on a hot evening and let your troubles fade away!

Makes 6 servings

FOR THE PEANUT SAUCE
6 tablespoons creamy peanut butter
6 tablespoons rice vinegar
¼ cup vegetable oil
¼ cup sugar
2 tablespoons kecap manis (Indonesian dark soy sauce, available at Asian or specialty markets)
2 tablespoons finely chopped gingerroot
1 tablespoon fish sauce (available at Asian and specialty markets)
2 teaspoons sesame oil

Put the peanut butter in a small bowl and gradually stir in all the remaining ingredients. The sauce can be kept covered in the refrigerator for up to 3 days.

FOR THE SPRING ROLLS
2 ounces dried vermicelli rice noodles
1 tablespoon sesame oil
2 lobsters, 1¼ pounds each, steamed and shelled (pages 18 and 19)
2 medium carrots, peeled
2 medium zucchini
2 medium yellow summer squash
2 ounces bean sprouts (½ cup)
24 (8- to 10-inch) round spring roll wrappers

¼ cup cilantro leaves
¼ cup basil leaves

1. Cook the rice noodles in boiling salted water until soft, 4 to 5 minutes. Drain in a colander and run under cold water. When cool, toss with the sesame oil.

2. Cut the lobster meat into ½-inch chunks.

3. Slice the carrots lengthwise into long, thin strips, then cut the strips into long, thin sticks.

4. Cut the skins with about ⅛ inch of the flesh in large strips from the zucchini and the summer squash. Discard the cores. Cut the strips into long, thin sticks.

5. In a bowl toss the carrots, zucchini, yellow squash, and bean sprouts with enough of the peanut sauce to coat them. In another bowl toss the lobster with enough of the peanut sauce to coat it.

6. Pour ½ inch warm water in a shallow dish. Submerge 2 of the wrappers in the water until they are soft and pliable, about 1 minute. Don't leave them in for too long or they will start to fall apart.

7. Transfer the soaked wrappers to a clean, dry kitchen towel. Arrange a thin line of the vegetables across the center of each wrapper. On top of the vegetables, arrange thin lines of lobster, cilantro, and basil, and finally a thin line of noodles. Tightly roll one side of the wrapper over the filling. Then, using both hands, roll the wrapper tightly into a long tube, pulling the filling toward you as you roll it away from you. Repeat the soaking, filling, and rolling with the remaining ingredients.

8. With a very sharp knife slice the spring rolls crosswise into 1-inch pieces. Arrange the rolls on a plate and serve, passing the remaining peanut sauce for dipping.

NOTE: Fresh spring rolls must be eaten the day they are made because the moist wrappers quickly dry out and become tough. But all the ingredients except for the noodles can be prepared a day ahead and kept carefully wrapped in the refrigerator. The rolls can then be assembled a few hours before your guests arrive and covered tightly with plastic wrap. It's also fun to let your guests help make the spring rolls in the kitchen.

Roasted Pepper Custard with Corn, Garlic, and Herb Ragoût

There are few things more amazing than watching bell peppers in the garden. One day they are little green nubs, then along comes some hot weather and you suddenly have huge, brilliantly colored bells. Serve this custard as a first course or a light main course. The custard can be made a day ahead and finished with the simple sauce just before serving.

Makes 6 servings

FOR THE CUSTARD
2 red bell peppers
1 tablespoon olive oil
4 large egg yolks
1 large egg
1 cup heavy cream
1 teaspoon kosher salt
1/4 teaspoon freshly ground black pepper

1. Preheat the oven to 450 degrees F. Butter six 4-ounce ceramic ramekins.

2. In a bowl toss the peppers with the oil. Transfer to a baking sheet and bake for 10 minutes. Turn the peppers over and cook for another 10 minutes until completely soft.

3. Remove the peppers from the oven. Reduce the oven heat to 350 degrees F. Transfer the peppers to a bowl, cover with plastic wrap, and set aside for 10 minutes. Remove the peppers from the bowl, and when they are cool enough to handle, remove as much of the skin as possible along with the stems and seeds. Purée the peppers in the jar of a blender until smooth, about 1 minute. Pass the purée through a fine sieve into a medium bowl.

4. Whisk together the egg yolks, egg, and cream. Add the bell pepper purée, salt, and pepper.

5. Divide the custard among the ramekins. Arrange the ramekins in a roasting pan, spacing them evenly apart. Carefully pour 1/2 inch hot water in the pan. Bake for 20 minutes until the custards seem firm when the ramekins are gently tapped. Serve at once, or cover and keep in a warm place for up to 1 hour. Alternatively, the custards can be cooked

a day ahead, cooled, covered, and refrigerated; reheat for 10 minutes in a water bath in an oven that has been preheated to 350 degrees F.

FOR THE CORN RAGOÛT

18 cloves garlic, peeled
½ cup Chicken or Vegetable Stock (page 23 or 24)
2 cups fresh corn kernels (cut from about 3 ears)
3 tablespoons unsalted butter
1 tablespoon chopped mixed herbs, such as tarragon, thyme,
    flat-leaf parsley, chives, or rosemary
1 teaspoon kosher salt
¼ teaspoon freshly ground black pepper

1. Put the garlic in a small saucepan and cover with cold water. Bring to a boil, reduce the heat to low, and simmer for 10 minutes until the garlic is soft. Drain the garlic and set aside.

2. Warm the stock in a large sauté pan over medium heat. Add the corn, cover, and cook for 3 minutes. Uncover and add the garlic, butter, herbs, salt, and pepper.

TO SERVE

1. Divide the corn ragoût among 6 warm plates.

2. Gently run a knife around the edge of each warm custard. Unmold a custard onto each plate and serve.

NOTE: You can use foil ramekins instead of ceramic ones. Once the custards are baked, let them set for 5 minutes. With a paring knife, poke a tiny slit in the bottom of each foil cup, then invert onto serving plates. Lift the foil cups off the custards and serve.

Heirloom Gardening

Gardeners debate the precise definition of heirloom plants because not all "heirlooms" are actually old. But everyone agrees that heirlooms are plants whose seeds are "true to type." That means the plant will produce seeds that will grow into the same plant again and again.

That simple notion might seem obvious unless you've ever planted seeds from a hybrid tomato and gotten a strange mutant. Hybrid seedlings—those commercially raised plants you see lined up in home centers, ready for your garden—are forcefully "inbred" to emphasize certain characteristics, like uniformity and resistance to a particular disease. (It's not genetic engineering because the genes themselves aren't altered.) In the process the plant generally loses the ability to reproduce.

Heirloom plants have also been crossed and "selected" for certain qualities over time but in a more natural way that doesn't distort the plant's reproductive code. So you can literally start with one tomato seed and grow the same tomatoes for the rest of your life as long as you save some seeds from every crop for the next year. (For details on seed saving, see page 319.)

Even if you don't care about saving seeds, you'll be fascinated by the history behind your heirloom plants. Many were brought here by immigrants, who needed to start new gardens and wanted a link to their former lives. The Mayflower bean came over with the first pilgrims. Others like Jimmy Nardello's sweet Italian frying pepper arrived at Ellis Island sewn into the hats of Italian *paesani*. In the last two decades, new seeds came with refugees from Cambodia, Vietnam, Laos, Cuba, and Haiti.

American farmers used to save their seeds, but as agriculture became more industrialized, hybrids took over. Hybrid tomatoes can be "programmed" to ripen all at once, with tough skins to survive mechanical harvesting and long-distance shipping. That's great if you own a ketchup factory, but not what you want in your home garden. You want tomatoes that ripen over time, so you can enjoy them all summer. You want tomatoes with interesting shapes and colors. Most of all, you want tomatoes that taste good. Heirlooms have what you want. (For a list of great heirloom tomatoes, see page 126.)

Even so, interest in heirlooms waned after World War II as Americans migrated to cities. Once people relied on grocery stores for all their food, they forgot about Grandpa's funny-looking tomatoes. Small seed companies kept some heirlooms alive, but many closed or consolidated. By 1984 the total number of nonhybrid vegetable varieties sold commercially dropped below 5,000, an all-time low.

But with Americans paying closer attention to the source and quality of their food, heirloom gardening is coming back. Over the last five years commercial seed companies—mostly small regional suppliers—have reintroduced some 2,000 nonhybrid varieties. This adds new meaning to the phrase "You haven't even touched your vegetables."

Eggplant Chips

One afternoon in the kitchen of Stars in San Francisco, a prep cook was set to work slicing and baking a case of eggplant. In his enthusiasm he managed to slice them too thin, so in the oven they turned crisp and brown instead of soft. Jeremiah Tower, the chef, was furious, and no one dared even to touch the offending eggplant. But gradually the mood changed, and over the course of the evening, one cook after another discreetly sampled the eggplant chips. Soon they were gone. Ever since that night, we have been making various renditions of these chips. They are great as a snack, as part of an antipasto platter, and with grilled fish.

Makes 6 servings

1 pound eggplant (see Note)
½ cup olive oil
Kosher salt
Freshly ground black pepper

1. Preheat the oven to 350 degrees F.

2. Cut the eggplant lengthwise in half, and with a very sharp serrated knife, cut crosswise into 1/16-inch slices. Transfer the sliced eggplant to a bowl, drizzle with the olive oil, and toss to coat well. Lay the eggplant slices on a rimmed baking sheet (do not overlap them) and sprinkle with salt and pepper.

3. Bake the eggplant, checking frequently, for about 10 minutes until golden brown. Some chips will be done before others; remove them with a spatula to a platter and return the pan to the oven until the remaining chips are ready. These are best served immediately, but you can store the cooled chips in a sealed container overnight.

NOTE: Western, Japanese, Chinese, and Turkish eggplants work very well for eggplant chips. White eggplants seem to have too many seeds and fall apart during cooking. Several types of eggplants will give you a variety of flavors if you're cooking a lot of chips; otherwise one type is fine.

 SALADS

How to Make a Real Garden Salad

"Garden salad" has become a tired cliché on restaurant menus. Yet making the real thing is not difficult, provided you have access to a garden or farmers' market. (Supermarket lettuce, mostly shipped from California, can make an excellent salad but lacks the spirit of a true garden salad.) The main thing is to use whatever looks best in the garden or greenmarket on that day. Herbs, field greens, and even flowers have different flavors that will transform a salad of simple lettuce from a monochromatic experience to a rich tapestry of flavors. Arugula adds a peppery flavor, citrus marigolds taste like oranges, and tarragon leaves wake up the palate. Toss the salad with some olive oil, vinegar, salt, and pepper, and enjoy. Figure on a handful or so of lettuce leaves or other greens per person; if you're shopping at a greenmarket, don't be afraid to buy several different lettuces; you'll use them up in a few days. For a nice presentation, toss the lettuce in the dressing, arrange it on plates (or in a salad bowl for the table), then sprinkle the herbs and flowers on top.

Some of our suggestions for a great salad:

HERBS	LETTUCES	FLOWERS	FIELD GREENS
tarragon	Lollo Rossa	nasturtiums	arugula
basil	oakleaf	rose petals	tatsoi
mint	Red Oakleaf	johnny jump-ups	mizuna
parsley	romaine	citrus marigolds	red mustard
cilantro	radicchio	sage flowers	mustard
thyme	frisée	thyme flowers	chicory
sorrel	butterhead	cilantro flowers	

Marinated Tomatoes

We whip up this quick salad whenever the tomatoes start to take over the garden. Tomatoes "marinate" in minutes, so you can put this salad together from start to finish while the main course is cooking.

Makes 6 servings

3 very ripe large tomatoes
¼ cup finely chopped flat-leaf parsley
Kosher salt
Freshly ground black pepper
¼ cup extra-virgin olive oil
2 tablespoons balsamic vinegar

Core the tomatoes and slice them into ⅛-inch rounds. Arrange the slices on a plate. Sprinkle with the parsley, salt, and pepper, then drizzle with the olive oil and vinegar. Serve immediately or let sit for up to 1 hour.

Tomatoes Forever

Tomatoes are the poster kids of the heirloom-gardening movement, which took off in the 1980s. Thanks to the efforts of dedicated seed savers around the world (and the interest of chefs), hundreds of old-time tomato varieties in every shape and color are now being grown in American gardens. (For more about heirloom gardening and seed saving, see pages 118 and 319.) Heirloom tomatoes come in purple, black, white, yellow—even red if you insist. They look like eggs, footballs, and chile peppers. Some are fuzzy as a peach, others small as a blueberry, still others big as a softball. They have names like Box Car Willie and Mortgage Lifter. Many of them have a taste that will remind you why you used to love tomatoes.

But the truth is not all heirloom tomatoes taste great, look great, or perform well. Many are subject to cracking at the stem end, which might not bother you much; others get blossom-end rot, which is worse. As our master gardener says, there's a reason some of them were forgotten. One problem is that unlike hybrid tomatoes, which are bred to grow in most climates, heirlooms can be quite picky about the type of weather they like, especially if the seeds come from a long line of plants grown in a specific climate. (They tend to adapt over time.) So try to buy seeds that were grown in your region, then save your own seeds for next year.

Don't get us wrong—we love heirlooms and grow dozens of them. (See our list of favorites on page 126.) And we want to encourage you to do the same, but be prepared for occasional disappointment. Just because a seed catalog raves about a tomato doesn't mean it's the best choice for your garden. Seed suppliers are constantly experimenting with obscure varieties from growers all over the place. They're not trying to pull the wool over your eyes, but watch out for phrases like "a little finicky," "sensitive to blight," or "needs coaxing in rainy weather." Those are major hints.

It can be even harder to get good information on which heirlooms don't have much taste. Many of the paste tomatoes are mild to the point of blandness, possibly because they are bred to be so dry. One exception is Amish Paste. And be careful of the green tomatoes, for it can be hard to tell when they're ripe.

To grow great tomatoes, start the seeds indoors six weeks before planting time—no sooner unless you have a greenhouse, because the plants get leggy under indoor light. Tomato seeds germinate best at a soil temperature of 70 to 75 degrees F, so be sure to start the seeds in a very warm place. (Use a sterile peat-based growing mix, not potting soil, which is too heavy.) After sprouting, the trick is to give them enough light, preferably in a south-facing window or under bright artificial light. After the first set of true leaves show, give them a good dose of fish emulsion or seaweed fertilizer; repeat every two weeks after that. As the plants gain more sets of leaves, pot them in bigger containers.

Many people have informal (okay, cutthroat) competitions with neighbors for the biggest tomato transplant or the first tomato harvested. Yes, we grow huge transplants in our greenhouse, all the way up to one-gallon pots. And, yes, our tomatoes have been featured on *Victory Garden*. But without a greenhouse you're better off keeping your seedlings on the small side. Don't be ashamed, for they'll catch up in the garden later. You'll enjoy wonderful tomatoes in August like everyone else on the block.

When it's time to move tomato seedlings outdoors, we dig a deep hole (about 1 foot) and add a handful of compost, ¼ cup bone meal, plus 2 tablespoons of Tomatoes Alive or some other balanced organic fertilizer. We then set the stem down low in the hole (any part that's underground will sprout roots, which makes the plant stronger) and water well. Two weeks after planting, we spray BTK (*Bacillus thuringiensis* var. *kurstaki*, often sold under the brand name Dipel), which is an organic-approved biological control to prevent tomato hornworm, capable of devastating a whole crop in a few days. (Hornworms seem to go in cycles. They disappear for several years and then return like the plague, as they did in Maine during the summer of 2002.) If it's cold and windy, apply a copper fungicide—but try not to plant tomatoes when it's cold and windy.

In Maine tomatoes are at the mercy of June weather. If June is cold and yucky, the tomato crop will be late, no matter what happens in July and August. But if June is hot, the tomatoes get off to a great start and will outshine anything mid-summer throws at them.

Cold or warm, soon enough tomato plants need staking. The easiest way to do it at home is to use wire cages. Many heirlooms get super tall and rangy, so get the big 54-inch cages for indeterminate varieties. (Indeterminates keep on growing and producing new fruit all season.) If you started your own seeds, you'll know from watching them grow which ones are

going to zoom high and which will be smaller. Plan accordingly, because you need to set up your staking system before the plants get big.

Tomato plant maintenance basically involves pruning out suckers once a week, catching them before they get big. Suckers are the shoots that grow from between a leaf and the main stem; they become branches and grow more tomatoes. If you don't twist them out, you'll end up with dozens of branches—and lots of teeny, tiny tomatoes. We like fewer larger tomatoes, so we keep an eye on those suckers. But if you miss a sucker and it turns into a branch (it happens), don't remove it because you could damage the plant.

Some gardeners let the first (lowest) sucker live on to become a second stem, which is okay, especially for determinate varieties that produce all their fruit at once. It isn't even strictly necessary to prune suckers from determinates, but we do. (One exception is currant-type cherry tomatoes where the whole point is to have zillions of tiny tomatoes.)

Pruning out suckers also promotes good air circulation, which is a key to avoiding blight and other soil- and waterborne diseases of late summer. Another good practice is to strip off the lowest leaves so they don't touch the ground. And be careful when watering not to let the soil splash up onto the lower leaves. By the end of the season, everybody who grows tomatoes has some blight problems—it's part of the tomato life cycle—but if you groom carefully once a week, it won't be a big problem. ⌒

8 GREAT HEIRLOOM TOMATOES

Brandywine This is the single most popular heirloom and with good reason. Introduced in 1889 by a Philadelphia seed company, it's a big, deep red, round, indeterminate, slicing tomato with a slightly tart taste. If you've never grown an heirloom tomato, start here. We also grow Yellow Brandywine.

Cherokee Purple The Cherokee Purple is another big slicing indeterminate from Tennessee (and may or may not be of Cherokee origin). Its brick-red color is distinctive,as is its smoky taste.

Currant Both Yellow and Red Currant tomatoes are from South America and descended from the original wild, berrylike tomatoes. (Later breeding made tomatoes big.) Kids enjoy picking and eating these little gems, and we love to sprinkle them over salads.

Black Krim Our gardener says these deep purple indeterminates look like bruises. They are definitely eye-catching, with a rich flavor in salads and sauces.

Arkansas Traveler These mild pink indeterminates were developed in the nineteenth century at the University of Arkansas for southern gardens, but they do well in Maine. The Arkansas Traveler is one of the few heirloom tomatoes that almost never cracks, so it looks great in a salad.

Orange Strawberry Here is truly a strange tomato: The earliest fruits are globe shaped, the late-season ones are strawberry shaped. All are orange in color. The Orange Strawberry is best used fresh in salads.

White Queen Heirloom-tomato doyenne Carolyn Male claims White Queen is the only "white" tomato (it's actually pale yellow) with flavor, and she may be right. We use them in salads, and you can also make an unusual "white" tomato sauce with them. The earliest harvest is paler than later growth, which becomes a deeper yellow.

Green Zebra This is a "modern" slicing heirloom developed by grower Tom Wagner in 1985. It's become quite popular because of its striking green-and-yellow pattern, but it also happens to taste great, and it doesn't crack.

...AND A FEW NOTABLE HYBRIDS

We also grow many hybrid tomatoes, which tend to be more reliable and uniform—an important consideration when your business depends on them! So over the years we've found some pretty tasty ones:

Sungold Quite simply the best cherry tomato.

Super Sweet Did we mention it's sweet?

Big Boy An excellent beefsteak, not mealy like some others.

Arrows Trio of Summer Salads

With this trio we highlight the flavors and textures of three different greens in an eye-catching first course or luncheon salad. If you prefer, you can double any one of these salads to make a single salad for four.

For the third salad, try to find white balsamic vinegar, available in many supermarkets and specialty markets. Because it is not aged, it is much lighter (and less viscous) than brown balsamic vinegar, although it is still more intense than conventional white wine vinegar. You can substitute a good-quality brown balsamic vinegar.

Makes 6 servings

Creamy Blue Cheese with Bacon Lardons

2 tablespoons finely crumbled blue cheese
2 tablespoons champagne vinegar
2 tablespoons sour cream
$\frac{1}{2}$ teaspoon kosher salt
$\frac{1}{2}$ teaspoon freshly ground black pepper
2 tablespoons extra-virgin olive oil
2 tablespoons olive oil
3 thick slices bacon, cut into $\frac{1}{2}$-inch pieces
6 ounces lettuce such as Bibb or romaine (about 1 medium head),
    leaves separated, washed and dried

1. Combine the blue cheese, vinegar, sour cream, salt, and pepper in a medium bowl and gradually whisk in both olive oils until emulsified. The vinaigrette will keep covered in the refrigerator for up to 3 days.

2. Warm a large sauté pan over high heat until it is quite hot. Add the bacon to the pan and toss. Reduce the heat to medium and cook, stirring occasionally, until the bacon lardons are crisp, about 5 minutes. Using a slotted spoon, transfer the bacon to a paper-towel-lined plate.

3. Toss the lettuce with the dressing, arrange on plates, and garnish with the lardons.

Garden Herb Vinaigrette with Sourdough Croutons

½ sourdough baguette (1 piece about 12 inches), cut into ½-inch cubes
½ cup olive oil
½ cup flat-leaf parsley plus 1 teaspoon finely chopped flat-leaf parsley
1 teaspoon finely chopped thyme leaves
1 teaspoon finely chopped rosemary leaves
¼ cup extra-virgin olive oil
¼ cup tarragon leaves
2 tablespoons red wine vinegar
1 teaspoon whole-grain mustard
1 teaspoon Dijon mustard
1 teaspoon kosher salt
10 whole black peppercorns
6 ounces lettuce such as oakleaf (about 1 medium head), leaves separated,
    washed and dried

1. Preheat the oven to 325 degrees F.
2. Toss the bread cubes in a bowl with ¼ cup of the olive oil and transfer to a baking pan. Bake until golden and crisp, about 15 minutes.
3. Remove the croutons from the oven, transfer to a bowl, and toss with the chopped parsley, thyme, and rosemary. Once cool, the croutons can be stored in an airtight container for up to 2 days.
4. Combine the remaining ¼ cup olive oil, the extra-virgin olive oil, ½ cup parsley, tarragon leaves, vinegar, both mustards, salt, and peppercorns in the jar of a blender and process for 1 minute until smooth. The vinaigrette will keep covered in the refrigerator for up to 3 days.
5. To serve, toss the lettuce with the dressing, arrange on plates, and garnish with the croutons.

White Balsamic Vinaigrette with Fresh Orange Sections

2 tablespoons balsamic vinegar, preferably white
1 teaspoon kosher salt
½ teaspoon freshly ground black pepper
2 tablespoons olive oil
2 tablespoons extra-virgin olive oil

6 ounces lettuce or greens such as arugula or baby spinach
   (about 6 handfuls), washed and dried
2 large oranges, peeled and sectioned (page 310)

1. Combine the vinegar, salt, and pepper in a medium bowl and gradually whisk in both olive oils. The vinaigrette will keep covered in the refrigerator for up to 3 days.

2. Toss the lettuce with the dressing, arrange on plates, and garnish with the orange sections.

NOTE: Serve with a sparkling wine or crisp Chablis.

Melon and Frisée Salad with Raspberry Vinaigrette

Watermelons are subtropical fruits from Africa that can be grown in Maine—although not those gigantic bombs you see in the supermarket, which come from Mexico or Texas and require too many frost-free days for us northerners. Instead we grow smaller varieties (about the size of a soccer ball) that mature in less than a hundred days, which pushes our season to the limit. They taste like watermelons did when you were a kid—dripping with more sweetness than you thought possible. Incidentally forget that old saw about judging a watermelon's ripeness by "thumping" it; that's about as useful as kicking the tire of a car. A garden watermelon is ripe when the first leaf (just before the stem enters the melon) turns brown.

We also grow succulent muskmelons—Golden Gopher is an heirloom favorite in Maine—which works if the summer stays relatively warm; every year it's a gamble. In the store or in the field, melons (as opposed to watermelons) are ripe when they yield to soft pressure and have a sweet, melony scent at the stem end. Contrary to popular belief, melons do not ripen off the vine; they merely get softer, which is a polite way of saying they start to decompose. They don't get any sweeter on the kitchen counter.

Bitter frisée and sweet melon contrast nicely in this salad. It's also beautiful on the plate with whole raspberries as garnish, but you could also dress it up with edible flowers (page 191) or toasted pecans (page 272). An assortment of melons is nice, which will leave you with plenty of extra melon for breakfast.

Makes 6 servings

1½ cups raspberries
¼ cup red wine vinegar
1 teaspoon kosher salt
½ teaspoon freshly ground black pepper
¼ cup extra-virgin olive oil
¼ cup olive oil
About 3 pounds melon, such as red or yellow watermelon, cantaloupe, honeydew, Crenshaw, and/or Golden Gopher
18 ounces frisée (about 3 medium heads), leaves separated, washed and dried

1. In the jar of a blender purée 1 cup of the raspberries, the vinegar, salt, and pepper. Add both olive oils and process briefly just until combined. The vinaigrette will keep covered in the refrigerator for up to 2 days.

2. Halve and seed the melons. Using a small melon-ball scoop, make 2 cups melon balls. Alternatively, you can cut the melons into ½-inch chunks.

3. Toss the frisée with some of the vinaigrette in a large bowl and divide it among 6 chilled plates. Toss the melon balls with the remaining vinaigrette and arrange on top of the frisée on each plate. Garnish with the remaining ½ cup raspberries and serve at once.

BEATING THE BUGS

Bugs have a way of driving otherwise calm gardeners into fits of frenzy. When your hard work is being devoured by six-legged creatures, it's tempting to reach for the nearest poison and blast them into oblivion. But there is almost always a better way. At Arrows we don't use any man-made chemicals other than mild insecticidal soap (available at garden centers), and we do a pretty good job of keeping the bugs at bay.

Our first line of defense is garden tidiness. By keeping the beds weeded and free of debris, we eliminate the breeding ground for many bugs. We also rotate crops, which confuses pests that stick around for the same treat year after year.

Many bugs can be controlled by timing your plantings. For example, holding off squash and pumpkin plantings until early summer can prevent a plague of striped cucumber beetles, which stunt plants by devouring their leaves and stems and also spread bacterial diseases. By mid-June the beetles have hatched and moved on.

During the growing season, we walk the garden every morning and carefully observe what's going on. We look for caterpillars on the broccoli or tomatoes and check squash and cucumbers for the first signs of squash beetles. We check the underside of potato leaves for the bright orange, caviarlike egg masses of the Colorado potato beetle. All these critters can be removed by hand; that's the least invasive method of control.

The next weapon is the garden hose. We have good luck with simply washing bugs off plants or spraying them with insecticidal soap, which is water soluble so it doesn't hang around in the soil.

Some plants can be protected with physical barriers. Plastic collars foil cutworms, ugly ground-burrowing caterpillars that chew through the stems of tender seedlings such as tomatoes and broccoli. (You can make collars by removing the bottoms of plastic cups. Slip them over the seedling when transplanting and push into the ground about ½ inch.) Row covers—lightweight sheets of polypropylene fabric that let in light and water but keep out bugs—are really effective against flea beetles, those tiny hopping insects that devour greens. Lay the covers down right after sowing the seeds because flea beetles don't waste any time.

Another poison-free way to control flea beetles is to coat the inside of a plastic bucket with Tanglefoot (this super-sticky goop that's used on flypaper can be bought at garden centers). Invert the bucket quickly over an infested plant and rap it; this startles the beetles and causes them to jump—right onto the sticky sides.

If a problem persists, we identify the pest and use a specific treatment, rather than a broad-based chemical that kills everything in sight. For example, certain types of BT (*bacillus thuringiensis*) kill the larvae of potato beetles; others eliminate corn borers or tomato hornworms. (BT is a biological control, actually a bacterium, that's harmless to humans, bees, and wildlife, although it can kill butterfly larvae. It's approved for organic farming. Buy it at home centers or from seed catalogs.)

The last resort are natural, plant-derived insecticides like rotenone or pyrethrin, which are approved for organic growers. They are much safer for the environment than man-made chemicals because they break down quickly before entering the watershed. But they are still neurotoxins, which means they kill brain cells; don't use them indiscriminately and never just before harvesting. ❧

Sweet-and-Sour Fennel Salad

With its feathery top, fennel is one of the most exotic-looking plants in the garden. This rendition of fennel is great by itself, or with chilled oysters, grilled fish, or Lobster and Fresh Vegetable Spring Rolls (page 114). Fennel grows slowly but is incredibly hardy. In a home garden, half a dozen fennel plants is plenty.

Makes 6 servings

½ cup rice vinegar
¼ cup sugar
2 tablespoons sweet chile paste (available at Asian and specialty markets)
2 tablespoons soy sauce
1 tablespoon chopped gingerroot
2 large bulbs fennel, halved lengthwise, cored, and thinly sliced crosswise
Kosher salt
Freshly ground black pepper

1. In a stainless-steel saucepan, bring the vinegar, sugar, chile paste, soy sauce, and ginger to a boil.
2. Put the fennel in a medium bowl and pour the hot liquid over it. Toss the fennel well and season with salt and pepper to taste. Chill the fennel in the refrigerator for 1 hour or up to 1 day.

Chilled Maine Lobster Salad
with Tomato–Tarragon Vinaigrette

Tarragon has a sweet, almost aniselike flavor that we love in chilled dishes like potato salad, lobster rolls, artichoke salads, or even on a simple plate of sliced tomatoes. Here we combine some of these favorite tastes into one dish. In the garden tarragon grows slowly and is best started from a small plant—it is propagated from cuttings, not seeds. It's a perennial, but in really cold climates be careful not to cut too much or it will die.

Makes 6 servings

FOR THE VINAIGRETTE
1 large tomato, peeled and seeded (page 179)
1 shallot, peeled
2 tablespoons freshly squeezed lemon juice
1 tablespoon tarragon leaves
1 teaspoon kosher salt
6 whole black peppercorns
½ teaspoon paprika
½ cup extra-virgin olive oil

Process all the vinaigrette ingredients except the olive oil in the jar of a blender for 30 seconds until smooth. With the blender running, gradually add the oil. Check the seasoning and add more salt and pepper as needed. The vinaigrette will keep covered in the refrigerator for up to 1 day.

FOR THE SALAD
2 lobsters, 1¼ pounds each, steamed and shelled (pages 18 and 19)
6 ounces frisée (about 1 medium head), leaves separated, washed and dried
3 tablespoons tarragon leaves

1. Slice each lobster tail into 6 medallions. Leave the claws and knuckle meat whole.
2. Toss the frisée with about ¼ cup of the vinaigrette in a large bowl, then arrange on 6 chilled plates. Toss the lobster with the rest of the vinaigrette and divide among the salads. Sprinkle with the tarragon and serve at once.

Sugar Snap Pea and Rock Shrimp Salad

A garden delivers so many little pleasures, and peas hidden behind the leaves is certainly one of them. Who can resist sugar snap peas right off the trellis? The challenge is to refrain from picking them too soon, before they've developed sweetness; when ready, the pods will be swelled with large peas. The Asian greens in this salad add a spicy note, and they're so easy to grow.

Rock shrimp, which come from the Gulf of Mexico, are small and delicate (similar to Maine shrimp, page 292), and they stay quite firm after cooking. Any small shrimp will work in this recipe.

Makes 6 servings

FOR THE VINAIGRETTE
⅓ cup rice vinegar
2 tablespoons soy sauce
2 tablespoons finely chopped gingerroot
2 tablespoons sugar
1 teaspoon sweet chile paste (available at Asian and specialty markets)
½ teaspoon kosher salt
½ teaspoon freshly ground black pepper
⅔ cup vegetable oil
1 tablespoon sesame oil

Combine the vinegar, soy sauce, ginger, sugar, chile paste, salt, and pepper in a small bowl. Gradually whisk in the vegetable and sesame oils. The vinaigrette will keep covered in the refrigerator for up to 3 days.

FOR THE SHRIMP AND PEAS
Kosher salt
8 ounces sugar snap peas (about 2 cups)
2 cups white wine
1 cup white wine vinegar
1 cup water
1 bunch scallions, finely chopped

4 bay leaves

1½ pounds rock or other small shrimp, peeled

1. In a large pot bring 2 quarts water and 1 tablespoon salt to a boil. Fill a medium bowl halfway with ice water.

2. While the water is heating, remove the fibrous strings from the peas; snap off the top of each one and the string will come with it. Plunge the peas into the boiling water for 20 seconds. Drain the peas in a sieve and submerge immediately in the ice bath. As soon as the peas are completely chilled, drain them, wrap them in a clean kitchen towel, and refrigerate.

3. Combine the wine, vinegar, water, scallions, bay leaves, and 2 tablespoons salt in a large stainless-steel saucepan and bring to a simmer over medium heat. Add the shrimp and cook for 2 minutes; do not let the liquid boil. Drain the shrimp (discard the poaching liquid), transfer to a large plate, and refrigerate. When the shrimp are completely chilled, cover the plate with plastic wrap and return to the refrigerator until ready to serve.

TO SERVE

2 ounces tatsoi (about 2 handfuls), washed and dried

2 ounces mizuna (about 2 handfuls), washed and dried

4 scallions, light and dark parts, finely chopped

Toss the tatsoi and mizuna with one-third of the vinaigrette and divide it among 6 chilled plates. Toss the shrimp and peas with the remaining vinaigrette and arrange on top of the greens. Garnish with the scallions and serve at once.

NOTES

1. The shrimp and sugar snap peas taste best when cooked the same day you serve them.

2. Serve with an Asian ale or an Alsatian white wine.

✑MAIN COURSES

Mushroom, Leek, and Potato Strudel

This is an ambitious vegetarian dish that's a real showstopper because of the way it towers above the plate. In summer we love cooking with golden chanterelle mushrooms, which are gathered wild in the Maine woods. Chanterelles also carpet many of the four thousand islands along the Maine coastline, where frequent fog creates the perfect growing environment. A sauce made from slow-roasted tomatoes lightens this substantial strudel.

Makes 6 servings

6 large Yukon Gold potatoes, peeled and cut into ¼-inch slices
Kosher salt
12 tablespoons (1½ sticks) unsalted butter
6 medium leeks, light part only, cut into ¼-inch rings, well washed
    and dried
1½ cups Vegetable or Chicken Stock (page 24 or 23)
Freshly ground black pepper
8 ounces chanterelle mushrooms—or a mix of button, cremini,
    and shiitake—cleaned and trimmed
1 (16-ounce) package phyllo dough, thawed
¼ cup tarragon leaves, plus additional for garnish
3 cups Slow-Roasted Tomato, Parmesan, and Basil Sauce (page 168)

    1. Put the potatoes in a saucepan with enough cold water to cover by 2 inches, add 2 teaspoons salt, and bring to a boil. Cook until the potatoes are just tender when pierced with a knife, about 10 minutes. Drain the potatoes and set aside to cool.

2. Melt 2 tablespoons of the butter in a medium sauté pan over medium heat. Add the leeks and stock, season with salt and pepper, and bring to a boil. Cover and braise over low heat until the leeks are soft, about 10 minutes. Drain the leeks if needed, transfer them to a plate, and allow to cool.

3. Cut the larger chanterelles into quarters; keep the small ones whole. Warm 2 tablespoons of the butter in a large sauté pan over medium heat. Add the chanterelles and cook, stirring occasionally, for about 5 minutes until they are soft. Season with salt and pepper and transfer the mushrooms to a plate to cool.

4. Preheat the oven to 350 degrees F. Line a baking sheet with parchment paper.

5. Unroll the phyllo dough on a worktable. Cover with plastic wrap topped with a damp towel. Melt the remaining 8 tablespoons butter. Transfer 1 sheet of phyllo to a clean countertop and brush lightly with butter. Top with another layer of phyllo and brush it with butter. Repeat until you have 6 layers of phyllo buttered and stacked together. Remember to work with 1 sheet at a time, keeping the remaining dough covered.

6. Arrange one-third of the potatoes in a line along one short end of the prepared phyllo. Sprinkle one-third of the tarragon leaves over the potatoes. Top with one-third of the leeks and finally one-third of the chanterelles. Using both hands, gently roll the filling up in the phyllo. Make 2 more strudels the same way, using 6 phyllo sheets for each strudel. Transfer the prepared strudels to the parchment-lined pan.

7. Bake for 8 to 10 minutes until golden brown. Remove from the oven and transfer the strudels to a cutting board. Cut each strudel into six 2-inch-long pieces with a serrated or electric knife.

8. Warm the tomato sauce in a medium saucepan over low heat, stirring to prevent scorching.

9. To serve, ladle a pool of tomato sauce on each of 6 warm plates. Stand 3 pieces of strudel up on each plate and garnish with tarragon.

Maine Sweet Clams with Risotto and Arugula

One of our favorite greens to grow is arugula, which is so versatile—delicious warm or chilled. Its sharp, peppery flavor complements the sweet, briny taste of Maine clams, which are similar to the tiny Adriatic clams favored in Italy.

Many people overcook risotto. In the classic dish each grain of rice still has a little bite. Another common mistake is undercooking the onions. Be patient—sauté them slowly until they are very soft but not browned. And make sure the stock you're adding is hot (keep it on a low flame next to the risotto pan). Cold stock takes too long to heat up, slowing the cooking process and making the rice glutinous.

Most recipes call for steaming clams open in advance. We think steaming toughens clams, so we prefer to shuck them raw (page 143) and cook the clams in the dish. If you prefer, you can steam well-scrubbed clams in a covered saucepan over medium-high heat for about 5 minutes, removing each clam as it opens with a slotted spoon and transferring it to a bowl. Once cool, scoop out the clams with your fingers, dipping them in the clam juice to wash off any grit. Strain the juice through a fine sieve, then add it to the chicken stock.

Makes 6 servings

FOR THE RISOTTO
2 quarts Chicken or Vegetable Stock (page 23 or 24)
1 tablespoon unsalted butter
1 tablespoon olive oil
½ small yellow onion, peeled and finely chopped
3 cups Arborio rice
¼ cup grated Reggiano Parmesan cheese
½ cup white wine
Kosher salt

1. In a medium saucepan bring the chicken stock to a simmer.

2. Warm the butter and olive oil in a large stainless-steel saucepan (at least 2 quarts) over medium-low heat. Add the onion and sauté, stirring frequently, until translucent, about 5 minutes. Add the rice and, using a wooden spoon, cook and stir for 2 minutes.

3. Add about ½ cup of the hot stock to the rice. Stir over medium heat until the rice

absorbs nearly all the stock. Continue to stir and add stock, about ½ cup at a time as needed, until the rice is just tender and still a bit soupy, 10 to 15 minutes. Stir in the Parmesan and white wine and cook for another minute. Add salt to taste. Cover the risotto and keep warm off the heat while quickly heating the clams and dressing the arugula.

FOR THE CLAMS AND ARUGULA
4 tablespoons (½ stick) unsalted butter
36 small clams, shucked (page 143)
2 teaspoons freshly squeezed lemon juice
2 bunches arugula, tough stems trimmed, washed and dried
1 tablespoon olive oil
Kosher salt
Freshly ground black pepper

1. Melt the butter in a large stainless-steel sauté pan over medium heat. Add the clams and 1 teaspoon of the lemon juice and cook gently for 2 minutes.

2. In a medium bowl toss the arugula with the olive oil, the remaining 1 teaspoon lemon juice, and salt and pepper to taste.

TO SERVE
Divide the risotto among 6 warm large bowls or plates. Arrange the arugula in a ring around the risotto. Spoon the clams over the risotto and serve at once.

NOTE: Pinot Gris is an excellent wine with this dish.

SHUCKING CLAMS

When we make a dish like Maine Sweet Clams with Risotto and Arugula (page 141), we look for the smallest clams, such as littlenecks, Maine mahogany, Manila, or cherrystones. Small clams are more tender, but, because they cook so quickly, the usual technique of steaming to get them open tends to overcook them. That's why we prefer to "shuck" our clams raw, then add the raw clams directly to the dish.

The first step is scrubbing whole clams clean of sand, using a kitchen brush (preferably brass, but bristle will do) and several changes of cold water. Discard any clams that don't close tightly when handled. Then put the clams in a pot of fresh water and let them soak for at least 10 minutes, which helps purge sand from inside.

The best tool for shucking clams is a clam knife: a simple, flexible, flat-bladed tool (available at most housewares stores or from catalogs), but you can substitute a strong, short knife such as a good-quality paring knife. Hold the clam in a folded towel in your left hand (if you're right-handed) with the "hinge" of the clam against your palm. Carefully insert the blade of the knife in between the two shells on the edge opposite the hinge. Don't poke with the tip of the knife; push the whole edge of the knife blade between the shells. Continue pushing the knife all the way into the clam and run the knife around the edge to separate the top and bottom shells. Once it is open, cut under the clam to remove it from the shell. Place the clam in a bowl and repeat the process until you have shucked all the clams that you need. Reserve the clam juice, straining it through a fine sieve lined with a paper towel.

Grilled Sea Scallops with Chile Pepper Sauce

Chiles were always part of the cooking at Stars in San Francisco. Many of the people working in the kitchen were Latino, and Chef Jeremiah Tower was also chef/owner of the Sante Fe Bar and Grill, where chiles were king. We both enjoyed learning the subtle and not-so-subtle differences between anaheims and serranos, chipotles and anchos.

Although our garden at Arrows is far north of the border, chiles grow quite successfully here. Today we grow more than a dozen different kinds. We particularly enjoy anaheims for their mild flavor and poblanos for their boldness. We're not alone, for even supermarkets in Maine stock these peppers. Combined, the two make a rich sauce, perfect with scallops as well as white fish such as halibut.

Makes 6 servings

1 cup heavy cream
6 green anaheim chiles
2 green poblano chiles
¼ cup plus 1 tablespoon olive oil
Kosher salt
Freshly ground black pepper
½ cup Chicken or Vegetable Stock (page 23 or 24)
2 tablespoons freshly squeezed lime juice
3 tablespoons unsalted butter
½ small yellow onion, peeled and finely chopped
1 cup cilantro leaves, plus additional for garnish
1 cup sour cream
18 large fresh sea scallops

1. Preheat the oven to 450 degrees F.

2. Pour the cream into a medium heavy saucepan and simmer over medium-low heat until it is reduced by half, about 30 minutes.

3. While the cream is reducing, toss the peppers in a bowl with the 1 tablespoon olive oil and some salt and pepper. Transfer to a baking sheet and bake for 10 minutes. Turn the peppers over and bake for another 10 minutes until completely soft.

4. Transfer the peppers to a bowl and cover with plastic wrap; set aside for 10 minutes.

Remove the peppers from the bowl, and when they are cool enough to handle, remove as much of the skin as possible along with the stems and seeds. Transfer the peppers to the jar of a blender. Add the chicken stock and lime juice and blend until smooth, about 1 minute.

5. Melt the butter in a sauté pan over medium heat. Add the onion and sauté, stirring frequently, until translucent, about 5 minutes. Scrape into the blender with the pepper purée, add the cilantro, and blend until smooth. The sauce should be the consistency of ketchup; if it is too thick, add a tablespoon or two of water.

6. Pour the pepper purée into a medium bowl and whisk in the sour cream. Then whisk the mixture into the reduced cream. Warm over low heat, stirring constantly, for about 5 minutes. The sauce can be kept covered for a couple of hours in a warm place. Alternatively, it will keep, cooled and tightly covered, in the refrigerator for up to 2 days. Warm gently before serving.

7. Start a charcoal or gas grill.

8. Toss the scallops with the remaining ¼ cup olive oil and salt and pepper to taste. Grill the scallops over a very hot fire for 1½ minutes. Turn the scallops and grill for another 1½ minutes until firm and translucent. (Alternatively, you can sear the scallops on top of the stove. Warm a nonstick sauté pan over high heat for several minutes until the surface is quite hot. Add the scallops and cook as for the grill, browning them on both sides.)

9. Divide the sauce equally among 6 warm plates. Arrange the scallops on top and serve at once.

Peppers

We grow lots of peppers, about a dozen varieties—everything from standard red and orange bells to the more flavorful poblanos and anaheims to the fiery serranos and Thai bird chiles. Watching them ripen in the garden is a gorgeous sight. And because most peppers don't lose any of their brilliant color with cooking, you can walk through the garden and imagine all sorts of colorful dishes! (The exceptions are purple peppers, which turn green when you peel or roast them.)

Bells that we like include Red Beauty, Ariane (an orange variety), and the unusual Bianca, which is ivory colored all the way through. Moderately spicy poblanos are the standard chile in Southwest cooking, and they are used both green (unripe) and red; when you dry the red ones, they become anchos, a key ingredient in many Mexican and Tex-Mex sauces. Small hot peppers like serranos and Thai bird chiles are incredibly prolific; one plant is plenty for a family, unless you make Lucia's Nuclear Pickled Serranos (page 255). We eat them at lunchtime, as many as we can stand. You can also freeze tiny fresh peppers in tightly sealed containers.

Growing these heat-loving veggies in northern New England requires selecting varieties that do well in our short season (we read seed catalogs carefully) and starting them indoors

early. Wherever you live, don't rush peppers into the garden; wait until the warm weather has really arrived. In Maine, that means mid-June!

Some peppers, like poblanos, grow on really tall plants that need staking to keep the weight of the peppers from toppling them. Keep an eye on them as the peppers grow. For cheap and effective stakes, buy bundles of 4-foot-long spruce lath at a home center. In the garden push a stake into the ground next to the pepper plant, then tie it with twine or plastic garden tape, available at nurseries.

We like to let our bell peppers ripen in the garden until they turn deep red and get really sweet. But sometimes an early frost kills the plant when many of the peppers are still green. Then we pull the plants out by the roots and hang them upside down indoors. In about a week the peppers turn at least partially red before they start drying out. ↶

Sautéed Halibut with Thai Red Curry

Halibut, the largest flatfish (a family that includes sole and flounder), range from the Arctic Sea to New Jersey. Most are caught in the frigid waters off Maine and Nova Scotia. We buy whole fish that weigh 40 to 50 pounds and measure 5 feet long without their heads. Halibut has a firm texture that makes it perfect for sautéing and grilling. Thai red curry is also delicious in stir-fries.

Makes 6 servings

¾ cup vegetable oil
2 tablespoons finely chopped gingerroot
2 tablespoons finely chopped lemongrass, yellow part only
1 cup basil leaves
1 tablespoon Thai red curry paste (available at Asian and specialty markets)
2 (13.5-ounce) cans unsweetened coconut milk
1 cup heavy cream
1 tablespoon sweet chile sauce (available at Asian and specialty markets)
½ cup cilantro leaves
1 tablespoon fish sauce (available at Asian and specialty markets)
2 tablespoons sugar
Juice of 1 lime
Kosher salt
Freshly ground black pepper
6 skinless halibut fillets, 6 ounces each

1. Heat ½ cup of the oil in a large stainless-steel saucepan over medium heat. Add the ginger, lemongrass, basil, and curry paste and sauté, stirring frequently, for 5 minutes. Add the coconut milk, cream, chile sauce, and cilantro and simmer for 15 minutes. Strain the sauce through a fine sieve into another saucepan and stir in the fish sauce, sugar, and lime juice. Add salt and pepper to taste. The curry can be made up to a day ahead, cooled, and stored tightly covered in the refrigerator. Warm over medium heat before serving.

2. Preheat the oven to 450 degrees F.

3. In a large, nonstick, ovenproof sauté pan, heat the remaining ¼ cup oil until it is

almost smoking. Sprinkle the halibut fillets with salt and pepper. Add the fillets to the pan and sauté for about 1 minute until the underside is golden brown. Turn them over and sauté the other side until brown. (Depending on the size of your pan, you may have to brown the halibut in 2 batches.) Transfer the pan to the oven and bake for 4 minutes until just firm. (If you browned the halibut in 2 batches, arrange them on a baking sheet large enough to hold them all.)

4. Ladle a pool of sauce on each of 6 warm plates and place a halibut fillet on each plate.

NOTE: You can substitute sea bass, cod, or a similar firm-fleshed white fish for the halibut.

HOT SAUCES AND CHILE PASTES

A few decades ago it would have been hard to find any spicy condiment other than Tabasco in Maine, which is not noted for its fiery native cuisine. Fortunately the "salsa revolution" has opened the door to all sorts of spicy preparations even in Maine, although it takes some searching to find really good ones.

We love Asian chile pastes and use them in recipes throughout the year—everything from Seared Orange and Cabbage Salad (page 174) and New Zealand Cockles with Chinese Dark Wine and Ham Sauce (page 304) to Maine Shrimp Dumplings with Cilantro (page 302). We collect lots of different Asian pastes, as well as both Asian and Latin American hot sauces. They last indefinitely, so you can amass quite a variety without worry that they'll go bad. (Some need refrigeration after opening.)

Pastes differ from sauces in both texture and flavor. Most hot sauces have a vinegar base, so when you add them to food, you're adding vinegar. That isn't always what you want. Chile pastes, on the other hand, are little more than pulverized chiles mixed with soy oil, salt, garlic, and sometimes sugar. The different flavors and heat levels come from the types of chiles used. Avoid brands, often sold in supermarkets, that have thickening agents and other unnecessary additives. The best varieties are sold in health-food stores or, better yet, Asian markets, where you can find all sorts of exotic brands from Thailand, Vietnam, and China. Some have rich, dark flavors that work well with meat; others are cleaner-tasting and more suitable for lighter dishes. One of our favorite pastes is Mae Ploy, a fairly sweet blend that the label helpfully advises is "For Chicken." The Rooster brand is a good Asian hot sauce—very spicy but meaty and vinegary.

Grilled Maine Bluefin Tuna with Tomatoes and Gremolata Aïoli

Wrestling with a 200-pound bluefin tuna isn't something we do on a regular basis. When we first opened Arrows, local fish purveyors couldn't get bluefin tuna, even though it is caught during summer off the coast of Maine and Canada. (The cold water accounts for bluefin's high fat content, which gives it a richer, meatier taste than other tuna, which prefer warmer seas.) Because gourmands in Japan are willing to pay an exorbitant price for bluefin, most Maine fishermen sell their catch to a broker, who promptly air freights it to Japan. But after much cajoling and pleading, we finally got one of the local fishermen to show up one morning with a beauty of a bluefin—such a beauty that it took several people to hoist it onto the kitchen counter. Fortunately, we can now get bluefin tuna—in more manageable pieces—from our purveyors.

When you purchase bluefin tuna, it will no doubt be filleted; your fishmonger can also cut it into steaks for you. (Yellowfin can be substituted.) Sliced tomatoes are the perfect accompaniment for this regal fish. We prefer coarse sea salt when grilling big fish steaks, but kosher salt is fine.

Makes 6 servings

1 cup Aïoli (page 158)
¼ cup chopped flat-leaf parsley
1 teaspoon finely grated lemon zest
¼ teaspoon anchovy paste, optional
6 bluefin tuna steaks, 6 ounces each
¼ cup olive oil
Coarse sea salt or kosher salt
Freshly ground black pepper
6 large tomatoes, preferably an assortment of garden varieties,
    cut into ¼-inch slices

1. Start a charcoal or gas grill.

2. In a medium bowl mix together the aïoli, parsley, lemon zest, and anchovy paste if using. Set aside.

3. Brush the tuna with the olive oil and sprinkle with salt and pepper. Grill the tuna over a hot fire for 2 minutes. Flip the steaks and grill for another 2 minutes for medium-rare fish. You'll know it's medium-rare from its pink hue.

4. Fan the tomatoes on 6 plates. Arrange the tuna steaks on top of the tomatoes, spoon a dollop of the gremolata aïoli on each steak, and serve at once.

How to Tell from Tuna

Bluefin is the best tuna you can buy, period. They don't head up the East Coast until summer, when they follow the Gulf Stream north, chasing after smaller prey like mackerel, a similar oily fish. We like to grill tuna steaks and garnish them simply. But not all bluefin cuts are created equal. We're incredibly picky about what we'll take, and you should be too because it's expensive. Look for loin pieces that are solid red. Avoid belly sections, which have white streaks or rings of tough, fatty connective tissue. (We call it *osso buco tuna* because it resembles veal shanks.) The loin actually looks like a tenderloin of beef and tastes even better. ⌒

Lemongrass and Lemon Roasted Chicken

People are always amazed that we can grow lemongrass, an essential ingredient of Southeast Asian cooking, in Maine. Actually it grows quite well here; it needs very little care and doesn't seem to interest Maine's many bugs.

Lemongrass is typically used in savory dishes, but we also make lemongrass tea, sorbet, and ice cream. This chicken is easy to prepare and perfect with steamed jasmine rice (page 104) and Sweet-and-Sour Fennel Salad (page 134).

Makes 6 servings

4 stalks lemongrass, yellow part only
1 large roasting chicken, about 5 pounds
4 kaffir lime leaves
Finely grated zest and juice of 2 lemons
1 tablespoon finely chopped gingerroot
2 tablespoons sugar
2 tablespoons sesame oil
2 tablespoons vegetable oil
2 tablespoons soy sauce

1. Cut the lemongrass into 1-inch sections, then cut the sections in half lengthwise.

2. Gently lift the skin of the chicken around the breast and insert half of the lemongrass under the skin. Put the remaining lemongrass and 2 of the lime leaves in the cavity.

3. Finely chop the remaining 2 lime leaves. Put them in a large shallow bowl and add the lemon zest and juice, ginger, sugar, sesame and vegetable oils, and soy sauce.

4. Add the chicken, turn it around in the marinade to coat, and cover with plastic wrap. Refrigerate for at least 2 hours or up to 6 hours, turning once during this time.

5. Preheat the oven to 350 degrees F.

6. Transfer the chicken to a roasting pan (discard the marinade) and roast for 1½ hours, basting occasionally, until the juices run clear when the meat is pricked with a knife. Remove the lemongrass and lime leaves from the cavity, cover the chicken with foil, and allow it to rest for 10 minutes. Carve the chicken and serve at once.

NOTES

1. Lemongrass and kaffir lime leaves can be found in Asian markets and many supermarkets.

2. A medium-bodied Pinot Noir or Burgundy such as a Gevrey Chambertin or Pommard is the perfect match with this chicken, but if you prefer a white, select a full-bodied California Chardonnay.

Grilled Rib-Eye Steak with Herbs and Caramelized Onions

Rib-eye steaks, which the French call *entrecôtes,* are richly marbled, which makes them quite juicy and full of flavor. Because they don't dry out over high heat, rib-eyes are our favorite cut of beef to throw on a searingly hot grill. Try to find aged rib-eye steaks, which are more tender and have a mellower flavor. Most aged beef is sold directly to restaurants, but good butchers and even some supermarkets stock aged beef, especially in the summer grilling season.

In this recipe, sweet caramelized onions stand up to the smoky flavor of the meat. Intensely aromatic herbs like tarragon (the foundation of that classic steak accompaniment, béarnaise sauce) also work well with grilled beef. Here we mix herbs into a salad that is sprinkled over the steaks.

Makes 6 servings

2 tablespoons unsalted butter
⅔ cup white wine
2 tablespoons balsamic vinegar
3 medium yellow onions, cut in half around the equator, skin on
Kosher salt
Freshly ground black pepper
6 rib-eye steaks, 7 ounces each, preferably aged
2 tablespoons olive oil
¼ cup extra-virgin olive oil
2 tablespoons red wine vinegar
¼ cup tarragon leaves
¼ cup flat-leaf parsley
¼ cup chervil leaves

1. Preheat the oven to 350 degrees F.
2. Cut the butter into small pieces and sprinkle it over the bottom of a small baking dish. Add the wine and balsamic vinegar. Sprinkle the flat side of the onions with salt and pepper and arrange them flat side down in the baking dish. Bake until the onions are very

soft and brown, about 45 minutes. Remove from the oven, cover with foil, and keep in a warm place until ready to serve. (The onions can be prepared up to 2 hours ahead.)

3. Start a gas or charcoal grill.

4. While the onions are cooking, brush the steaks on both sides with the 2 tablespoons olive oil, season with salt and pepper, and set aside at room temperature for up to 30 minutes or in the refrigerator for up to 4 hours.

5. When the coals are white hot and you can barely hold your hand over the fire for a second, grill the steaks for about 3 minutes on each side until medium-rare.

6. While the steaks are grilling, whisk together the extra-virgin olive oil and red wine vinegar in a small bowl. Toss in the herbs and season with salt and pepper.

7. Put a steak on each of 6 plates and add an onion half flat side up. Drizzle the steaks with some of the cooking liquid from the baking dish and top with the herb salad. Serve at once.

SAUCES

Green Goddess Dressing

In our rendition of this classic San Francisco dressing, we use a greater variety of herbs than traditional recipes. Green Goddess goes well with just about any lettuce, but we prefer Lollo Rossa, a frilly red-tinged variety that stands up well to heavier dressings like this. It's best made the same day you serve it.

Makes about 1 cup

½ cup Mayonnaise (page 158)
2 tablespoons champagne vinegar
2 anchovy fillets, mashed
1 scallion, finely chopped
2 tablespoons finely chopped tarragon leaves
2 tablespoons finely chopped flat-leaf parsley
2 tablespoons finely chopped chervil leaves
2 tablespoons finely chopped chives
2 tablespoons finely chopped dill
1 teaspoon kosher salt
1½ teaspoons freshly ground black pepper
2 tablespoons extra-virgin olive oil
2 tablespoons olive oil

Combine the mayonnaise with the vinegar, anchovies, scallion, all the herbs, salt, and pepper in a medium bowl. Gradually whisk in both oils. The dressing can be covered and stored in the refrigerator for up to 1 day.

Aïoli or Mayonnaise

Aïoli, the simple, yet assertive, garlic mayonnaise of Mediterranean cuisine, is a natural accompaniment to spontaneous summer meals like grilled fish or steak. The traditional way to make aïoli is with a mortar and pestle, first crushing the garlic with the egg yolks and lemon juice and gradually adding the olive oil. Many chefs use a standing mixer with a whisk, but we prefer a food processor. It's not quite as romantic either way, but it certainly is a lot faster. You can also make aïoli with a hand whisk. In recipes that call for mayonnaise, simply eliminate the garlic.

Makes about 1½ cups

5 large egg yolks
3 cloves garlic, peeled and finely chopped (omit if making mayonnaise)
Juice of 1 lemon
¾ cup olive oil
¼ cup extra-virgin olive oil
Ice water
Kosher salt
Freshly ground black pepper

1. Combine the egg yolks, garlic, and lemon juice in the bowl of a food processor fitted with the metal blade. Process for 20 seconds. With the machine running, add both of the olive oils drop by drop, then slowly increase to a steady stream as the eggs and oil become emulsified. As the emulsion gets thick and starts to bind into a ball, thin it with a teaspoon or two of ice water. The final consistency should be a little thinner than store-bought mayonnaise.

2. Season the aïoli with salt and pepper. Store in a tightly sealed nonreactive container in the refrigerator for up to 1 day.

Clark's Mom's Salmon Vinaigrette

This simple all-in-one vinaigrette is both a marinade and a sauce for grilled salmon. The acidity is a perfect balance for the rich flavor of salmon. Use about ½ cup to marinate salmon steaks or fillets for 15 minutes at room temperature or 1 hour in the refrigerator. Baste the fish with marinade as it grills. When you are ready to serve, spoon some of the remaining 1 cup vinaigrette on each plate and top with the salmon. It's also tasty with roasted fowl and pork.

Makes about 1½ cups

3 tablespoons brown sugar
2 tablespoons red wine vinegar
2 tablespoons balsamic vinegar
1 tablespoon whole-grain mustard
1 tablespoon Dijon mustard
2 sprigs rosemary, leaves only, finely chopped
1 teaspoon kosher salt
½ teaspoon freshly ground black pepper
3 tablespoons Worcestershire sauce
2 tablespoons soy sauce
½ cup olive oil
¼ cup extra-virgin olive oil

Combine the sugar, both vinegars, both mustards, rosemary, salt, and pepper in a medium bowl. Stir in the Worcestershire and soy sauces. Gradually whisk in both oils. The vinaigrette will keep covered in the refrigerator for up to 2 days.

Spicy Cilantro and Basil Sauce

Serve this sauce at summer barbecues. Its spicy tang and cool temperature is perfect in hot weather. Try it with grilled shrimp, tuna, and chicken. In Maine we love it on an August night with steamed or grilled lobster.

Makes about 1½ cups

1 cup canned unsweetened coconut milk
½ cup cilantro leaves
¼ cup basil leaves
¼ cup flat-leaf parsley
¼ cup vegetable oil
2 shallots, peeled
3 tablespoons freshly squeezed lime juice
2 tablespoons sugar
1 serrano chile, stemmed and seeded
2 teaspoons finely chopped gingerroot
1 teaspoon kosher salt

Combine all the ingredients in the jar of a blender and process for 30 seconds until smooth. Cover and refrigerate or keep at room temperature until serving. It is best used the same day it is made.

FRESH HERBS

Fresh herbs from the garden can transform a weeknight meal into a memorable occasion with virtually no effort. One of our favorite quick summer dinners is pasta tossed with olive oil, fresh herbs, and chopped ripe tomatoes. The proportion of oil, tomatoes, and herbs scarcely matters—use as much of whatever you like, tossing it all together with the hot pasta. We use whatever is coming out of the garden, mixing tarragon, parsley, chives, thyme, basil, oregano, marjoram, even dill or mint. Add some crumbled feta or Parmesan cheese and you've got a meal. Add grilled jumbo shrimp and you've got a dinner fit for company. Assuming your ingredients are impeccably fresh and ripe, this will impress guests as much as a dish you slaved over all day.

Marinades are another good way to get the flavor of herbs into every dish. The simplest version doesn't require a recipe: Just add a few tablespoons of herbs to a few tablespoons of olive oil and brush it over vegetables, fish, poultry, or meat before cooking. Try tarragon and thyme for roasted chicken or grilled vegetables like squash, eggplant, bell peppers, scallions, and leeks. An easy marinade for grilled steak or seafood is to warm a few tablespoons of olive oil with several sprigs of rosemary for about 5 minutes. Let it cool, then brush it over the meat before grilling. (For an even more flavorful take on this idea, see Clark's Mom's Salmon Vinaigrette, page 159.)

Vietnamese Clear Dipping Sauce

Our version of this standard Vietnamese table condiment includes Vietnamese coriander, which is very different from cilantro, the common Mexican variety of coriander sold in most stores. Vietnamese coriander has long, pointed leaves and a strong lemony taste that is almost as aromatic as perfume. It's easy to grow from seed, and you can bring it indoors for the winter. A decent substitute in this recipe is lemon verbena or mint. Serve this sauce with meat or fish.

Makes about 1½ cups

½ cup sugar
1 serrano chile, stemmed and finely chopped
1 tablespoon finely chopped gingerroot
1 tablespoon finely chopped basil leaves
1 tablespoon finely chopped Vietnamese coriander leaves,
    or lemon verbena or mint leaves
1 tablespoon finely chopped cilantro leaves
1 cup rice vinegar
¼ cup freshly squeezed lime juice
1 tablespoon fish sauce (available at Asian and specialty markets)

Combine the sugar, chile, ginger, basil, coriander, and cilantro in a medium bowl. Add the vinegar, lime juice, and fish sauce and stir until the sugar is dissolved. Alternatively, you can put all the ingredients in a tightly sealed jar and shake well. The sauce is best used on the day it is made, but it will keep in a sealed container in the refrigerator for up to 2 days.

Cool Cucumber Coulis

When he was a kid, Clark started a garden, which, like a typical kid, he promptly neglected. The one crop that survived and even flourished was cucumbers. At Arrows, too, they grow like weeds. One summer we were afraid they might invade the neighborhood, so we came up with this "cool" cucumber coulis. It's a perfect balance for all kinds of spicy food and is great paired as a double condiment with a spicy chile sauce and served with Lobster and Fresh Vegetable Spring Rolls (page 114). Best of all, it's easy to make.

Makes about 2 cups

1 large cucumber
$\frac{1}{2}$ cup cilantro leaves
$\frac{1}{4}$ cup rice vinegar
1 tablespoon finely chopped gingerroot
2 teaspoons kosher salt
$\frac{1}{2}$ cup sour cream or crème fraîche

1. Peel and halve the cucumber lengthwise. With a spoon, scrape out the seeds. Cut the cucumber into 1-inch pieces and put these into the jar of a blender. Add the cilantro, vinegar, ginger, and salt and purée until smooth.

2. Pour the cucumber purée into a bowl and whisk in the sour cream. Cover and refrigerate until needed for up to 1 day.

Creamy Corn Sauce

The essence of good cooking is simplicity and, in our opinion, nowhere is that more true than with corn. At the height of summer, corn is so sweet that it doesn't need a lot of fussing. This sauce, which we serve with lobster or halibut, is about as simple as it gets. The sauce plays off traditional creamy New England chowders—but without the bacon and potatoes—leaving the corn to stand on its own.

Makes about 3 cups

Kosher salt
2 cups fresh corn (cut from about 3 ears)
1 cup Chicken or Vegetable Stock (page 23 or 24)
$\frac{1}{2}$ cup heavy cream
Freshly ground black pepper

1. In a medium saucepan bring 2 quarts water and 1 tablespoon salt to a boil. Add the corn to the water, cook for 1 minute, and drain. Working in batches, purée the corn with the chicken stock in the jar of a blender until smooth; use about 1 cup corn and $\frac{1}{2}$ cup stock at a time. Transfer the purée to a bowl as you go.

2. Stir the cream into the corn and season with salt and pepper to taste. If not serving immediately, cool, cover, and refrigerate for up to 1 day.

3. When ready to serve, pour the sauce into a heavy saucepan and warm over medium heat, stirring occasionally to prevent scorching.

Roasted Pepper Pesto

This variation on classic pesto is a rich accompaniment to lamb and veal.

Makes about 2 cups

4 red bell peppers
$\frac{2}{3}$ cup plus 1 tablespoon olive oil
$\frac{1}{4}$ cup toasted pine nuts (page 272)
2 tablespoons finely grated Reggiano Parmesan
2 tablespoons freshly squeezed lemon juice
1 clove garlic, peeled
Kosher salt
Freshly ground black pepper

1. Preheat the oven to 450 degrees F.
2. In a bowl toss the peppers with the 1 tablespoon oil. Transfer to a baking sheet and bake for 10 minutes. Turn the peppers over and cook for another 10 minutes until completely soft.
3. Remove the peppers from the oven. Transfer the peppers to a bowl and cover with plastic wrap; set aside for 10 minutes. Remove the peppers from the bowl, and when they are cool enough to handle, remove the stems, seeds, and as much of the skin as possible.
4. Combine the roasted peppers in the jar of a blender with $\frac{2}{3}$ cup oil, the pine nuts, Parmesan, lemon juice, and garlic and process until smooth. Season with salt and pepper. Cover and refrigerate until needed, for up to 2 days.

Fast Tomato Sauce

The faster you cook tomatoes, the fresher the sauce tastes. So fast cooking is what you want in August, when the tomatoes are at their natural ripest and are flying out of the garden. This sauce is made in about 20 minutes—the time it takes water to boil for pasta. It's not necessary to peel the tomatoes; as generations of Italian grandmothers have known, the skin adds a rustic bite to the sauce.

Makes about 4 cups

12 medium tomatoes (about 3 pounds)
½ cup olive oil
1 medium onion, peeled and finely chopped
4 cloves garlic, peeled and finely chopped
1 cup basil leaves
1 cup chopped flat-leaf parsley
1 tablespoon chopped rosemary leaves
Kosher salt
Freshly ground black pepper
1 cup red wine

1. Cut the tomatoes in half around the circumference and squeeze out the seeds. Coarsely chop the tomatoes into ½-inch pieces.

2. In a large stainless-steel saucepan, warm the olive oil over medium heat. Add the onion and garlic and cook, stirring frequently, until the onion is soft and translucent, 5 to 7 minutes. Add the tomatoes; cover and cook for 5 minutes.

3. Remove the cover and add the herbs. Sprinkle lightly with salt and pepper and add the red wine. Cover again and cook for another 5 minutes. Stir the sauce and taste. Season with salt and pepper as needed. Serve at once or let cool, then refrigerate in a tightly sealed nonreactive container for up to 2 days. It will also keep frozen for up to 1 month.

Ways to Water

We're big believers in underground irrigation with soaker hoses, those leaky black hoses that sweat water right into the ground. (You can buy them at any hardware store or home center.) We use them on everything except herbs and lettuces, which don't mind overhead water. Almost everything else can get all sorts of diseases when the leaves get wet, especially around coastal Maine, where the foggy air is wet enough to touch most days anyway.

Besides keeping plants dry and disease free, soaker hoses conserve water because none is wasted by evaporation; what comes out goes down to the roots, period. They also save time. Although they take some initial effort to set up, it's nothing compared to the hours later spent dragging around sprinklers or standing in the garden like a scarecrow with a hose in your hand.

To make sure no water evaporates, we lay the soaker hoses around our garden beds right after planting, then mulch over them with landscape cloth that lets moisture through, followed by salt marsh hay (available at good garden centers), which has no weed seeds. It's expensive hay, but it should last four years if you pull it back in fall and keep it dry over the winter.

The main thing to understand about soaker hoses is that you can't string hundreds of feet together in one long snake, or the water will never reach the end of the line. It is better to connect several soaker hoses to an inexpensive splitter valve, which allows running four or more hoses off one spigot, so the water is distributed evenly to all the hoses at once.

It's hard to say how long to leave the hoses running because everything depends on your setup, climate, and water pressure. But figure that an average vegetable garden needs about an inch of water per week. (Herbs need less; watery crops like cucumbers need more.) If your soil feels dry at the depth of your finger (beyond where the dew keeps the surface moist), you need to water.

If you must water with a sprinkler, do it early in the morning; running a sprinkler at midday shocks plants because half the water evaporates off them in minutes. It's a waste to boot. ᴓ

Slow-Roasted Tomato, Parmesan, and Basil Sauce

When Mark was a beginning chef at Maine's famous old restaurant the Whistling Oyster, he spent a few days working with an accomplished Italian chef visiting from Rome. One of the best things he learned was this elegant slow-roasted tomato and basil cream sauce. Slow-roasting concentrates the flavor of tomatoes, and it's easy to do. This sauce adds richness to vegetarian main courses such as Mushroom, Leek, and Potato Strudel (page 139) or a simple pasta dish.

Makes about 3 cups

8 medium tomatoes, cored
1 tablespoon olive oil
Kosher salt
Freshly ground black pepper
1 cup basil leaves
1 cup heavy cream
$^{1}/_{4}$ cup grated Reggiano Parmesan

1. Preheat the oven to 300 degrees F.
2. Toss the tomatoes with the olive oil, sprinkle with salt and pepper, and transfer to a baking dish. Cover with foil and roast for 2 hours until very soft.
3. Remove the tomatoes from the oven and pour the liquid from the baking dish into a measuring cup. Put the tomatoes and basil leaves in the jar of a blender and add about $^{1}/_{2}$ cup of the tomato liquid, just enough to get the mixture moving in the blender. (Discard the rest of the liquid.) Process for 1 minute. Pass the purée through a fine sieve, pushing the pulp through with the back of a spoon or ladle, into a bowl. Set aside.
4. In a medium stainless-steel saucepan bring the cream to a simmer over medium heat, then reduce the heat to low. Cook, stirring occasionally, until the cream is reduced by half, about 30 minutes.
5. Add the tomato purée and Parmesan to the cream. Increase the heat to medium and bring the mixture to a simmer, stirring constantly so that the sauce does not scorch. Season with salt and pepper to taste. Serve at once or cool, cover, and refrigerate for up to 1 day. Before serving, warm the sauce over low heat.

Spicy Corn Relish

We created our own rendition of this old southern staple, which can be served with grilled fish or chicken, as well as many other main courses.

Makes about 3 cups

½ cup champagne or cider vinegar
½ cup sugar
2 cups fresh corn kernels (cut from about 3 ears)
1 small red onion, peeled and finely chopped
1 small red bell pepper, stemmed, seeded, and finely diced
½ serrano or jalapeño chile, stemmed, seeded, and finely chopped
2 teaspoons kosher salt

1. Put the vinegar and sugar in a stainless-steel saucepan and bring to a boil.

2. Add the corn, onion, bell pepper, chile, and salt and return to a boil. Reduce the heat and simmer for 3 minutes. Remove the pan from the heat, transfer the relish to a bowl, and refrigerate. Once cool, the relish can be kept covered in the refrigerator for up to 1 week.

Tomatillo Salsa

Even as far north as Maine, tomatillos grow like weeds. Although they are in the same family as tomatoes (*Solanaceae*), they are more closely related (by genus *Physalis*) to the decorative Chinese Lantern and some types of gooseberry. But we grow them just like tomatoes: Start the seeds indoors and transplant them outside after all danger of frost has passed. The husk-covered fruit ripens in mid-summer on vigorous, upright vines; pick when the fruit turns from green to light yellow and the fruit fills the husk. One or two tomatillo plants will keep your family in salsa until the first frost.

This salsa is light and healthy. We serve it with grilled fish, roast pork, and grilled steaks.

Makes about 2 cups

12 tomatillos, husked and finely diced
1 large red onion, peeled and finely chopped
2 tablespoons finely chopped cilantro leaves
1 tablespoon olive oil
1 tablespoon freshly squeezed lime juice
1 teaspoon finely chopped serrano chile
1 teaspoon kosher salt
1 teaspoon freshly ground black pepper

Put all the ingredients in a medium bowl and mix together. Cover and refrigerate until needed for up to 1 day.

SIDE DISHES

Thai-Style Corn-on-the-Cob

The natural sugar in corn starts to convert to starch as soon as it's picked, which is why local corn from a garden or farmers' market always tastes sweeter than that from the supermarket. Corn takes up a lot of space in the garden; if you don't have much room, you can grow baby corn and still have the pleasure of shucking your own corn crop. Best of all, you can eat the whole tender ear. If you want to try this Thai-inspired grill recipe with baby corn, just thread several of the small cobs on a skewer. Serve with grilled tuna or roasted pork.

Makes 6 servings

Kosher salt
6 ears corn, shucked
$\frac{1}{2}$ cup canned unsweetened coconut milk
3 tablespoons clarified butter (page 44), melted
1 teaspoon freshly ground black pepper
6 sturdy bamboo chopsticks, soaked in water for at least 30 minutes

1. In a large pot bring 2 quarts water and 1 tablespoon salt to a boil. Add the corn, cook for 3 minutes, and drain.

2. Toss the corn in a bowl with the coconut milk, the butter, 1 tablespoon salt, and the pepper.

3. Start a charcoal or gas grill.

4. Using an ice pick, awl, or small, sturdy knife, make a $1\frac{1}{2}$-inch-deep hole in the stalk end of each ear of corn and insert a chopstick. Grill the corn, turning it regularly so as not to burn it, for 2 to 4 minutes until lightly browned. Serve at once.

Mom's Market–Basket Ratatouille

Clark's mother often made this perfect summer vegetable dish after a morning spent at the farmers' market. There, as in our own garden, peppers, eggplants, and squash are on brilliant display during late summer. Perhaps no dish better exemplifies the principal of cooking with the season than ratatouille. We serve ours with roasted or grilled lamb and with "big" fish such as tuna or salmon.

Makes 6 servings

1 medium zucchini
1 medium yellow summer squash
½ cup olive oil
6 cloves garlic, peeled and finely chopped
1 large red onion, peeled, halved, and thinly sliced
Kosher salt
Freshly ground black pepper
1 small Italian eggplant, cut into ½-inch pieces
1 medium red bell pepper, stemmed, seeded, and thinly sliced
1 medium yellow bell pepper, stemmed, seeded, and thinly sliced
¼ cup red wine vinegar

1. Cut the skins with about ⅛ inch of the flesh from the zucchini and the summer squash. Discard the cores. Slice the squash skins crosswise ½ inch thick.

2. Warm the olive oil in a large stainless-steel sauté pan over medium heat. Add the garlic, onion, and salt and pepper to taste. Sauté for 5 minutes, stirring frequently.

3. Add the eggplant, red and yellow peppers, and sliced zucchini and yellow squash. Sauté, stirring frequently, over medium-low heat until the vegetables are just tender, about 10 minutes.

4. Stir in the vinegar, add more salt and pepper if needed, and remove from the heat. Serve warm, at room temperature, or slightly chilled. Once cooled, the ratatouille can be covered and refrigerated for up to 1 day.

THE ZUCCHINI THAT ATE MAINE

They say that in Maine the only reason to lock your car is to keep other folks from tossing in their zucchini. Anyone who gardens knows the feeling. Somehow those few seeds morph into a bumper crop that could feed a small country. One way to control the zucchini invasion is to pick the squash when quite small and tender. Left on the vine, zukes can double in size seemingly before your eyes. But sooner or later you'll neglect the garden for a couple days and return to find several of these monsters hiding under the leaves. Remain calm. Stay in your home. And get out the frying pan. Here are some of our favorite ways to deal with the zucchini invasion.

- We love to make zucchini pancakes, which we serve with duck, grilled fish, and roast chicken. Grate just the outside part (including the peel) and toss the cores, which are full of seeds and don't have much flavor. Salt the shredded zukes and let rest for 30 minutes, then rinse and squeeze out the moisture. Shred in some onion, carrots, and cabbage if you like, bind it with some flour (about $1/4$ cup per 2 cups of vegetable) and eggs (1 per 2 cups of vegetable), add salt and pepper, then brown in hot olive oil. To make them Asian style, use rice flour and add some shredded ginger and chile paste. Or simply substitute zucchini for the parsnips and carrots in Lentil, Root Vegetable, and Herb Cakes (page 260).
- Small zucchini can be transformed quickly into an exotic salad. First cut the zucchini into matchsticks about 3 inches long and $1/8$ inch wide. (A mandoline fitted with the 5mm blade works perfectly, or just use a knife.) For a Near Eastern flavor, toss the zucchini matchsticks with mint leaves, lemon juice, cashews, and currants. Or for a Southeast Asian version, toss with lime juice, basil and cilantro leaves, peanuts, chopped fresh chiles, and a dash of fish sauce.
- Make a quick Italian antipasto by slicing zucchini lengthwise, tossing with olive oil, salt, and pepper, and grilling until golden.
- Thinly slice zucchini and sauté with garlic, rosemary, and olive oil, or your favorite herbs and butter.
- Make zucchini "cutlets" by slicing crosswise about $1/2$ inch thick; coat the slices with flour, then egg, then bread crumbs, and sauté until golden brown on both sides.
- Thinly slice zucchini and serve raw with tomatoes, basil, and goat cheese.

Seared Orange and Cabbage Salad

One summer our garden produced a bumper crop of Chinese and Napa cabbages, which are huge. We used the cabbage in many ways, but this was the most popular. Cooking with dried orange peel—which in this recipe is accomplished by searing a fresh peel—is a classic technique in Chinese cooking. Here the orange adds another dimension to the traditional Asian method of pickling cabbage. Serve with both meat and fish.

Makes 6 servings

3 large oranges
1 large head Napa cabbage
2 teaspoons kosher salt
2 tablespoons vegetable oil
1 teaspoon finely chopped garlic
¼ cup rice vinegar
¼ cup sugar
1 tablespoon finely chopped gingerroot
1 tablespoon sweet chile paste (available at Asian and specialty markets)
1 tablespoon sesame oil
1 tablespoon soy sauce

1. With a vegetable peeler, remove the zest from the oranges in long strips, avoiding the white pith underneath. Squeeze the juice from the oranges and set aside.

2. Wash, dry, and cut the cabbage lengthwise into quarters. Remove the core and slice the quarters crosswise 1 inch thick. Transfer the cabbage to a large bowl, sprinkle with the salt, and toss to combine.

3. Heat the vegetable oil in a heavy stainless-steel saucepan over high heat until smoking hot. Add the orange zest and stir vigorously for about 1 minute, being careful not to blacken the peel.

4. Reduce the heat to medium, add the garlic, and stir until it is slightly brown. Add the orange juice, vinegar, sugar, ginger, chile paste, sesame oil, and soy sauce. Increase the heat and bring to a boil. Pour the boiling liquid over the cabbage and allow it to cool, stirring occasionally. Once cool, the cabbage can be covered and refrigerated for up to 1 day.

Chive Mashed Potatoes

Mashed potatoes are an American classic; when Mark was growing up, they appeared on the dinner table at least once a week. We make an indulgent version at Arrows, opting for cream, but milk works well too. Chopped chives, abundant in summer, add wonderful flavor.

Makes 6 servings

2 pounds Yukon Gold or white potatoes, peeled and cut
    into 1½-inch cubes
Kosher salt
4 tablespoons (½ stick) unsalted butter, at room temperature
1 cup heavy cream or whole milk, at room temperature
¼ cup finely chopped chives

1. Put the potatoes in a medium saucepan. Add 2 tablespoons salt and enough cold water to cover the potatoes by 2 inches. Bring to a boil and cook until the potatoes are very soft when pierced by a knife, about 20 minutes.

2. Drain the potatoes and immediately transfer them to a standing mixer fitted with the whisk attachment. Whip the potatoes on medium speed, gradually adding the butter, cream, and, finally, the chives. (Alternatively, pass the potatoes through a potato ricer or food mill into a bowl, then whisk in the other ingredients.) Season with salt to taste. Serve at once or cover and keep warm for an hour in a double boiler set over very low heat.

5 WAYS TO STRETCH YOUR GARDEN

Until they start giving away land, most gardeners will have to make do with less space than they'd like. At Arrows we're experts on maximizing garden space. With three gardeners working less than an acre of land, we keep our beds busy. Some plots get rotated several times during the same season, lying "fallow" for all of 24 hours. You probably don't need to garden as intensively as we do, but here are some ways to make sure something is always coming up.

- Plant beets or parsnips in pea beds after the peas are finished in July. The root crops will be ready to harvest in late fall.
- Stagger lettuce plantings, starting new seeds every three weeks or so. Otherwise you'll have bushels of lettuce in spring and none in late summer to go with your tomatoes.
- After harvesting garlic in August, sow a fall crop of spinach or chard, which will last until frost. Or sow fall peas by the end of August, but use varieties like Eclipse that are resistant to powdery mildew.
- Plant kale and spinach in late fall for an early spring crop.
- Sow radishes between rows of slower growing plants like leeks. By the time the leeks need space, the radishes will be gone.

Yam and Leek Gratin

This late-summer gratin is inspired by childhood family meals. It's simple to make and beautiful too, with its multiple orange layers. The crispy, caramelized top layer gives way to the velvety sweetness of the yams and leeks. The dish is always a favorite at Arrows because of the rich and mellow flavors, which work well with both meat and fish. It can also serve as the centerpiece of a vegetarian dinner.

Makes 6 servings

Kosher salt
3 large leeks, light part only, cut into ¼-inch rings, well washed
6 medium yams, peeled and very thinly sliced (no thicker than ⅛ inch)
Freshly ground black pepper
1 cup heavy cream

1. Preheat the oven to 350 degrees F.
2. In a large pot bring 2 quarts water and 1 tablespoon salt to a boil. Fill a medium bowl halfway with ice water. Drop the leeks into the boiling water and cook for 15 seconds. Drain the leeks in a colander, then immediately submerge them in the ice bath. Let cool, drain, and wrap in a clean kitchen towel to dry.
3. Butter an 8-inch square, 2-quart baking dish. In the bottom of the dish, arrange a layer of one-third of the yams slightly overlapping each other. Sprinkle lightly with salt and pepper. Arrange half the leeks over the yams. Repeat the yam layer, the leek layer, then top with a final layer of yams. Do not put pepper on the last layer.
4. Pour the heavy cream into the baking dish and cover with foil. Bake for 1 hour.
5. Remove the foil and bake for 20 minutes more until the yams have absorbed almost all the liquid and are golden brown. Remove the gratin from the oven and let sit for 10 minutes. Cut the gratin into 6 squares and transfer the squares to plates with a metal spatula. Serve at once.

NOTE: A mandoline is a handy tool for thinly slicing yams.

Arrows Yellow Curry with Summer Vegetables

When your tomatoes and squash get away from you in August, here's a way to use them. The spiciness of the curry is nicely balanced by the cooling coconut milk. Serve with Lemongrass and Lemon Roasted Chicken (page 152) or Crispy Trout with Ginger and Lemongrass (page 47).

Makes 6 servings

1 tablespoon vegetable oil
2 stalks lemongrass, yellow part only, cut into 1-inch pieces
1 tablespoon finely chopped gingerroot
1 tablespoon Thai yellow curry paste (available at Asian and specialty markets)
2 teaspoons turmeric
2 (13.5-ounce) cans unsweetened coconut milk
6 kaffir lime leaves (available at Asian and specialty markets)
½ cup heavy cream
2 teaspoons fish sauce (available at Asian and specialty markets)
2 teaspoons freshly squeezed lime juice
2 tablespoons sugar
1 medium zucchini, cut into ¼-inch cubes
1 medium yellow summer squash, cut into ¼-inch cubes
¼ cup basil leaves
¼ cup cilantro leaves
½ cup Tomato Concassé (page 179)

1. Warm the vegetable oil in a large sauté pan over medium heat. Add the lemongrass, ginger, curry paste, and turmeric and sauté for 5 minutes. Add the coconut milk and lime leaves and simmer for 10 minutes. Add the cream, fish sauce, lime juice, and sugar and simmer for 10 minutes more.

2. Strain the curry through a fine sieve into a medium stainless-steel saucepan. Add the zucchini and summer squash and simmer for 4 minutes until tender. Add the basil, cilantro, and tomato concassé and serve at once.

Tomato Concassé

Tomato concassé—chopped, peeled, and seeded tomato—adds color and flavor to pastas and makes a brilliant garnish for many dishes. We also use it in salads. It's easy to make if you have ripe, firm tomatoes. It can be stored in a sealed nonreactive container in the refrigerator for up to 1 day or in the freezer for up to 1 month.

Makes about 2 cups

Kosher salt
6 large tomatoes

1. Bring 2 quarts water and 1 teaspoon salt to a boil in a large pot. Prepare an ice bath by filling a medium bowl halfway with ice water. Add the tomatoes to the boiling water and cook for 10 seconds. Transfer the tomatoes with a slotted spoon to the ice bath and allow them to chill completely.

2. Remove the tomatoes from the ice bath and slip off the peels. Cut through the equator of each tomato and squeeze out the seeds.

3. Place the tomatoes cut side down on a cutting board, flatten them with the palm of your hand, then cut the tomatoes into ½-inch dice.

Onion and Rosemary Focaccia

The onions in this rich, yeasty dough caramelize on top during baking, filling the kitchen with their sweet smell. Rosemary, one of the most intensely aromatic herbs, holds its own against the onions. Serve with pasta or a salad and make sandwiches with any leftovers the next day.

Makes 24 pieces, about 12 servings

2 (¼-ounce) envelopes active dry yeast
6 cups bread flour
2 cups lukewarm water
1 medium onion, peeled and finely chopped
1 tablespoon kosher salt
2 rosemary sprigs, leaves only, finely chopped
¾ cup olive oil, plus additional for topping
Cornmeal for dusting
Coarse sea salt, optional

1. Combine the yeast and 2 tablespoons of the flour in a small bowl. Add ½ cup of the water and mix lightly. Set aside until bubbly on top, 5 to 10 minutes.

2. Put the remaining flour in the bowl of a standing mixer fitted with the dough hook. Add the yeast mixture and remaining 1½ cups water and mix on medium-low speed until the mixture forms a stiff dough, 1 to 2 minutes. (Alternatively, stir the yeast mixture and flour together in a large bowl.) Cover the dough with plastic wrap and let rise until doubled in size, about 1 hour.

3. In a small bowl mix together the onion, kosher salt, rosemary, and half of the oil. Set aside.

4. Once the dough has risen, return the bowl to the mixer. With the mixer on low speed, slowly drizzle in the remaining oil, allowing it to be absorbed. Stop the machine, add the onion mixture, and mix the dough on medium-low speed for 4 to 6 minutes, until shiny. (Alternatively, combine the oil, onion mixture, and dough in a large bowl, then turn it out onto a lightly floured board and knead by hand for 6 minutes until smooth and elastic.) Transfer the dough to a well-oiled bowl and let rise, covered with plastic wrap, for 30 minutes until almost doubled in size.

5. Preheat the oven to 400 degrees F. Oil a 16 x 12-inch rimmed baking sheet and dust with cornmeal; shake off the excess.

6. Turn the dough onto a worktable, form it into a rectangle the size of the prepared pan, and fit it in the pan. Brush the top with olive oil and let the dough rise in a warm place until almost doubled in size.

7. With your fingers, press dimples about 1 inch apart all over the dough. Sprinkle with sea salt if using. Bake for 20 to 25 minutes until golden.

8. Remove from the oven and cut into 24 rectangles. Serve hot from the oven or at room temperature. Once cool, the focaccia will keep well wrapped at room temperature for up to 2 days.

DESSERTS

Cinnamon Basil Shortcakes with Peaches

Using herbs in desserts will change the way you think about the last course, and change the way you garden as well. Many exotic herbs, including cinnamon basil, lemon basil, chocolate mint, orange mint, and lemon verbena, actually taste like classic dessert ingredients. And sugar helps bring out these unexpected flavors. Although unusual, these herbs are easy to grow yourself; in fact, most need almost no care at all. (Looking for them in supermarkets is hit-or-miss, but herb purveyors at greenmarkets often carry some of them.) For this recipe, you could substitute regular basil.

Makes 12 servings

2½ cups all-purpose flour
12 tablespoons (1½ sticks) unsalted butter, cold, cut into small cubes
⅓ cup plus 7 tablespoons sugar
2½ teaspoons baking powder
½ teaspoon baking soda
¼ teaspoon kosher salt
12 large cinnamon basil leaves, finely chopped
2 large eggs
About ½ cup buttermilk
1 tablespoon ground cinnamon
8 peaches
¾ cup heavy cream, cold

1. Preheat the oven to 400 degrees F.
2. In the bowl of a food processor fitted with the metal blade, pulse the flour, butter,

⅓ cup sugar, baking powder, baking soda, salt, and basil, until the mixture resembles corn-meal. (Alternatively, combine the ingredients by hand or with a pastry cutter in a large bowl.)

3. Crack the eggs into a measuring cup and add enough buttermilk to measure ¾ cup; beat with a fork to combine. Add the buttermilk mixture to the dough in the food proces-sor and pulse just until the dough starts to come together. Turn the dough onto a lightly floured worktable and gently knead about 12 times to bring everything together. Cover the dough with plastic wrap and let rest for 5 minutes.

4. Mix together the remaining 7 tablespoons sugar and the cinnamon. Set aside.

5. Roll or pat the dough about ¾ inch thick and cut it with a 2½-inch biscuit cutter or thin-lipped glass. After cutting, reroll the scraps and cut more rounds. Continue this process once or twice until all the dough has been cut. You should have 12 rounds.

6. Transfer the rounds to a cookie sheet lined with parchment paper and brush them lightly with water. Sprinkle them with 2 tablespoons of the cinnamon sugar. Bake the shortcakes for 10 minutes until golden brown. Remove the shortcakes from the oven, transfer to a rack, and let cool. If you are not using the shortcakes right away, store them in an airtight container for up to 1 day.

7. Slice the peaches and place them in a bowl. Sprinkle the remaining cinnamon sugar over the peaches and toss them to coat. Let the peaches sit for 30 minutes.

8. With an electric mixer (or by hand using a wire whisk), whip the cream on medium speed until soft peaks form. Use immediately or cover and refrigerate for up to 3 hours.

9. To serve, split the shortcakes horizontally. (If desired, you can warm them for 5 minutes in an oven that has been preheated to 400 degrees F.) Put the bottom half of each cake on one of 12 plates. Spoon the peaches and half of their juice over the bottom halves of the cakes, dot with whipped cream, and cover with the top halves of the cakes. Drizzle the plates with the remaining peach juice.

NOTE: You can substitute strawberries in season for the peaches; prepare them the same way.

COMMUNITY-SUPPORTED AGRICULTURE

If you don't have room for a garden of your own, you can still get involved in local food production—and learn to think like a chef-gardener—by joining a local Community Supported Agriculture (CSA) farm. In return for buying a "share" in a CSA, members receive a selection of fresh, healthy vegetables delivered (usually to a specified location in town) every week. Because the selection is based on what's ripe and ready, you never know exactly what you're getting. (Count on lots of chard but expect tomatoes in August.) It's great fun to arrive at the pick-up site and be surprised by the harvest of the week. Because it probably includes at least a few things you wouldn't have thought to buy in the store, you'll be forced to get creative in the kitchen, as chefs do. You'll also learn a lot about what grows—and when—in your area and have the satisfaction of knowing that you are supporting local farmers.

The cost of a CSA membership varies by region and services—some have options to purchase locally raised meat, eggs, and cut flowers—but it's typically a fraction of what you already spend at the supermarket. Go to www.biodynamics.com/usda to find organic CSAs in your area.

If you live anywhere near a rural area, you can find local farmers to supply you with meat and dairy products. Most farmers have limited marketing budgets, to put it mildly, often consisting of a hand-lettered sign in the front yard, so you need to be diligent and keep looking. Just about every working farm has animals that must occasionally be culled, such as male sheep (they're called rams), which can be dangerously feisty. Many farms sell butchered lamb or mutton for much cheaper than the grocery store, and it's almost always better. Ask what the animals have been fed; you want naturally raised, grass-fed meat. You'll have the most luck if you buy in quantity because most farmers don't have the time to package and sell individual cuts. (Owning a chest or upright freezer is a real advantage here.)

Pork is even easier to find in the countryside, because pigs don't need much room and aren't too finicky about food. Best of all, local farm pigs usually have much more fat than commercially raised pigs, which unfortunately have been bred and fed to be as lean as chicken. This is not a virtue: When it comes to pork, the fat is where the flavor is.

Beef is harder to find locally because the animals are simply too big to be slaughtered easily. But you can probably find fresh local milk and cream. Look for farmers who raise Jersey cows, which produce very rich milk often used in cheese making. (Jersey cows are uniformly tan in color; avoid milk from Holsteins, the common black-and-white cows that produce most commercial milk, which is thin and watery by comparison.)

To learn even more about food production spend some time working on a local farm. Most farms need able-bodied helpers at some time of the year (usually in summer). The pay is low but the experience, especially for young people, will be memorable. Contact your agricultural extension service; every state has one, affiliated with land-grant universities.

Orange-Blackberry Tart

We love the crunchy and smooth textures in this tart, which also combines two of our favorite dessert flavors—citrus and berries. Several of the steps can be done in stages. The tart dough and filling can be made up to 2 days ahead, but don't place the blackberries on top until a few hours before serving.

Makes 10 servings

FOR THE TART DOUGH

16 tablespoons (2 sticks) unsalted butter, cold, cut into small cubes
½ cup sugar
1 large egg
1 teaspoon finely grated lemon zest
2½ cups all-purpose flour

1. Pulse the butter, sugar, egg, and lemon zest in the bowl of a food processor fitted with the metal blade just a few times to break up the butter a bit. With the machine off, add the flour. Pulse again just until the ingredients form a dough. (Alternatively, combine the ingredients by hand or with a pastry cutter in a large bowl.)

2. Transfer the dough to a floured worktable and gently knead just a few times to bring it together. Wrap the dough in plastic wrap and refrigerate until firm, about 1 hour, or for up to 1 day.

3. On a floured table, roll the dough into a circle ⅛ inch thick. Fit the dough into a 10-inch tart pan with a removable bottom, pressing the dough to the bottom of the pan to eliminate air bubbles. Trim the excess dough from the edges and prick the bottom a dozen times with a fork. Refrigerate until firm, about 1 hour.

4. Preheat the oven to 350 degrees F.

5. Put the tart shell on a baking sheet. Line the dough with foil and fill with dried beans or pie weights. Bake for 15 minutes. Carefully remove the foil with the weights and bake the shell for another 15 minutes until golden brown. Let cool in the pan. The tart shell will keep, well wrapped, for up to 1 day.

8 tablespoons (1 stick) unsalted butter, at room temperature

⅔ cup sugar

3 large eggs, at room temperature

2 large yolks, at room temperature

1 cup freshly squeezed orange juice, at room temperature

3 tablespoons freshly squeezed lemon juice

1 teaspoon unflavored powdered gelatin

Finely grated zest of 1 orange

1. In a large mixer bowl beat the butter and sugar until light and creamy, 3 to 5 minutes. Beat in the eggs and yolks one by one, scraping down the bowl between additions. Beat the mixture for a few minutes before gradually beating in the orange juice. The mixture may look slightly curdled, but do not worry; it will become smooth when it cooks.

2. Pour the lemon juice into a small bowl and sprinkle the gelatin on top. Set aside.

3. Pour the butter mixture into a medium stainless-steel saucepan and add the orange zest. Cook, whisking constantly, over medium heat until it thickens enough to coat the back of a spoon and the temperature reaches 170 degrees F on a kitchen thermometer. Do not let it boil. Take the pan off the heat, add the gelatin, and stir until the gelatin dissolves. Strain the mixture through a fine sieve into a bowl and let cool for about 30 minutes.

4. Pour the mixture into the baked shell. Refrigerate until set, about 3 hours, or for up to 1 day.

TO SERVE

1 cup heavy cream, cold

4 cups blackberries

1. With an electric mixer (or by hand using a wire whisk), whip the cream on medium speed until soft peaks form. Use immediately or refrigerate for up to 3 hours.

2. Arrange the blackberries on top of the orange filling in a pretty pattern. Cut the tart into 10 slices. Top each slice with whipped cream or serve the cream on the side.

Steamed Raspberry Pudding

Steamed puddings are a classic Yankee dessert. They tend to be served around the holidays, when they are made with pumpkin or molasses. This version is lighter and more suitable for summer.

Makes 6 servings

1½ cups fresh or frozen raspberries
1 cup sugar
12 tablespoons (1½ sticks) unsalted butter, at room temperature
2 large eggs
1½ cups all-purpose flour
1¼ teaspoons baking powder
1 teaspoon finely grated lemon zest
½ teaspoon ground cinnamon
⅔ cup whole milk

1. Preheat the oven to 350 degrees F.
2. Generously butter the inside of six 6-ounce round ramekins, then sprinkle with a little sugar and tap out the excess.
3. Toss the raspberries with ½ cup of the sugar and divide the mixture among the ramekins, arranging them to cover the bottom of each mold.
4. In a large mixer bowl beat together the butter and remaining ½ cup sugar on medium speed until light in color, 3 to 5 minutes. Beat in the eggs one at a time.
5. Mix together the flour, baking powder, lemon zest, and cinnamon in a bowl. Stir the dry ingredients, alternately with the milk, into the butter mixture, to make a smooth batter. Divide the batter equally among the ramekins, filling them to ¼ inch from the top.
6. Place the ramekins in a roasting pan, spacing them evenly. Add enough hot water to the pan to come halfway up the side of the molds. Butter a large piece of aluminum foil and place the foil, butter side down, on top of the pan. Seal it tightly around the edges.
7. Bake for about 35 minutes until a toothpick inserted into the center of the puddings comes out clean. Remove from the oven and allow the puddings to cool for 10 minutes in the water.
8. Remove the puddings from the molds by inverting them onto a rack. Serve the pud-

dings on warm plates. (If not serving immediately, cool the puddings completely in their molds, individually wrap them in plastic wrap, and refrigerate for up to 2 days. Before serving, unwrap the puddings, place them on a cookie sheet, and warm them for 5 minutes in an oven that has been preheated to 350 degrees F, then unmold.)

NOTES

1. You can serve the puddings in the molds, though they won't look as spectacular.

2. You can use foil ramekins instead of ceramic ones. Once the custards are baked, let them set for 5 minutes after removing them from the hot water. With a paring knife, poke a tiny slit in the bottom of each foil cup, then invert onto serving plates. Lift the foil cups off of the custards and serve.

Blackberry Compote

At Arrows we grow our own blueberries, strawberries, and raspberries. We also buy wild Maine blueberries as well as local blackberries for this compote. Serve it chilled with vanilla or a berry ice cream (page 198) and garnish it with edible orange or yellow flowers like calendula, nasturtium, or citrus marigold. The dark color of the berries contrasts boldly with the flower petals.

Makes about 1 quart

½ cup water
½ cup sugar
4 cups blackberries
Juice of 1 lemon

1. Combine the water and sugar in a medium stainless-steel saucepan.
2. Cut a circle of parchment paper that will cover the berries and liquid in the saucepan, and cut a half-inch hole in the center of the circle to vent steam; set aside. Bring the sugar and water to a boil over high heat and cook for 5 minutes. Remove the saucepan from the heat and add the berries. Cover the berries with the paper and set the saucepan back on the stove over medium-low heat. Simmer for 10 minutes; do not let the mixture boil. Remove the saucepan from the heat, remove the parchment paper, and gently stir in the lemon juice.
3. Cool the berry compote in the refrigerator. Once it is cool, cover and refrigerate in a nonreactive container for up to 3 days.

8 EDIBLE FLOWERS YOU CAN GROW

Some people are nervous about eating flowers, afraid they'll get sick. Indeed, there are many poisonous garden flowers—including larkspur, delphinium, and morning glory—but if you stick to the well-known edibles, you can relax and enjoy them.

Borage   Related to the popular forget-me-not, borage is an annual with small, star-shaped blue and pink flowers. We like small amounts of this strong-flavored herb in salads or in herb rubs for roast meat.

Calendula   These long-blooming orange flowers on 18- to 20-inch stalks are aromatic and slightly bitter. They can be dried like an herb and added to soups, or used fresh in summer salads. The plants self-sow like nothing else and will come back every year. We can't imagine a kitchen garden without them.

Chrysanthemum and Marigold   Separate but sympathetic branches of the Aster family, chrysanthemums and marigolds are grown mainly as ornamentals, but a few are considered edible. A type of Japanese chrysanthemum called *shungiku* (a variety of *Chrysanthemum coronarium*) is grown specifically as a vegetable. Its aromatic serrated leaves are harvested young for use in *oden,* a Japanese stew. But the 5-inch yellow flowers are edible too; they have a spicy, citrusy taste. You can also eat the flowers of smaller citrus marigold varieties, such as Lemon Gem and Orange Gem, which we like to grow.

Herb Flowers   Virtually all herbs have edible flowers, most of which taste stronger than the leaves. We use the tiny flowers of basil and thyme wherever we'd use the leaves. Bright-blue sage blossoms are a dramatic garnish for roast pork. Chives are generally grown for the green stalks, but the marble-size purple flower heads are also edible. They taste like the stalks only a bit spicier. Sprinkle the fine petals over soups or salads, just as you would the stalks.

Lavender   Fragrant lavender blossoms can make you sleepy, cure a headache, and soothe a burn. Do you need anything else? If that weren't enough, we make tea of lavender flowers (page 273), roast them with shallots (page 258), and add them to ice cream (page 98).

Nasturtium   Nasturtium's bright-orange flowers and 2- to 3-inch round leaves add a delicious peppery taste to salads. And they grow just about anywhere, actually preferring rather poor soil. What a miracle!

Rose   All roses are edible, but not all have much taste or fragrance. The best are the so-called old varieties—hardy rugosas and other bush-types that add an incredible perfume to ice cream. Avoid hybrid tea roses, which don't have much flavor. One of our favorite edible roses is a majestic heirloom climber called New Dawn, which we have trained over a trellis in our garden. We tend to use rose petals to flavor desserts and teas, but you can also sprinkle them on salads.

Viola Violas are one of the hardiest annual flowers, blooming brilliant purple and orange in early spring, when lettuce is also at its peak. Sprinkled over salads, viola blossoms add wintergreen flavor as well as rich color. ❧

Berry Sorbet with Orange Crisps

We love mixing different types of berries, which is also quite practical because you don't always have a lot of one type to harvest. This refreshing high-summer sorbet is great with orange crisps, which look like stained glass after they've baked. Use any combination of berries you like. You can also substitute thawed frozen berries.

Makes about 1 quart sorbet and about 3 dozen cookies, or 6 servings

FOR THE BERRY SORBET
3 cups mixed berries, such as raspberries, blueberries, and strawberries,
    plus additional for garnish
1½ cups sugar, plus more if needed
½ cup water
3 tablespoons freshly squeezed lemon juice
¼ teaspoon ground cinnamon

1. Fill a large bowl halfway with ice water. Have ready a smaller stainless-steel bowl that will sit in the ice bath.

2. Combine the berries, sugar, water, lemon juice, and cinnamon in a medium stainless-steel saucepan. Put the pan on the stove over low heat and cook, stirring occasionally, until the berries are soft and falling apart, about 10 minutes. Remove from the heat and cool slightly.

3. Transfer the mixture to the jar of a blender (work in batches if necessary) and purée until completely smooth. Strain through a fine sieve, pressing as much of the pulp through as possible. Discard the solids.

4. Taste the mixture; it should be very sweet and syrupy. (The sorbet will taste less sweet after it is frozen.) Depending on the sweetness of your berries, you might need to add as much as another ½ cup sugar; stir to dissolve it completely. Pour the berry syrup into the small bowl and place it in the ice bath to chill. Chill thoroughly, stirring occasionally.

5. Freeze the mixture in an ice cream machine, following the manufacturer's instructions.

6. Transfer the sorbet to a nonreactive container. Cover the surface of the sorbet with plastic wrap, then top with a lid. Freeze for at least 3 hours, or up to 1 week. If the sorbet gets too hard to scoop, break it up, transfer it to a food processor fitted with the

metal blade, and pulse a few times to soften it. Or if you have time, let it sit in the refrigerator for 30 minutes before serving.

FOR THE ORANGE CRISPS
8 tablespoons (1 stick) unsalted butter
½ cup sugar
3 tablespoons light corn syrup
½ cup plus 2 tablespoons all-purpose flour
Finely grated zest of 1 orange
1 tablespoon freshly squeezed orange juice

1. Combine the butter, sugar, and corn syrup in a medium saucepan; bring to a boil over medium heat, stirring occasionally.

2. Remove the saucepan from the stove and whisk in the flour, orange zest, and juice. Return the saucepan to medium heat and bring back to a boil while stirring. Boil and stir for 1 minute, then pour the mixture into a heatproof shallow dish. Refrigerate until the mixture can be formed into small balls, about 1 hour, or for up to 2 days.

3. Preheat the oven to 350 degrees F.

4. Scoop ½ teaspoon of the cookie dough and roll it into a little ball. Place 12 balls on an ungreased cookie sheet, leaving plenty of room between the balls as they will spread considerably in the oven. Bake for about 8 minutes until golden brown.

5. Remove the cookie sheet from the oven and let the cookies cool for 30 seconds. Remove the cookies with a thin metal spatula and place them on parchment paper or paper towels. Wipe the pan clean with a paper towel and let it cool completely before baking the next batch of cookies. Once completely cool, the cookies can be stored in an airtight container for 1 day. These cookies do not hold up well under humid conditions.

6. To serve, place 2 scoops of the sorbet into each of 6 chilled martini glasses or bowls and top each serving with 2 orange crisps. Garnish with fresh berries.

HOW TO FREEZE BERRIES

To freeze summer berries for later use, cover a rimmed baking sheet or shallow dish that fits in your freezer with plastic wrap and spread clean berries on it in a single layer, trying not to crowd them. Freeze for at least 2 hours. Check the berries to make sure they are frozen, then transfer them to a freezer bag, squeezing out any air from the bag. They will keep frozen for up to 2 months and retain their original shape, color, and flavor once thawed in the refrigerator. The texture will be less crisp, however. We use frozen berries in Blueberry Ice Cream (page 198) and as an informal topping for pound cake (page 345).

Cantaloupe Sorbet with Butter Cookies

Our pastry kitchen is right off the garden, which gives the pastry chef a definite advantage in scoping out the melon crop during late summer. Although we like to use melons in salads (page 130), we have to act fast if we hope to beat her to the melon patch. But when she turns melons into this tantalizing sorbet, we don't complain.

Makes about 1 quart sorbet and 4 dozen cookies, or 6 servings

FOR THE SORBET

2 medium cantaloupes
1 cup sugar, plus more if needed
$\frac{1}{4}$ cup water
$1\frac{1}{2}$ tablespoons freshly squeezed lime juice
$\frac{1}{4}$ teaspoon kosher salt

1. Quarter and seed the cantaloupes. Cut the flesh from the rinds and cut the flesh into 1-inch chunks. Measure about 8 cups cantaloupe chunks.

2. Put half of the melon, half of the sugar, and half of the water in the jar of a blender. Add the lime juice and salt and purée until silky smooth. Repeat the process with the remaining melon, sugar, and water.

3. Pass all the melon mixture through a fine sieve into a large nonreactive container, pressing as much of the pulp through as possible. Taste the mixture, it should be very sweet. (The sorbet will taste less sweet after it has frozen.) Depending on the sweetness of your melons, you might need to add as much as another $\frac{1}{2}$ cup of sugar.

4. Fill a large bowl halfway with ice water. Transfer the cantaloupe purée to a smaller stainless-steel bowl that sits in the ice bath. Chill the purée until very cold, stirring occasionally.

5. Freeze in an ice cream maker, following the manufacturer's instructions.

6. Transfer the sorbet to a nonreactive container. Cover the surface of the sorbet with plastic wrap, then top with a lid. Freeze for at least 3 hours, or up to 1 week. If the sorbet gets too hard to scoop, break it up, transfer it to a food processor fitted with a metal blade, and pulse a few times to soften it. Or if you have time, let it sit in the refrigerator for 30 minutes before serving.

FOR THE COOKIES

20 tablespoons (2½ sticks) unsalted butter, at room temperature
½ cup sugar
4 large egg yolks
1 tablespoon pure vanilla extract
3½ cups all-purpose flour
48 pecan halves, about 2 cups
1 large egg, for glazing

1. Preheat the oven to 350 degrees F.

2. In a large mixer bowl beat the butter until it is very light in color, 3 to 5 minutes. Add the sugar, egg yolks, and vanilla and mix very well, scraping down the bowl as needed. Add the flour to the butter mixture and mix slowly just until it forms a soft dough.

3. Form the dough with your hands into 48 balls, each 1 inch in diameter. Arrange them about 2 inches apart on cookie sheets lined with parchment paper. Flatten the cookies a little and push a pecan half onto each cookie.

4. Whisk the egg in a small bowl. Lightly brush each cookie with beaten egg.

5. Bake the cookies for about 10 minutes, rotating the pans halfway through this time if the cookies are baking unevenly, until deep golden brown. Cool them on a rack and store in a tightly sealed container for up to 1 week—if they last that long!

TO SERVE

Place 2 scoops of the sorbet in each of 6 chilled martini glasses or bowls and top each serving with 2 cookies.

NOTE: The cookie dough can be flavored with 1 tablespoon grated lemon zest, 1 teaspoon almond extract, or ½ cup toasted shredded coconut.

Blueberry Ice Cream

At Arrows we make everything from scratch, including this rich, fruity ice cream that tastes like the essence of summer. To make raspberry or vanilla ice cream, see the Note that follows.

Makes about 1 quart, or 6 servings

3 cups blueberries, plus a few additional for garnish
¼ cup water
2 cups heavy cream
1 cup sugar
Zest of 1 small lemon, removed in strips using a peeler
5 large egg yolks

1. Put the blueberries and water in a medium stainless-steel saucepan and cook over very low heat until the berries soften, about 5 minutes. Remove the pan from the heat and set aside to cool.

2. Transfer the berries to the jar of a blender and purée until completely smooth. Cover and refrigerate until needed or up to 1 day.

3. Fill a large bowl halfway with ice water. Have ready a smaller stainless-steel bowl that will sit in the ice bath.

4. Combine the cream, sugar, and lemon zest in a medium saucepan and cook over medium heat, stirring until the sugar dissolves. Bring the liquid to a simmer and turn off the heat.

5. Whisk the egg yolks in a medium bowl until light in color. Slowly add the hot cream while whisking constantly. Return the liquid to the saucepan and cook, stirring constantly with a wooden spoon, over medium heat until it reaches a temperature of 180 degrees F on a kitchen thermometer or it coats the back of the spoon. Strain the mixture through a fine sieve into the small bowl and place the bowl in the ice bath.

6. Stir the mixture until it cools slightly, then stir in the blueberry purée. Chill thoroughly, stirring occasionally.

7. Freeze the mixture in an ice cream machine, following the manufacturer's instructions. Serve at once or store the ice cream in a sealed container in the freezer for up to 1 week.

Place 2 scoops of ice cream in each of 6 chilled bowls. Garnish with fresh blueberries.

NOTES

1. To make red, white, and blue ice cream for the Fourth of July, make one batch of blueberry, another batch substituting raspberries for blueberries, and a third batch of vanilla ice cream. Serve as triple scoops in ice cream cones or in bowls.

When making raspberry ice cream, cook the berries for just 3 minutes and pass the berry purée through a fine sieve after puréeing to remove the tiny seeds.

2. To make vanilla ice cream, omit the berries and lemon zest. In Step 4, increase the cream to 3 cups and add the seeds from 1 vanilla bean. (Instead of vanilla seeds, you could add 2 teaspoons pure vanilla extract at the end of Step 5.)

BLUEBERRY HEAVEN

Blueberries are an important cash crop in Maine, which has the acidic soil and cold winters they love. (Our soil became acidic from eons of decomposing conifer forests.) The commercial crop is harvested from wild, low-bush blueberries, which are biennial and spread like ground cover across rocky fields called barrens. To clear weeds and encourage new growth, farmers burn their fields after the harvest in November or the following spring. (Native Americans were the first to notice that blueberries came back more vigorously after a forest fire.) The blackened, scorched barrens stretching to the horizon are striking—and very different from the same fields in fall, when the leaves turn bright red.

At Arrows we grow so-called high-bush blueberries, which produce large fruit every year on 4-foot-tall bushes. Easy to grow and care for, they're more suited to home gardening than the wild, spreading type. It's great fun to walk through the blueberry garden in August, plucking the juicy fruits. Kids love to help, but don't expect them to save many for your dessert.

If your soil is not acidic enough for blueberries (4.5 to 5.6 pH), consider yourself lucky! Few plants like soil that sour—azaleas and rhododendrons, actually related to blueberries, are exceptions. But you can easily bring down your pH by adding sulfur and mulching with peat moss. And in recent years, growers have introduced new blueberry varieties that perform well in warm climates. As long as you have the space (each bush needs about 25 square feet), there's very little excuse not to grow a few blueberry bushes.

And you won't need many, for the plants tend to overproduce, which leads to lots of smaller berries. To encourage bigger fruit, we prune out as many as one-quarter of the branches in early spring. We share our crop with the birds and still have plenty for ourselves, but some people cover their bushes with bird netting.

Blueberries can fool you at harvest time; they often look ripe before they are ripe. So inspect each berry carefully before picking. Really ripe ones have turned from shiny purple to dull blue and practically fall off the stem. If you have to actually tug, stop—and try again next weekend. ❧

FALL

LATE HARVEST

Fall comes fast in Maine. Suddenly it's September, and you see faint wisps of your breath in the garden one morning. Sweaters go on at night, even though the dahlias are reaching to the sky and the peppers are bright red. It's easy to deny summer is ending: Swimming is at its warmest around Labor Day (water cools more slowly than air), and kids are still doing cannonballs off the dock and spitting watermelon seeds, trying to put off the inevitable.

It's hard to say goodbye to fresh tomatoes, berries, and melons, and we savor those last tastes of summer long into September, even though the ripening winter squash tells us it's time to move on. So does the sun: It gets dark by dinnertime after Labor Day, and barbecuing must move under lantern light. We mourn the shorter days but revel in the crisp night air. As much as we enjoy the fruits of summer, fall is welcome at Arrows. It's the season to get serious again, and we're ready for something more substantial.

One thing we take seriously at Arrows is our apple crop, which has been ripening all summer in our orchard. Our apple trees were planted more than a hundred years ago and lived through a long period of neglect. Throughout Maine you can find forgotten orchards—some of them now deep in the forest, where they survive by growing straight up to the sky. It's amazing to walk in the woods and find an apple tree towering over the hemlocks, bearing fruit that only a monkey could reach.

We carefully prune and maintain our own apple trees, and every fall we harvest dozens of bushels of apples—far more than we can use. We serve them in every course, from Smoked Trout and Apple Salad with Horseradish Crème Fraîche (page 232) to Orchard

Apple Crisp (page 274). Apples are great with other fall crops (see Napa Cabbage and Apple Cole Slaw, page 229), and meat dishes that are inspired by ancient preservation techniques, such as Pork Loin Confit (page 244).

Maine is rightly proud of its heirloom apple orchards, but it's the maple trees that bring in thousands of tourists every October. These "leaf peepers" are fairly new to Maine; until the 1980s, our brilliant fall foliage displays were left largely to the locals.

Bringing that fiery display into our dining room is tricky. Maple leaves lose their color after a day or two, so it's not possible to use them as the basic structure of Big Bertha's fall arrangement. Instead we stick with the tried-and-true oak "skeleton" and use maple branches like cut flowers, changing them every day. Beech leaves animate a fall arrangement because you can bring them in green and they'll gradually turn yellow over a few days.

The leaf peepers bring a very different energy than do the summer crowds. One obvious change is that kids are back in school, so family vacationers are long gone. The local papers aren't listing as many public suppers, pie sales, and chowder contests. It's a time to slow down, greet old friends, and fire up the outdoor meat smoker. Smoking is a traditional fall activity that grew from necessity. Animals that grazed all summer in lush, green fields would have to be fed expensive grain and hay during winter. It often made more sense to butcher the animals in fall, rather than use precious resources feeding them. Smoking preserved the meat until the weather got cold enough to take over.

Today we smoke meat and seafood for the concentrated flavor it imparts. But the truth is we just love gathering around the warm, cozy meat smoker on brisk fall days. We consider it the autumn version of the summer barbecue, and you can do the same thing at home. (See How to Smoke Trout, page 233, and Smoked Duck Breasts with Swiss Chard and Pearl Onions, page 54.)

One day in fall we'll be rubbing our hands and stamping our feet around the smoker, trying to keep warm, then suddenly the next day the temperature climbs to seventy—Indian summer has arrived. The slower pace of autumn lets us enjoy these last shirtsleeve days. We hop in the car and drive to Boston or Camden, a storybook village hemmed in by mountains and the sea, two hours up the coast. Field trips give us a chance to taste what's cooking at other New England restaurants, and they reenergize us.

Fall is also melancholic. The blazing leaves wither and drop, extinguishing the last embers of summer. "A-yuh, we're headed into the tunnel," one knowing Mainer will say to another. We pay close attention to the weather forecast in fall, and especially to predictions of the first frost.

There are those who argue that autumn in Maine really lasts just one night—the night of the killing frost that separates summer from winter. Whether or not you believe that, it's certainly true that at Arrows the frost defines the season. After all, our menu is closely tied to our garden. The frost puts an end to tomatoes, peppers, basil, eggplant, sunflowers, and a host of other tender annual vegetables and flowers.

The amazing thing about the first frost is that it almost always precedes a month of frost-free weather. So, like most gardeners, we try to cheat that first cold snap to gain an extra month of growing. That means covering everything in sight with plastic sheets at the first hint of frost—a big job in a garden our size.

Long before the killing frost, we freeze whatever berries we haven't managed to eat fresh (page 195) and bring in bushels of herbs for drying, freezing, and making into flavored oils and vinegars (page 41). Used within a few months, dried herbs from the garden taste infinitely fresher than supermarket versions, and they are free for the taking.

Our bush beans turn brown by late September—a good sign, since the whole idea is to let the beans dry completely for optimal winter storage. (For more on growing beans, see page 85.) Once the beans start to rattle in the pods, they're ready to be harvested. Then we shuck them into burlap sacks and store them in the cellar until a really crisp day, when we make Escarole and White Bean Soup (page 295). One of our favorite soup beans is Maine Yellow Eye, a popular white heirloom with a pale yellow "eye" that disappears in cooking.

The last crops to come in are the pumpkins, gourds, and other winter squash. These quintessential fall crops require lots of garden space—the huge, spiky vines spread from here to Paducah. But they are simple to grow as long as you give them lots of compost. (Old-timers dropped the seeds right into piles of aged cow manure.) Once the vines take off, squash plants require almost no weeding because the massive leaves shade out competition.

After the squash comes in, the summer garden really starts to fade, and our greenhouse and raised beds again take center stage. Both extend the season when it gets cold in Maine, and we fill them with lettuce, greens, and herbs. Fortunately there are still hardy plants like kale, leeks, and parsnips in the outdoor garden, so we have an excuse to go out and walk through the rows. Soon even that simple pleasure will end; the forecast is calling for snow.

# APPETIZERS

Pumpkin Soup with Curried Pumpkin Seeds

Whenever we walk into our pumpkin patch, we feel like we've stepped into *Alice's Adventures in Wonderland*. The giant leaves, prickly vines, and massive pumpkins always seem a bit unreal—especially in fall, when the pumpkins ripen and turn the garden bright orange. That's when we feel Maine nights getting colder, and we start to crave hearty soups like this one. In France pumpkin is used almost exclusively in soup, so it seems natural to combine it with those other classic French soup ingredients—potatoes and leeks. You can also serve this soup chilled as pumpkin vichyssoise.

Most commercial pumpkins are grown for Halloween decorations and are too dry for cooking. Check fall greenmarkets for old-fashioned cooking varieties like Long Island Cheese, a popular blue-green American heirloom; Long Pie, an heirloom from northern Maine that looks like a giant zucchini; and Rouge Vif d'Etampes, the bright-orange French soup pumpkin. Seed catalogs carry these and many others. You can also substitute any large winter squash.

Curried pumpkin seeds add a crunchy texture and spicy flavor to the soup. They're also great on their own as a snack for a cocktail party. (To make as a snack, save 2 cups or more of the seeds, increasing the other ingredients for the curried pumpkin seeds accordingly.)

Makes 6 servings

FOR THE SOUP
1 pumpkin or other large winter squash, about 6 pounds
4 tablespoons olive oil
Kosher salt
Freshly ground black pepper

2 medium leeks, light part only, cut into ¼-inch rings,
    well washed and dried
2 large Yukon Gold or white potatoes, peeled and cut into 1-inch cubes
3 cups Chicken or Vegetable Stock (page 23 or 24)
2 cups heavy cream
2 tablespoons freshly squeezed lemon juice

1. Preheat the oven to 375 degrees F.

2. Cut the pumpkin in half. Scoop out the seeds and reserve ½ cup. Drizzle the meat sides of the pumpkin with 2 tablespoons of the olive oil and sprinkle with salt and pepper. Place the pumpkin cut side down on a cookie sheet and roast until the meat is very soft, about 30 minutes. Remove the pumpkin from the oven and scoop the flesh out of the skins.

3. While the pumpkin is roasting, warm the remaining 2 tablespoons olive oil in a large saucepan over medium heat. Add the leeks, reduce the heat, and cover the pan. Cook the leeks, stirring occasionally, until very soft, 3 to 5 minutes.

4. Add the potatoes, chicken stock, and 2 teaspoons salt to the leeks. Increase the heat to medium-high, bring to a boil, and cook until the potatoes are very soft when pierced with the tip of a knife, 15 to 20 minutes.

5. Working in batches, purée the potatoes and leeks with their cooking liquid and the pumpkin in the jar of a blender until very smooth. Combine the batches in a large bowl and whisk in the cream and lemon juice. Season with salt and pepper to taste. Refrigerate to cool, then cover and refrigerate for up to 2 days. When ready to serve, warm the soup over medium heat, stirring occasionally.

FOR THE PUMPKIN SEEDS
½ cup pumpkin or squash seeds
2 tablespoons olive oil
Finely grated zest of 1 orange
1 tablespoon Madras curry powder
2 teaspoons turmeric
1 teaspoon paprika
1 teaspoon kosher salt
½ teaspoon cayenne

1. Clean the pumpkin seeds of any string and flesh and spread out on a plate to dry for about 1 hour. (Do not dry on paper towels, which will stick to the seeds.)

2. Warm the olive oil in heavy sauté pan over medium heat. Add the orange zest and cook for 1 minute. Add the pumpkin seeds, curry powder, turmeric, paprika, salt, and

cayenne. Cook, stirring occasionally, until the seeds are crisp, about 8 minutes. Serve immediately or set aside to cool, then store in an airtight container for up to 3 days.

TO SERVE
½ cup crème fraîche, optional

Ladle the hot soup into 6 warm bowls. Drizzle with crème fraîche if using, and sprinkle the toasted pumpkin seeds on top. Serve at once.

Roasted Eggplant and Lentil Soup
with Sage Butter

This easy-to-prepare and robust soup is perfect for early fall, when the eggplants need to be picked before the frost. Puréeing the lentils and roasted eggplant gives this soup a more refined texture than traditional lentil soup.

Makes 6 servings

FOR THE SOUP
1 large eggplant
1 tablespoon olive oil
Kosher salt
Freshly ground black pepper
1 cup green lentils
2 cups Chicken or Vegetable Stock (page 23 or 24)
1 cup heavy cream
1 tablespoon freshly squeezed lemon juice

1. Preheat the oven to 400 degrees F.
2. Cut the eggplant lengthwise into quarters. Put the eggplant skin side down on a rimmed cookie sheet. Drizzle the eggplant with the olive oil and sprinkle with salt and pepper. Roast until the flesh is very soft, about 15 minutes. Remove from the oven and set aside.
3. Put the lentils and ½ teaspoon salt in a medium saucepan and add enough cold water to cover them by 2 inches. Bring to a boil, reduce the heat, and simmer until the lentils are soft, about 20 minutes. Drain the lentils, discarding the cooking liquid.
4. Scoop the eggplant flesh from the shells. Working in batches, purée the eggplant, lentils, and stock in the jar of a blender until very smooth. Combine the batches in a large bowl.
5. Whisk the cream and lemon juice into the soup. Add salt and pepper to taste. Refrigerate until cool, then cover and refrigerate for up to 1 day. When ready to serve, warm the soup over medium heat, stirring occasionally.

8 tablespoons (1 stick) unsalted butter, at room temperature
2 tablespoons finely chopped flat-leaf parsley
1 tablespoon finely chopped sage leaves
2 teaspoons freshly squeezed lemon juice
Kosher salt
Freshly ground black pepper

Beat all the ingredients together in a bowl with a spoon. Wrap the butter in wax paper, forming it into a cylinder about 1 inch thick, and twist the ends to seal. Wrap in plastic wrap and refrigerate for up to 2 days. Before serving, cut into 12 equal slices.

TO SERVE
6 small sprigs sage, optional

Ladle the hot soup into 6 warm bowls and top with a slice or two of sage butter. Garnish with a sprig of sage if using. Serve at once.

EGGPLANTS

Eggplants originated in India, spread to the Middle East, and arrived in Europe during the Middle Ages. The earliest varieties were white and shaped like eggs, which explains the name, despite the massive purple ones we are most familiar with. (We grow a white egg-shaped heirloom called Osterei.) Europeans at first refused to eat eggplants, regarding them as strictly ornamental. (Their broad foliage and deep-purple flowers make them among the most beautiful plants in the vegetable garden.) American colonists believed they caused insanity, which could be true: We're crazy about them, and we grow some fifteen different types.

For purées we grow lots of big Italian-style eggplants, including Black Bell, Nadia, and Zebra, a purple-and-white-striped version. The best way to purée these giant vegetables is to roast them (see page 210) until they are soft to the touch, then scoop out the flesh. Run it through a food processor fitted with the metal blade, or finely chop it by hand. Add salt, pepper, a little chopped garlic, a dash of lemon juice, and the purée is ready to be spread on bread.

When grilling eggplants, we like to mix shapes and colors, like the bright-pink Neon (a heavy producer in the garden); the long, black, Asian variety called Orient Express; and Little Turkish Orange. We also like Violeta di Firenze, a grooved purple fruit with white

splotches. To grill, slice the eggplants into ½-inch rounds, brush with olive oil, sprinkle with salt and pepper, and cook over a medium fire until browned on both sides, a few minutes.

Eggplants are heat lovers and can be a challenge to grow in cold climates. But we grow many varieties with no problem. The secret is starting the seeds at least two months before planting season, indoors or in a greenhouse. And if you live in a cold region, be sure to buy types suitable for your climate. You can also buy seedlings at planting time (pick the largest, stockiest ones), but you won't find the interesting varieties you can grow from seed. ⌒

Poached Garlic Soup with Thyme and Red Pepper Creams

This is one of our favorite soups for fall. It is robust and rich and certainly keeps the vampires away. The call for twelve heads—not cloves—of garlic is correct, but don't worry, poaching the garlic in chicken stock both concentrates and mellows the flavor.

Makes 6 servings

6 cups Vegetable or Chicken Stock (page 24 or 23)
12 heads garlic, cloves pulled apart but not peeled
    (discard excess papery covering)
1 tablespoon kosher salt
1½ cups heavy cream
2 tablespoons freshly squeezed lemon juice

1. Combine the stock, garlic, and salt in a large saucepan and bring to a boil. Reduce the heat and simmer for 1 hour until the garlic is very soft.

2. Strain the contents of the pan through a fine sieve, reserving the liquid and garlic separately. Pop the garlic cloves out of their skins and push the pulp through the sieve.

3. Whisk the garlic purée into the reserved poaching liquid and add the cream and lemon juice. Warm the soup over medium heat, stirring frequently. Alternatively, you can cool the soup, then keep it covered in the refrigerator for up to 1 day. Reheat before serving.

FOR THE THYME AND PEPPER CREAMS
1 red bell pepper
2 teaspoons olive oil
½ cup heavy cream
1 teaspoon freshly squeezed lemon juice
Kosher salt
Freshly ground black pepper
1 teaspoon chopped thyme leaves

1. Preheat the oven to 375 degrees F.

2. In a bowl toss the bell pepper with the olive oil. Transfer to a baking sheet and bake for 10 minutes. Turn the pepper over and cook for another 10 minutes until completely soft.

3. Remove the pepper from oven. Transfer to a bowl and cover with plastic wrap; set aside for 10 minutes. Remove the pepper from the bowl, and when it is cool enough to handle, remove as much of the skin as possible along with the stem and seeds. Push the pepper through a heavy-duty sieve into a bowl and set aside.

4. Whisk the cream in a bowl until it holds very soft peaks but is not too stiff. With a rubber spatula, fold half of the cream into the pepper purée and add ½ teaspoon of the lemon juice. Season with salt and pepper.

5. Stir the thyme and remaining ½ teaspoon lemon juice into the rest of the cream. Season with salt and pepper. Use immediately or cover and refrigerate the creams separately for up to 3 hours.

TO SERVE

Ladle the hot soup into 6 warm bowls, drizzle both creams on top, and serve at once.

Pumpkin Empanadas

Easy to grow and suitable for long storage, pumpkin and other winter squash were cultivated by virtually all the indigenous peoples of the New World, from the Penobscot Indians of Maine to the Aztecs of Mexico. This dish is inspired by traditional Mexican stuffed pastries, similar to pierogis. In Mexico pumpkin empanadas can be sweet or savory, depending on the spices you add. They are usually deep-fried, but here we bake them. Save the seeds to make Curried Pumpkin Seeds (page 207), a great snack.

Makes about 32 small empanadas, or 6 servings

FOR THE DOUGH
2 cups all-purpose flour
1 teaspoon kosher salt
½ teaspoon sugar
12 tablespoons (1½ sticks) unsalted butter, cut into small squares
2 large egg yolks
2 to 3 tablespoons ice water

1. Combine the flour, salt, and sugar in the bowl of a food processor fitted with the metal blade. Pulse to combine. Add the butter and pulse a few times to cut the butter into the flour, making pieces the size of peas. Add the egg yolks and pulse a few times to combine. Slowly, while pulsing the machine, add the water until the ingredients start to gather. (Alternatively, combine the ingredients by hand or with a pastry cutter in a large bowl.)

2. Transfer the dough to a floured work surface and gently knead it a few times to bring it together. Roll the dough into a cylinder about 1 inch in diameter. Wrap the dough in plastic wrap and refrigerate until firm, about 1 hour, or for up to 1 day. It can also be frozen for up to 2 weeks; thaw in the refrigerator overnight.

FOR THE FILLING
1 small pumpkin or other winter squash, about 3 pounds
2 tablespoons olive oil
Kosher salt
Freshly ground black pepper

4 medium shallots, peeled and finely chopped
1 teaspoon finely chopped thyme leaves

1. Preheat the oven to 375 degrees F.

2. Cut the pumpkin in half and scoop out the seeds. Drizzle the pumpkin flesh with 1 tablespoon of the olive oil and sprinkle with salt and pepper. Place the pumpkin skin side up on a cookie sheet and roast until the flesh is very soft, about 30 minutes.

3. Scoop the flesh out of the skins and purée in a food processor fitted with the metal blade, or a blender, until smooth. Measure 2 cups purée and transfer it to a bowl. (Use any excess purée in Pumpkin Soup, page 207.)

4. Warm the remaining 1 tablespoon olive oil in a small sauté pan over medium heat. Add the shallots and cook, stirring, until translucent, about 4 minutes. Scrape the shallots into the pumpkin purée, add the thyme, and season with salt and pepper if needed. Press a piece of plastic wrap directly on the purée and refrigerate until cool or for up to 1 day.

TO ASSEMBLE AND COOK THE EMPANADAS
1 large egg, lightly beaten

1. On a floured work surface, cut the dough cylinder into 1-inch sections. Put the pieces of dough on one of their flat ends and, using a rolling pin, roll each one into a round about ⅛ inch thick and 3 inches in diameter.

2. Put 1 tablespoon pumpkin purée in the center of each dough round. Brush the edge of each circle with the egg, then fold the circles in half, pressing out any air. Carefully crimp the edges together with the back of a fork.

3. Line 1 or 2 cookie sheets with parchment paper and arrange the empanadas ½ inch apart on the sheets. Bake until golden brown, 10 to 15 minutes. Serve warm, or cool completely, wrap in plastic wrap, and freeze for up to 1 week. Before serving, bring to room temperature and warm for 5 minutes in an oven that has been preheated to 350 degrees F.

Radicchio Gratin with Gruyère Cheese and Bacon

An early snow came to the Arrows garden one fall, blanketing our radicchio. Fortunately radicchio is very cold hardy, and the snow did not affect it at all, except to slow its growth. From this we learned that radicchio is a terrific late-fall crop. With raised beds or row covers, your garden can keep producing radicchio year-long, even in a harsh climate like Maine's. Most people associate radicchio with raw salads, but roasting radicchio takes the edge off its natural bitterness.

Makes 6 servings

12 slices bacon, cut into 1-inch pieces
½ cup balsamic vinegar
2 teaspoons soy sauce
1 teaspoon finely chopped tarragon leaves
2 teaspoons kosher salt
1 teaspoon freshly ground black pepper
½ cup olive oil
½ cup extra-virgin olive oil
4 large heads radicchio, leaves pulled apart
8 ounces Gruyère cheese, thinly sliced

1. In a large sauté pan over medium heat, cook the bacon until crisp, about 5 minutes. Transfer the bacon to a paper-towel-lined plate.

2. In a large bowl combine the vinegar, soy sauce, tarragon, salt, and pepper. Whisk in both olive oils. The vinaigrette will keep covered in the refrigerator for up to 3 days.

3. Preheat the broiler.

4. Add the radicchio leaves to the vinaigrette and toss to coat. Transfer the leaves to a large baking dish, about 13 x 11 inches. Sprinkle the radicchio with the bacon, then cover with the cheese. Broil until the radicchio is wilted and the cheese is melted, 3 to 5 minutes. Serve immediately.

Bourbon and Brown Sugar Gravlax

After making gravlax, the Scandinavian salt-cured salmon, the traditional way for years, we decided to experiment. This became our favorite flavor combination. The brown sugar and bourbon complement salmon, which has a natural sweetness as well. Serve with Horseradish Crème Fraîche (page 251) and thin slices of red onion and Granny Smith or other crisp apple.

Makes 6 servings

2 salmon fillets cut from the tail end, skin on but scaled,
    about 1 pound each and 8 inches long
¼ cup bourbon
3 tablespoons brown sugar
¼ cup kosher salt
3 tablespoons freshly ground black pepper
1 Granny Smith apple, peeled, halved, cored, and thinly sliced

1. Remove any small pin bones from the salmon fillets. Put the fillets skin side down on a rimmed cookie sheet or in a large, shallow, nonreactive dish. Pour the bourbon over the fillets. Spread the sugar, then the salt, and then the pepper evenly over the meat side of each fillet. Arrange the apple slices evenly over just 1 fillet.

2. Take the fillet that is not covered with apples and invert it over the other one. Place another cookie sheet or dish on top of the fish and place a weight of at least 2 pounds, such as a brick or several cans, on top.

3. Refrigerate the entire setup for 3 days, draining off and discarding the liquid once a day.

4. On the fourth day the salmon will feel very firm to the touch. With a sharp slicing knife, scrape the apples and pepper off the salmon. Then, starting with the tail ends, slice the gravlax on a bias as thin as possible. Gravlax can be kept refrigerated for 3 to 4 days after curing. Wrap the fillets in parchment paper, then in plastic wrap.

Potato Gnocchi with Six Herbs

The secret to making these tasty potato dumplings is a gentle hand. Overworking the dough makes the dumplings tough. What makes this recipe perfect for early fall is the way it unites so many different herbs from your garden. Don't be afraid to substitute others.

Makes 6 servings

Kosher salt
2 pounds Yukon Gold or white potatoes, peeled and cut
    into 2-inch chunks
1 cup all-purpose flour
2 large eggs, lightly beaten
1 tablespoon finely chopped flat-leaf parsley, plus ½ cup flat-leaf
    parsley for serving
1 teaspoon finely chopped thyme leaves
1 teaspoon finely chopped rosemary leaves
1 teaspoon finely chopped tarragon leaves
1 teaspoon finely chopped chives
1 teaspoon finely chopped marjoram leaves
3 tablespoons olive oil
½ cup extra-virgin olive oil
2 medium shallots, peeled and finely chopped

1. Combine the potatoes with 1 quart water and 2 teaspoons salt in a medium saucepan. Bring to a boil and cook until the potatoes can be pierced easily with a knife, about 25 minutes. Drain the potatoes well and pass them through a potato ricer or food mill.

2. Sift the flour into a large bowl and make a well in the middle. Add the potato, eggs, 1 teaspoon salt, the chopped herbs, and 1 tablespoon of the olive oil to the well. Using your hands, bring the dough together by lightly kneading and gathering the mixture, working from the well out to the edges.

3. Sprinkle a work surface with flour and use your hands to roll the dough into a long ½-inch-wide cylinder. Cut into 1-inch lengths. Gently press the back of a fork into each

dumpling to shape it. Covered with a clean kitchen towel, the dumplings will keep at room temperature for up to 1 hour.

4. In a large pot bring 3 quarts water, 2 teaspoons salt, and 1 tablespoon of the olive oil to a boil over high heat. Brush a large heatproof plate or dish with the remaining 1 tablespoon olive oil. Add the gnocchi to the boiling water and cook until they float to the top, 1 to 2 minutes. Remove the gnocchi with a slotted spoon and transfer to the oiled plate.

5. In a large, preferably nonstick, sauté pan, warm the extra-virgin olive oil over medium heat. Add the shallots and cook until golden brown, about 5 minutes. Add the gnocchi and warm them for a minute. Divide the gnocchi among 6 shallow bowls, sprinkle with the whole parsley leaves, and serve at once.

SALADS

Cucumber and Cherry Tomato Salad

If we're lucky and the killing frost comes late, we can harvest tomatoes well into October in Maine. Until then, the plants can be protected from light frosts by covering them with plastic sheets overnight. But sooner or later the real thing comes—a deep, penetrating frost that shrivels the vines, leaving green tomatoes to dangle helplessly in the cold. We console ourselves with the knowledge that as annuals, tomatoes must die at the end of the season; in frost-free climates they simply burn out, succumbing to wilt or other infirmities of age.

We use lemon cucumbers, which are small and round, as well as regular cucumbers, in this recipe, but you can use either alone.

Makes 6 servings

¼ cup freshly squeezed lemon juice
2 tablespoons finely chopped basil leaves
Kosher salt
Freshly ground black pepper
¼ cup olive oil
¼ cup extra-virgin olive oil
2 large cucumbers
3 lemon cucumbers, or 1 additional large cucumber
4 ounces lettuce, such as Red Oakleaf and frisée (about 1 medium head),
    leaves separated, washed and dried
2 pints cherry tomatoes, washed and quartered
½ cup cilantro leaves
½ cup flat-leaf parsley

1. Combine the lemon juice and basil in a large bowl. Season with salt and pepper and whisk in both olive oils.

2. Peel the large cucumbers and halve lengthwise. Cut the lemon cucumbers in half. With a teaspoon, scoop out and discard the seeds from all the cucumbers. Cut the cucumbers into ¼-inch half-rounds.

3. Toss the lettuce leaves with one-third of the lemon dressing, and arrange on 6 chilled plates.

4. In the same bowl you used to season the lettuce, combine the tomatoes, cucumbers, cilantro, and parsley. Add the rest of the dressing and toss gently. Spoon the cucumbers and tomatoes on top of the lettuce and serve.

CUCUMBERS

Cucumbers have become so common that Americans have almost stopped thinking about them. They just seem to exist, in every salad. But when you start growing your own, you discover an amazing variety of cukes that are anything but boring. Some are relatively dry and small, which is what you want for pickling—like the Maine-developed Northern Pickling, which bears zillions of cukes in cool climates. Even smaller is Vert de Massy, a 1- to 2-inch French pickling heirloom used for cornichons.

Our favorite salad cucumbers include Boothby Blond (a Maine heirloom), which is yellow with black spines; the lemon cucumber, also yellow and lemon shaped; and the long, striped Armenian cucumber, which looks more like a zucchini. We grow about eight different cukes, including Asian varieties. Unlike most cucumbers, which rely on insects to pollinate the flowers, the Japanese variety Tasty Jade can be grown year-round in a greenhouse because the all-female flowers are parthenocarpic—meaning they don't need pollination. Talk about cool.

Great ways to use up lots of cukes include Cucumber and Cherry Tomato Salad (page 223), which you could eat every day in summer, and Cool Cucumber Coulis (page 163), a sauce that's great with grilled chicken or fish. ⌒

Red and Golden Beet Salad
with Sherry-Shallot Vinaigrette

This is a beautiful salad with a lot of different flavors: sweet beets, salty cheese, and tangy vinaigrette. Beets are easy to grow. Just sprinkle the oddly shaped seeds, which look like bread crumbs, right onto the ground, then cover with a ½ inch or so of soil. Water daily until they sprout. Be sure to harvest beets before they get too big. Giant, softball-size orbs are mealy and taste like dirt. If you can't find golden beets, use all red beets instead.

For this recipe we use farmer's cheese, a fresh, crumbly white cheese available at specialty food stores. You can substitute a good feta.

Makes 6 servings

FOR THE VINAIGRETTE
¾ cup extra-virgin olive oil
¼ cup sherry vinegar
1 tablespoon balsamic vinegar
3 large shallots, peeled and coarsely chopped
1 teaspoon kosher salt
12 whole black peppercorns

Combine all the ingredients in the jar of a blender and process until smooth. The vinaigrette will keep covered in the refrigerator for up to 3 days.

FOR THE SALAD
2 medium yellow beets, trimmed
2 medium red beets, trimmed
Kosher salt
3 ounces butterhead lettuce (about ½ head), leaves separated, washed and dried
3 ounces mixed greens such as arugula and mizuna (about 3 handfuls), washed and dried
8 ounces farmer's or feta cheese, crumbled

1. Put the yellow and red beets in separate medium saucepans with enough cold water to cover them by 2 inches and add 2 teaspoons salt to each pan. Bring both pans to a boil over high heat. Cook until the beets are easily pierced with a small knife, about 20 minutes.

2. Drain the beets and submerge them in ice water until cool. Using your fingers, slip the skins from the beets and discard. Slice the beets into $\frac{1}{8}$-inch rounds.

3. In a large bowl toss the lettuce and greens with half of the vinaigrette. Arrange on 6 chilled plates. Put the yellow beets in the same bowl, drizzle with half of the remaining vinaigrette, and arrange on the plates. Repeat with the red beets. Sprinkle the cheese over the salads and serve.

NOTE: We like to make this salad with a mix of red and yellow beets. Be sure to cook them separately, and toss the yellow beets first, so the red beets don't stain the yellow ones.

Red Oakleaf Salad with Pistachio Toasts and Red Wine Vinaigrette

Red Oakleaf, with its delicate, deeply lobed leaves, is one of the prettiest lettuces we grow. And because it grows so fast, we always have a lot of it. Here we pair Red Oakleaf with pistachio butter spread over small pieces of toasted baguette—a contrast in textures.

Makes 6 servings

2 tablespoons red wine vinegar
Kosher salt
Freshly ground black pepper
$\frac{1}{2}$ cup olive oil
$\frac{1}{4}$ cup extra-virgin olive oil
$\frac{3}{4}$ cup toasted pistachio nuts (page 272)
4 tablespoons ($\frac{1}{2}$ stick) unsalted butter, at room temperature
12 thin slices sourdough baguette
6 ounces Red Oakleaf lettuce (about 1 medium head), washed and dried

1. In a bowl combine the vinegar, 1 teaspoon salt, and $\frac{1}{4}$ teaspoon pepper. Whisk in $\frac{1}{4}$ cup of the olive oil and all the extra-virgin olive oil. The vinaigrette will keep covered in the refrigerator for up to 3 days.

2. In a food processor fitted with the metal blade, grind $\frac{1}{2}$ cup of the pistachios until smooth and pastelike. Add the butter and season with salt and pepper to taste. Process briefly just to combine. Scrape the pistachio butter into a small bowl and set aside. The pistachio butter can be made a day in advance and kept covered in the refrigerator. Bring to room temperature before using.

3. Preheat the oven to 300 degrees F.

4. Toss the bread in a bowl with the remaining $\frac{1}{4}$ cup olive oil. Transfer to a cookie sheet and toast in the oven until golden brown, about 5 minutes. Remove from the oven and set aside to cool.

5. Toss the lettuce with the vinaigrette and arrange on 6 chilled plates. Spread the pistachio butter on the toasts and put 2 slices on each plate. Put the remaining $\frac{1}{4}$ cup pistachios in the bowl in which you tossed the lettuce. Toss the nuts in the vinaigrette still clinging to the bowl. Sprinkle over the salad and serve.

Chicory Salad
with Creamy Mustard Vinaigrette

In the fall and early winter chicory is a stubborn survivor in the garden. But as it grows more slowly, its bitterness intensifies. This creamy mustard vinaigrette cuts the bitterness. Add some crispy bacon, croutons, and tomatoes if you want a more substantial salad.

Makes 6 servings

½ cup Aïoli (page 158)
2 tablespoons champagne or white wine vinegar
2 tablespoons whole-grain mustard
2 teaspoons Dijon mustard
1 tablespoon finely chopped tarragon leaves
1 teaspoon kosher salt
¼ teaspoon freshly ground black pepper
2 tablespoons olive oil
2 tablespoons extra-virgin olive oil
6 ounces chicory (about 1 medium head), leaves separated,
    washed and dried

1. In a large bowl mix together the aïoli, vinegar, both mustards, the tarragon, salt, and pepper. Slowly whisk in both olive oils. The vinaigrette will keep covered in the refrigerator for up to 3 days.

2. Just before serving, toss the chicory with the vinaigrette. Arrange on 6 chilled plates and serve.

Napa Cabbage and Apple Cole Slaw

The Maine woods are dotted with ancient apple trees, a reminder that much of today's forest was once cultivated land. Pastures, hayfields, and orchards reverted to woods when farming waned. Using our own apples in new and different ways is always a challenge. For this recipe, the tart, crunchy Granny Smith apple works well. Serve this slaw with Roast Pork Loin with Rosemary and Garlic (page 242) or Bourbon and Brown Sugar Gravlax (page 219).

Makes 6 servings

1 large head Napa cabbage
1 cup Mayonnaise (page 158)
½ cup red wine vinegar
3 tablespoons whole-grain mustard
2 Granny Smith apples, peeled, halved, cored, and thinly sliced
1 large red onion, peeled, halved, and thinly sliced
Kosher salt
Freshly ground black pepper

1. Cut the cabbage lengthwise in half and remove the core. Finely shred the cabbage with a sharp knife.

2. Whisk the mayonnaise, vinegar, and mustard together in a large bowl. Add the cabbage, apples, and onion and toss to coat well. Season with salt and pepper to taste. Serve at once or cover and refrigerate for up to 1 day.

Warm Beet Greens and Beets

By late fall we start pulling up all our beets before the real freezing weather sets in. Although the beets themselves will keep for many days before getting soft, the greens should be used right away, and there is no better way than in a warm salad. Beet greens are so good that many gardeners grow beets just for the greens, harvesting them when the beets are still marble sized. If you have a garden, try this recipe with baby beets and their super-tender greens.

Makes 6 servings

2 pounds medium beets with greens attached
Kosher salt
½ cup olive oil
¼ cup red wine vinegar
Freshly ground black pepper
6 ounces Dry Jack cheese or Reggiano Parmesan, thinly sliced

1. Cut off the beet greens and stalks, wash them, cut into 1-inch pieces, and set aside. Put the beets in a medium saucepan with enough cold water to cover them by 2 inches and add 2 teaspoons salt. Bring the water to a boil over high heat. Cook until the beets are easily pierced with a small knife, about 20 minutes.

2. Drain the beets and submerge them in ice water until cool. Using your fingers, slip the skins from the beets and discard. Slice the beets into ¼-inch-thick rounds.

3. Warm the olive oil in a large sauté pan over medium heat. Add the beets and cook for several minutes until warm.

4. Toss the beet greens in a medium bowl with the vinegar and season with salt and pepper. Add the greens to the beets and cook, stirring continuously, until the greens are just wilted, about 2 minutes. Divide the greens and beets among 6 warm plates. Sprinkle with the cheese and serve at once.

Warm Salads

In late fall we're getting tons of leeks and Brussels sprouts out of our garden, just in time for warm salads. The basic technique calls for blanching (page 67) the vegetables for a minute or two in boiling water (first clean and slice leeks, or clean and pull Brussels sprouts apart to get loose leaves), then tossing them with vinegar, salt, and pepper. Just before serving, quickly warm the vinegar-coated leaves in a little hot olive oil. That's it! For tender greens that are too delicate for direct heat, simply put the leaves in a bowl, add vinegar, salt, and pepper, drizzle over a little hot olive oil, and toss. (Be careful: Here is one salad we don't toss by hand.) ✏

Smoked Trout and Apple Salad
with Horseradish Crème Fraîche

The intense flavor of smoked trout contrasts with tangy apples and bitter frisée in this unusual salad. It might seem strange to have both vinaigrette and horseradish crème fraîche in one dish, but the combination works because of the many flavors and textures in the salad itself.

Makes 6 servings

3 smoked trout fillets, about 1½ pounds (page 233)
3 Granny Smith apples, peeled, halved, cored, and thinly sliced
1 red onion, peeled, halved, and thinly sliced
1 tablespoon freshly squeezed lemon juice
2 tablespoons red wine vinegar
1 teaspoon kosher salt
¼ teaspoon freshly ground black pepper
¼ cup olive oil
¼ cup extra-virgin olive oil
4 ounces frisée (about 1 small head), leaves separated, washed and dried
½ cup Horseradish Crème Fraîche (page 251)

1. Remove the skin and any bones from the trout fillets. Cut or break the trout into finger-size pieces and set aside.

2. Toss the apples and onion with the lemon juice in a small bowl.

3. In a large bowl mix together the vinegar, salt, and pepper. Whisk in both olive oils.

4. Toss the frisée with the vinaigrette and divide among 6 chilled plates. Arrange the onion and apples on the edge of the plates and sprinkle the trout on top of the frisée. Drizzle with horseradish crème fraîche and serve.

HOW TO SMOKE TROUT

Clark learned how to smoke trout from his dad with fish they had caught on Loon Lake in Washington State. Smoked trout tastes great on its own as an appetizer and as an ingredient in other dishes, like Smoked Trout and Apple Salad with Horseradish Crème Fraîche (page 232). Nothing beats the fresh, grassy taste of wild trout, but perhaps smoking makes even more sense with farm-raised trout because it adds so much flavor to what is often a rather bland fish.

Smoking is an easy weekend project that requires a smoker (available almost anyplace that sells barbecue equipment) or a kettle grill. The type of wood chips you use largely determines the taste. Hickory imparts a strong flavor. Apple and cherry wood are less intense and sweeter. Mesquite is quite spicy. Virtually all supermarkets these days sell hickory and mesquite chips, especially in summer. You can order other types of wood from kitchen supply catalogs, or gather your own. If you have an apple tree, save the pruned wood for your grill—the greener the better. (Lay the branches right down on the coals.) Grape wood is also sweetly aromatic, so if you have grapevines, save those cuttings.

Makes 8 smoked fillets

4 whole boneless trout, 8 to 10 ounces each, heads removed
¼ cup light brown sugar
1½ tablespoons kosher salt
2 cups wood chips, such as hickory, mesquite, apple, or cherry, soaked in cold
    water for at least 1 hour

1. Put the trout on a rimmed cookie sheet and open them to expose the flesh. Sprinkle the flesh with the brown sugar, then the salt. Wrap the pan with plastic wrap and refrigerate for at least 6 hours or overnight.

2. Light a small charcoal fire in your smoker firebox or in the middle of your kettle grill. Allow the coals to become white-hot. Drain and add about ¼ cup of the wood chips to the fire. Put the trout skin side down on the smoker, or on the outside edge of the kettle grill as far from the fire as possible. Close the smoker or cover the grill with the lid.

3. Check the smoker every 30 minutes, adding small amounts of charcoal and wood chips as needed to keep the fire burning and smoking. Continue this process for at least 4 hours until the trout are very firm and golden.

4. Remove the trout from the smoker, bring them inside, and cool at room temperature for about 10 minutes. Transfer the trout to a cookie sheet and refrigerate uncovered for 30 minutes.

5. With a sharp knife, split each trout lengthwise in half to yield 8 fillets total. Wrap each fillet tightly in plastic wrap, then put them in a large plastic freezer bag. The smoked trout

will keep in the refrigerator for up to 1 week or in the freezer for 1 month. If freezing, thaw in the refrigerator overnight before proceeding.

6. To serve, remove the skin by carefully peeling it away from the flesh, starting at the narrow tail end.

MAIN COURSES

Polenta Lasagna

This lasagna can serve as a first course, an accompaniment to a main dish, or the centerpiece of a vegetarian meal. Add an arugula salad tossed with a vinaigrette (page 40) or Sherry-Shallot Vinaigrette (page 225) perhaps, and you have a complete dinner. Instant polenta works well for this dish and is easier to use than regular polenta, which takes longer to cook.

Makes 6 main-course or 12 appetizer servings

1 (12-ounce) box instant polenta
1 medium eggplant, cut into $\frac{1}{8}$-inch rounds
4 tablespoons olive oil
Kosher salt
Freshly ground black pepper
1 red bell pepper
1 yellow bell pepper
2 tablespoons unsalted butter
1 large red onion, peeled and finely chopped
2 ounces white mushrooms, thinly sliced (about $\frac{1}{2}$ cup)
2 cloves garlic, peeled and finely chopped
2 tablespoons finely chopped flat-leaf parsley
1 teaspoon finely chopped rosemary leaves
1 cup mascarpone cheese
4 tablespoons finely grated Reggiano Parmesan
$\frac{1}{4}$ cup sun-dried tomatoes, cut into thin strips

1. Butter two 13 x 9-inch baking pans. Cook the polenta according to the directions on the box. When the polenta is cooked, divide it between the prepared pans. Smooth the top of the polenta with the flat side of a chilled stick of butter (this really works well) or a spatula. Refrigerate the polenta uncovered for at least 2 hours.

2. Preheat the oven to 450 degrees F.

3. Toss the eggplant rounds with 3 tablespoons of the olive oil, then sprinkle with 1 teaspoon each salt and pepper. Lay the rounds out on a cookie sheet and bake for 15 minutes until soft and lightly browned. Remove the eggplant from the oven and set aside to cool.

4. In a bowl toss the peppers with the remaining 1 tablespoon olive oil and sprinkle with salt and pepper. Transfer to a baking sheet and bake for 10 minutes. Turn the peppers over and cook for another 10 minutes until completely soft.

5. Remove the peppers from the oven. Transfer the peppers to a bowl and cover with plastic wrap; set aside for 10 minutes. Remove the peppers from the bowl, and when they are cool enough to handle, remove as much of the skin as possible along with the stems and seeds. Cut the peppers into ¼-inch strips and set aside.

6. In a large sauté pan melt the butter over medium heat. Add the onion, mushrooms, garlic, parsley, rosemary, and 1 teaspoon salt. Sauté until the onion is lightly browned and the mushrooms are cooked through, about 10 minutes. Transfer to a bowl and set aside to cool.

7. Cover the polenta pans with plastic wrap and invert onto a countertop so that the polenta falls out of the pans and onto the plastic wrap. You may need to tap the bottoms of the pans to get the polenta out. Cut each polenta cake crosswise in half. Transfer one piece to a buttered rimmed cookie sheet, using the plastic wrap to move it to the sheet. Remove and discard the plastic wrap.

8. Spread ¼ cup of the mascarpone over the polenta piece and sprinkle with 1 tablespoon of the Parmesan. Arrange one-third of the eggplant, peppers, mushroom mixture, and sun-dried tomatoes on top, cover with a second piece of polenta, and complete the layering until you have 3 layers of polenta, cheese, and vegetables. Put the last piece of polenta on top. Spread with the remaining ¼ cup mascarpone and sprinkle with the remaining 1 tablespoon Parmesan. (The lasagna can be wrapped in plastic and refrigerated for up to 1 day. Unwrap and bring to room temperature before proceeding.)

TO BAKE AND SERVE

1. Preheat the oven to 325 degrees F.

2. Transfer the lasagna to the oven and bake for 30 minutes until warmed through. Cut into 6 or 12 pieces and serve at once.

NOTE: A robust Italian wine such as an Amarone or a Barolo is the perfect match.

Sautéed Turbot with Lemon–Parsley Butter

Turbot is a delicate white fish; if you like halibut and Dover sole, you should enjoy turbot as well. Only buy the freshest; it should be displayed as a whole fish and still have a bit of a sheen to it. Have your fishmonger skin and fillet the turbot. For this type of fish, simple flavors—just lemon and parsley—are perfect.

Makes 6 servings

½ cup freshly squeezed lemon juice
12 tablespoons (1½ sticks) unsalted butter
1 teaspoon finely chopped lemon zest
2 tablespoons finely chopped flat-leaf parsley
Kosher salt
Freshly ground black pepper
2 tablespoons clarified butter (page 44) or olive oil
6 skinless turbot fillets, 4 to 6 ounces each
1 lemon, cut into 6 wedges

1. Pour the lemon juice into a medium stainless-steel saucepan and bring to a boil over medium heat. Cook until the liquid is reduced by half.

2. Reduce the heat to medium-low and gradually whisk the butter into the reduced lemon juice. Make sure the mixture does not boil or the butter will separate. Remove from the heat and stir in the lemon zest, parsley, 1 teaspoon salt, and ½ teaspoon pepper. Cover the sauce and set in a warm place, such as the back of the stove, for up to 1 hour.

3. Preheat the oven to 450 degrees F.

4. Heat the clarified butter in a large sauté pan over medium-high heat. Salt and pepper the fish lightly on both sides. When the clarified butter is very hot but not smoking, gently place the fillets in the pan. Brown for about half a minute on each side, flipping them with a large spatula. (Depending on the size of your pan, you may have to brown the fillets in 2 batches.) Transfer the pan to the oven and bake for 2 minutes until just firm. (If you browned the turbot in 2 batches, arrange them on a baking sheet large enough to hold them all.)

5. Ladle the lemon-parsley sauce onto 6 warm plates. Place a turbot fillet on each plate and garnish with the lemon wedges.

Hickory-Roasted Black Sea Bass
with Mushroom Broth and Thyme Crème Fraîche

This is a great way to infuse fish quickly with the smoky flavor of hickory. The technique grew out of our desire to serve a sautéed fish with a subtle, smoky flavor—not the heaviness of genuine slow smoking. You can do it right in your oven with no special equipment. It's an ambitious recipe, but each of the components is quite simple, and several can be done ahead of time.

Black sea bass has more flavor and firmness than many white fish, lending it to accompaniments typical of red meat, such as mushrooms and thyme. This recipe calls for fillets, but black bass is also excellent served whole because it has a simple bone structure.

Chive Mashed Potatoes (page 175) make a nice side dish to this recipe.

Makes 6 servings

FOR THE MUSHROOM BROTH
3 ounces shiitake mushrooms (about 1 cup)
2 cups Chicken or Vegetable Stock (page 23 or 24)
10 sprigs thyme

1. Trim the mushroom stems, reserving the caps, and combine the stems with the stock in a medium saucepan. Pick the leaves from the thyme sprigs. Add the thyme stems to the stock, reserving the leaves for the crème fraîche.

2. Gently heat the stock over very low heat for 1 hour. Remove from the heat and refrigerate. When it is cool, strain it, discarding the solids. Cover the broth and refrigerate for up to 3 days.

3. When ready to serve, bring the broth to a simmer in a medium saucepan. Thinly slice the mushroom caps and add them to the broth. Simmer for 2 minutes.

FOR THE THYME CRÈME FRAÎCHE
½ cup crème fraîche or sour cream
1 tablespoon finely chopped thyme leaves
1 teaspoon freshly squeezed lemon juice

Kosher salt
Freshly ground black pepper

Combine the crème fraîche, thyme, and lemon juice in a bowl and season with salt and pepper. Cover and refrigerate for up to 1 day.

FOR THE BASS
$1/4$ cup olive oil
6 skinless black sea bass fillets, about 6 ounces each
Kosher salt
Freshly ground black pepper
$1/2$ cup hickory chips, soaked in water for at least 1 hour

1. Preheat the oven to 425 degrees F.
2. Warm the olive oil in a large sauté pan over medium-high heat. (Depending on the size of your pan, you may have to cook the bass in 2 pans.) Sprinkle the bass fillets lightly with salt and pepper. When the oil is very hot but not smoking, add the fillets to the pan. Cook until the underside is browned, about 1 minute, then gently turn the fillets over.
3. Drain and add the hickory chips to the pan. Cover and bake in the oven for 3 minutes until the bass is just firm.

TO SERVE
$1/2$ cup toasted walnuts (page 272)

Remove the fish from the oven, discard the wood chips, and put 1 bass fillet on each of 6 plates or shallow soup bowls. Spoon the mushrooms and broth around the fish. Sprinkle the toasted walnuts on top of the fish and drizzle with the crème fraîche. Serve at once.

PRESERVING HERBS

Preserving herbs is a great way to keep the fragrance of the summer garden all year. The three basic techniques we use are drying, freezing, and infusing them in oils and vinegar.

DRYING HERBS

The best herbs to dry are rosemary, sage, lavender, thyme, oregano, and marjoram. Simply tie several herb sprigs together with kitchen twine and hang them upside down in a dry place. Allow the herbs to dry for several weeks before using. You can leave the herbs hanging and use as needed or take them down and store them in plastic bags or glass jars.

Another easy drying project is harvesting basil plants after the frost and allowing the stems to dry over the winter. (Remove the leaves and store the stems in a dry, well-ventilated place like a porch or attic.) Next summer you'll have basil twigs that can be used as fragrant skewers for grilling meats (page 32), scallops, or vegetables. For a great outdoor party appetizer, thread basil skewers with balls of fresh mozzarella, fresh basil leaves, and cherry tomatoes. Drizzle with olive oil (if you made some basil oil, all the better) and sprinkle with sea salt.

FREEZING HERBS

Most herbs are better dried than frozen, but mint and parsley (especially the curly variety) hold up well to freezing. Simply wash and spin-dry parsley sprigs before storing in plastic freezer bags. When you need some parsley, just remove a few sprigs and chop them up. In the fall we pick lots of mint before the frost. After washing and drying the leaves, purée them in a food processor fitted with the metal blade or finely chop by hand. Freeze the purée in ice cube trays, then wrap the cubes in heavy freezer bags. When you need mint for a recipe, just take out a cube. Months later, it still tastes amazingly fresh.

HERB-INFUSED VINEGAR

To make herb-infused vinegar for salads, start with top-quality vinegar from a health-food or specialty market; herbs will not mask the harshness of cheap vinegar. Be sure to pick the best herbs you can find, avoiding discolored leaves or those that have been eaten by pests. For 2 cups vinegar, use about 1½ cups herbs. Put the herbs in a clear glass bottle or jar, add the vinegar, and seal tightly with a lid or stopper. Set the bottles in a sunny place for about three weeks, then strain the vinegar and discard the herbs. Transfer the vinegar to a clean bottle with a fresh herb sprig for decoration. Here are some of our favorite combinations:

tarragon	red wine vinegar
lemon thyme	champagne vinegar
rosemary	apple cider vinegar

dill or fennel

sage, oregano, or marjoram

white wine vinegar

sherry vinegar

HERB OILS

Herb oils are great in pastas, salads, marinades, or drizzled over fresh vegetables and mild fresh cheeses. One of our favorites is garlic and thyme oil with grilled shrimp. (Oils made with garlic should be kept refrigerated and used within a month to avoid the risk of botulism.) To make herb oils, use good-quality olive oil but not extra-virgin, which has too strong a flavor. Figure about 1 cup herbs to 2 cups oil. For sturdy herbs such as rosemary, sage, and thyme, gently warm the oil in a saucepan over low heat, then remove from the heat and add the herbs. For more delicate herbs like cilantro, basil, and lemon verbena, start with room-temperature oil. Either way, transfer the herbs and oil to clean glass bottles and keep in a warm place like a windowsill (unless you've added garlic; refrigerate the oil instead) for several weeks to infuse the flavor. Strain if you like. ༄

Roast Pork Loin with Rosemary and Garlic

Few dishes fill the kitchen with such tantalizing aromas as a pork roast, especially when cooked with lots of garlic and rosemary. The loin is a very tender cut, but it can become too dry when cooked. To add moisture, we soak the loin in a simple brine overnight. Serve with Chive Mashed Potatoes (page 175), Braised Red Cabbage (page 336), and Mustard-Rosemary Sauce (page 254).

Makes 6 servings

2 quarts cold water
Kosher salt
1 tablespoon sugar
6 bay leaves
1 teaspoon whole black peppercorns
1 pork loin, bone in, about 4 pounds
2 tablespoons olive oil
4 cloves garlic, peeled and thinly sliced
¼ cup rosemary leaves
Freshly ground black pepper
½ cup Chicken Stock (page 23)

1. In a large bowl or pot combine the water, ¼ cup salt, the sugar, bay leaves, and whole peppercorns. Stir until the salt is dissolved. Add the pork loin; it should be completely submerged in the brine. (If not, add more water.) Cover with plastic wrap or a lid and refrigerate overnight.

2. Remove the loin from the liquid and pat dry. Discard the brine. Transfer the loin to a roasting pan and rub the meat all over with the olive oil, garlic, and rosemary. Cover with plastic wrap and refrigerate for at least 1 hour or up to 24 hours.

3. One hour before roasting, remove the loin from the refrigerator to bring it to room temperature and season with salt and pepper.

4. Preheat the oven to 325 degrees F.

5. Pour the stock around the loin, cover with foil or a lid, and cook for about 2 hours until a kitchen thermometer inserted in the center reads 150 degrees F.

6. Remove the pork from the oven and allow it to rest for 10 minutes. Transfer to a cutting board and thinly slice. Serve at once.

Pork Loin Confit

Many people are familiar with duck confit and how delicious, tender, and moist it can be, but few think of making a confit of pork. The results are similar. You can have your butcher get rendered pork, duck, or even goose fat for this preparation, or make your own as we do. Don't worry—the fat cooks the meat and preserves it, but the meat itself is not at all fatty. We modernize confit a bit by using less salt than in traditional recipes. Serve this pork with Mustard-Rosemary Sauce (page 254) and Warm Red Cabbage Slaw with Creamy Herbed Goat Cheese (page 314).

Makes 6 to 8 servings

1 boneless pork loin, 3 to 4 pounds
3 tablespoons kosher salt
4 cloves garlic, peeled and thinly sliced
2 tablespoons rosemary leaves
2 tablespoons crushed bay leaves
1 tablespoon whole black peppercorns
About 2 quarts rendered fat (page 245), melted

1. Starting a day in advance, sprinkle the pork with the salt, and shake off and discard any excess. Fit into a shallow casserole, and rub the pork with the garlic, rosemary, bay leaves, and peppercorns. Put another casserole on top of the pork, then place in the top casserole a weight of at least 2 pounds, such as a brick or several cans, to press the pork. Refrigerate overnight.

2. The following day, preheat the oven to 325 degrees F.

3. Remove the pork loin from the casserole and discard the garlic, herbs, and peppercorns. Transfer the pork to a deep roasting pan just larger than the meat. Pour the rendered fat into the pan to cover the pork completely. Cover the pan and cook in the oven for about 2 hours until a metal skewer or thin knife inserted into the pork loin feels hot to the touch. The internal temperature should register 170 degrees F on a kitchen thermometer.

4. Carefully remove the pork loin from the fat, transfer it to a cutting board, and thinly slice. Serve at once. Alternatively, you can cool the loin, transfer it to a large container, and cover with the fat. Refrigerate for up to 1 week. When ready to serve, transfer the loin

to a roasting pan, cover with foil, and warm for about 1 hour in an oven that has been pre-heated to 350 degrees F. (The fat can be reused: Pour it through a fine sieve lined with 2 layers of cheesecloth and refrigerate for up to 2 weeks or freeze for about 6 months.)

RENDERED FAT

You can buy melted and clarified fat or "rendered" fat from your butcher for making Pork Loin Confit (page 244), but it's also easy to render it yourself. We use duck fat, because it's what we have on hand at the restaurant, but you can also use goose fat or even pork lard, which is already rendered and available at supermarkets. (A caveat: Supermarket lard is highly processed and often contains preservatives. It won't taste nearly as pure as home-rendered duck or goose fat.)

Finely chop the duck or goose fat in a food processor or meat grinder (or by hand) and transfer to a heavy-bottomed saucepan. Add a tablespoon or two of water and melt the fat slowly over the lowest possible heat for several hours until it is clear. Allow the fat to cool a bit, then strain it through a fine sieve. Refrigerate for up to 4 months or freeze nearly indefinitely.

As wonderful as rendered fat is for making confit, it's also great for browning foods. Because rendered fat has a much higher smoking point than butter or oil, you can get it much hotter before it starts to burn, which means food browns more quickly, without overcooking. Try using rendered fat in place of olive oil or clarified butter when browning meats, root vegetables, and potatoes. ∾

Braised Lamb Shanks

Slow-braising is one of our favorite methods of cooking. Tougher cuts of meat usually have much more flavor than tender cuts like the loin, and braising breaks down the muscle tissue, making these cuts delectable. If you add aromatics like rosemary, sage, and thyme, the meat will become infused with their flavor. Braising is also very easy because the process is largely unattended. Aïoli (page 158) is a perfect sauce for lamb shanks, and Herb-Roasted Fennel with Pancetta (page 259) makes an excellent side dish.

Makes 6 servings

5 tablespoons olive oil
6 lamb shanks, about 1 pound each
Kosher salt
Freshly ground black pepper
3 stalks celery, coarsely chopped
2 large carrots, peeled and coarsely chopped
1 medium yellow onion, peeled and coarsely chopped
4 sprigs rosemary
4 sprigs thyme
3 sprigs sage
2 cups white wine
4 cups Chicken Stock (page 23)

1. In a large sauté pan heat 1 tablespoon of the olive oil over medium-high heat. Sprinkle the shanks with salt and pepper. When the oil is hot but not smoking, add 2 shanks and brown on all sides, about 5 minutes. Transfer the shanks to a large roasting pan, wipe the sauté pan clean, and repeat the process twice more until all the shanks are browned.

2. Preheat the oven to 325 degrees F.

3. In the same sauté pan warm the remaining 2 tablespoons olive oil over medium heat. Add the celery, carrots, and onion and cook, stirring, until the onion is translucent, about 4 minutes. Scrape the vegetables into the pan around the shanks. Add the herbs and pour in the wine and stock. Cover with foil and transfer to the oven. Braise the shanks until the meat is very tender and almost falling off the bone, 1½ to 2 hours.

4. Remove the shanks from the oven and serve immediately.

NOTE: Because lamb fat is rather strong tasting, we generally don't serve the braising liquid. But if you want to serve it, the process is simple: Transfer the cooked shanks to a serving platter and cover with foil to keep warm. Strain the braising liquid through a fine sieve into a small saucepan. Spoon off and discard the fat from the top. Cook the liquid over medium-high heat, skimming the fat that rises to the surface, until the sauce is slightly reduced, about 10 minutes. Ladle some of the sauce onto each of 6 plates and put the shanks on top.

Herb-Braised Rabbit

Braising fills the air with wonderful, rich aromas. If you have never cooked rabbit, this is one of the best ways to do it. There are four easy steps to preparing this dish: two marinades (the first in wine, the second in oil), then sautéing and braising. The marinades, which infuse the meat with flavor and make it moist and very tender, should be done the day before serving.

We recommend serving this dish with Celery Root and Sour Cream Sauce (page 253).

Makes 6 servings

FOR THE FIRST MARINADE
3 rabbits, about 2 pounds each
2 (750-ml) bottles inexpensive white wine
20 juniper berries
2 tablespoons whole black peppercorns
1 red onion, peeled and coarsely chopped

Fit the rabbits into a large wide casserole or baking dish and add all the remaining ingredients. Refrigerate, turning the rabbits every 30 minutes or so, for 4 hours. Remove the rabbits and discard the marinade. Wash the casserole, then return the rabbits to it.

FOR THE SECOND MARINADE
¾ cup extra-virgin olive oil
½ cup tarragon leaves

Coat the rabbits with the olive oil and sprinkle with tarragon. Cover with plastic wrap and refrigerate overnight.

TO COOK
5 tablespoons olive oil
2 medium carrots, peeled and chopped
1 medium yellow onion, peeled and chopped
1 stalk celery, chopped

Kosher salt

Freshly ground black pepper

4 cups Chicken Stock (page 23)

1 (750-ml) bottle dry white wine, such as a Chardonnay or Pinot Grigio

6 sprigs tarragon

6 sprigs thyme

4 sprigs rosemary

2 cups Celery Root and Sour Cream Sauce (page 253), optional

1. Preheat the oven to 325 degrees F.

2. Remove the rabbits from the second marinade, place them in a large dish, and discard the marinade. Wash and dry the casserole and set aside while you prepare the vegetables.

3. Warm 2 tablespoons of the oil in a large sauté pan over medium heat. Add the carrots, onion, and celery and cook, stirring occasionally, until the vegetables are soft, about 10 minutes. Transfer the vegetables to the casserole. Wipe out the sauté pan.

4. Warm 1 tablespoon of the oil in the sauté pan over medium-high heat. Sprinkle the rabbits with salt and pepper. When the oil is hot but not smoking, add 1 rabbit and brown on each side until golden brown, about 3 minutes per side. Transfer the rabbit to the casserole with the vegetables. Wipe out the sauté pan and repeat with the other 2 rabbits, using the remaining 2 tablespoons oil.

5. Add the chicken stock, wine, tarragon, thyme, and rosemary to the casserole. Cover with foil and braise in the oven until the meat is very tender, 1½ to 2 hours.

6. Remove the casserole from the oven. Transfer the rabbits to a large cutting board. Strain the braising liquid through a fine sieve and discard the vegetables. Reduce the liquid and use it as a sauce (see Note), or cool, cover, and refrigerate for up to 3 days or freeze for up to 2 months to use as stock in other recipes.

7. Using a boning knife, remove the hind legs of the rabbits. Next, cutting along the backbone, remove the loin or saddle meat. Arrange a leg and loin on each of 6 plates. Ladle some sauce on top and serve at once.

NOTE: If you would like to serve the braising liquid as a sauce, cover the rabbits with a piece of foil to keep them warm. Pour the liquid into a small saucepan. Spoon off and discard the fat from the top. Cook the liquid over medium-high heat, skimming the fat that rises to the surface, until the sauce is slightly reduced, about 10 minutes.

# SAUCES

Horseradish Crème Fraîche

Horseradish grows slowly in the garden, but in the fall when this gnarled root is pulled from the soil, the long wait is worth it. No preserved horseradish compares to the clean zing of freshly grated horseradish. This sauce is perfect with Bourbon and Brown Sugar Gravlax (page 219) or with chilled fresh oysters.

Makes about 2 cups

1½ cups crème fraîche or sour cream
2 tablespoons grated fresh horseradish
1 tablespoon freshly squeezed lemon juice
Kosher salt
Freshly ground black pepper

Whisk together the crème fraîche, horseradish, and lemon juice in a medium bowl and season with salt and pepper to taste. Cover and refrigerate for up to 2 days.

Tomato Chutney

When the tomato vines wither with frost, the last tomatoes must be picked at once before they, too, start to freeze. That final harvest always yields a mix of ripe, partially ripe, and just plain green tomatoes. You can use them all in this sweet-sour, ginger-laced chutney, which we serve as a condiment with grilled tuna.

Makes about 3 cups

2 tablespoons vegetable oil
1 medium red onion, peeled and finely chopped
1 tablespoon gingerroot, finely chopped
1 teaspoon kosher salt
¼ teaspoon freshly ground black pepper
2 cups Tomato Concassé (page 179), made with ripe or green tomatoes
½ cup brown sugar
¼ cup red wine vinegar

1. Warm the oil in a medium stainless-steel saucepan over medium heat. Add the onion and cook, stirring, until the onion is translucent, about 5 minutes. Add the ginger, salt, and pepper and sauté for 1 minute.

2. Add the tomato concassé and cook for 1 minute. Add the brown sugar and vinegar, reduce the heat to low, and cook for 3 minutes more until thick. Remove the chutney from the heat, transfer to a bowl, and chill in the refrigerator. When it is cool, cover it and refrigerate for up to 1 day. Serve well chilled.

Celery Root and Sour Cream Sauce

Celery root looks like something from another planet. Yet watching the celery roots peek above the soil is exciting because we know how versatile and delicious they are. This sublime, creamy sauce is modified from traditional Russian cooking and has an unexpectedly rich, Old World flavor. You can use Enriched Stock (page 325) or Chicken or Vegetable Stock (page 23 or 24) as the base. Serve with Boiled Dinner, Our Way (page 326), Herb-Braised Rabbit (page 248), or Sautéed Turbot (page 237) as a substitute for the lemon-parsley butter.

Makes about 3 cups

1 medium celery root (about 1 pound), peeled and coarsely cut into 1-inch
    cubes
1½ tablespoons olive oil
Kosher salt
Freshly ground black pepper
1 cup Enriched Stock (page 325) or Chicken or Vegetable Stock
    (page 23 or 24)
½ cup sour cream
1 tablespoon finely chopped flat-leaf parsley
2 teaspoons freshly squeezed lemon juice

1. Preheat the oven to 350 degrees F.
2. In a medium casserole, toss the celery root with the olive oil and sprinkle with salt and pepper. Cover with foil or a lid, and roast until the celery root can be easily pierced with a knife, about 45 minutes.
3. Bring the stock to a boil. Working in batches, purée the celery root with the stock in the jar of a blender until smooth. Combine the batches in a bowl and whisk in the sour cream. Stir in the parsley and lemon juice, and season with salt and pepper if needed. Serve immediately or keep warm in a double boiler for up to 1 hour.

Mustard-Rosemary Sauce

This sauce goes well with Roast Pork Loin with Rosemary and Garlic (page 242), chicken, or salmon.

Makes about 2 cups

2 sprigs rosemary
½ cup white wine
¼ cup white wine vinegar
12 whole black peppercorns
16 tablespoons (2 sticks) unsalted butter, at room temperature
2 tablespoons Dijon mustard
1 tablespoon whole-grain mustard
Kosher salt
Freshly ground black pepper

1. Pull the leaves off the rosemary sprigs, finely chop the leaves, and set aside. Put the stems in a medium stainless-steel saucepan and add the white wine, vinegar, and peppercorns. Simmer over low heat until the liquid is reduced to about ¼ cup. Discard the rosemary stems.

2. Increase the heat to medium and whisk in the butter 1 tablespoon at a time. Do not boil the sauce once the butter has been added. Turn off the heat and add the chopped rosemary, both mustards, and salt and pepper to taste. Serve immediately or keep warm in a double boiler for up to 1 hour.

SIDE DISHES

Lucia's Nuclear Pickled Serranos

Serranos are just about the hottest peppers you'd ever want to eat whole. (Other peppers are hotter but tend to be used sparingly in sauces.) Pickled serranos (or slightly milder jalapeños) are great to pass at the table with grilled meat and seafood dishes. We eat them—but not too many—at our staff lunches.

Makes about 1 quart

¼ cup olive oil
8 ounces fresh serrano chiles
5 pearl onions, peeled, or 1 small onion, peeled and cut into 6 wedges
1 medium carrot, peeled and thinly sliced
6 cloves garlic, peeled
2 sprigs marjoram
2 sprigs thyme
2 sprigs oregano
3 bay leaves
1½ tablespoons kosher salt
1 teaspoon sugar
1 cup distilled white vinegar
1 cup water

1. Warm the oil in a large sauté pan over medium heat. Add the chiles, onions, carrot, and garlic. Cook, stirring frequently, until fragrant, 3 to 5 minutes. Do not brown.
2. Add the herb sprigs, bay leaves, salt, and sugar and stir until the herbs wilt. Add

the vinegar and water, increase the heat, and bring the mixture to a boil. Reduce the heat to low and simmer for 5 minutes.

3. Remove the pan from the heat. Transfer the mixture to a 1-quart Mason jar, cover, and refrigerate for at least 12 hours to allow the peppers to macerate. The peppers will keep refrigerated for up to 1 month.

Green and Yellow Beans with Toasted Pine Nuts

We're still getting lots of beans out of our garden in early fall, but after eating them with fresh herbs all summer, we're ready for something different. Pine nuts make the dish more substantial and autumn like. You can serve this dish with just about every type of main course, from meat to fish.

Makes 6 servings

Kosher salt
3 ounces yellow beans, ends trimmed
3 ounces green beans, ends trimmed
3 tablespoons unsalted butter
¼ cup toasted pine nuts (page 272)
Freshly ground black pepper

1. In a large pot bring 2 quarts water and 1 tablespoon salt to a boil. Fill a medium bowl halfway with ice water. Add the yellow and green beans to the boiling water and cook for 1 minute. Drain the beans in a colander and plunge them into the ice bath. After the beans are completely cool, drain them and wrap in a clean kitchen towel to dry.

2. Melt the butter in a medium saucepan over medium heat. Cook for a minute or two until the butter turns golden brown. Add the pine nuts and cook for another minute, stirring to coat them with the butter.

3. Add the beans to the saucepan, season with salt and pepper, and cook, stirring occasionally, until they are hot, about 2 minutes. Serve at once.

Honey and Lavender Roasted Shallots

Shallots are most often used to enhance the flavor of other foods, but here they take center stage in a dish that goes well with Roast Pork Loin with Rosemary and Garlic (page 242) and even Grilled Maine Bluefin Tuna (page 150). You can substitute just about any kind of small onion, such as pearl, cippoline, or Egyptian.

We also grow lavender, which has a lovely fragrance and makes a beautiful border to a flower garden. Most people think of lavender as the scent of soap and sachets, but we like its aroma in ice cream, pastries, and even savory dishes like this.

Makes 6 servings

2 tablespoons honey
2 tablespoons lavender tops, or 1 tablespoon dried lavender
3 tablespoons olive oil
18 large shallots, peeled
1 teaspoon kosher salt
$\frac{1}{2}$ teaspoon freshly ground black pepper

1. Preheat the oven to 325 degrees F.
2. Put the honey and lavender in a medium bowl and whisk in the olive oil. Add the shallots, sprinkle with the salt and pepper, and toss to coat.
3. Transfer the mixture to a shallow baking dish, cover with foil or a lid, and roast until the shallots are soft, about 20 minutes.
4. Remove from the oven. Serve the shallots immediately or keep warm for up to 1 hour. Alternatively, the shallots can be cooled, covered, and refrigerated for up to 1 day. Warm before serving.

Herb-Roasted Fennel with Pancetta

Technically fennel isn't a root vegetable because the bulb grows above ground, but it can be treated like one in the kitchen. In the fall that means roasting, which caramelizes the fennel, giving it a deliciously sweet aroma. Here we pair roasted fennel with pancetta, unsmoked Italian bacon. Feel free to substitute good-quality, thick-sliced American bacon.

Makes 6 servings

4 medium bulbs fennel, stalks trimmed
3 tablespoons olive oil
2 tablespoons chopped tarragon leaves
1 teaspoon chopped thyme leaves
Kosher salt
Freshly ground black pepper
6 slices pancetta or bacon

1. Preheat the oven to 375 degrees F.

2. Cut the fennel bulbs lengthwise in half, then cut each half into 3 wedges. Do not cut out the core as it holds the wedges together.

3. Toss the fennel wedges with the oil in a large baking dish. Sprinkle with the herbs and salt and pepper to taste, and arrange the pancetta on top of the fennel. Cover the dish with foil or a lid. Roast until the fennel can be easily pierced with the tip of a knife, about 30 minutes. Remove from the oven and serve at once. Alternatively, cool the dish, cover, and refrigerate for up to 1 day. Before serving, warm in an oven that has been preheated to 350 degrees F.

Lentil, Root Vegetable, and Herb Cakes

Serve these cakes with Spring Lamb Loin with Rosemary (page 57) or Plank-Roasted Salmon with Rosemary-Mustard Vinaigrette (page 317). They also work well as an appetizer or as a light vegetarian dinner.

Makes 6 servings

1 cup lentils
Kosher salt
3 tablespoons unsalted butter
1 small parsnip, peeled and cut into ¼-inch dice (about ¼ cup)
1 small carrot, peeled and cut into ¼-inch dice (about ¼ cup)
2 tablespoons finely chopped yellow onion
2 tablespoons finely chopped celery
Freshly ground black pepper
1 large egg, lightly beaten
2 tablespoons all-purpose flour
1 tablespoon finely chopped flat-leaf parsley
2 teaspoons finely chopped tarragon leaves
1 teaspoon finely chopped thyme leaves
1 teaspoon olive oil

1. Put the lentils and 1 teaspoon salt in a medium saucepan. Add enough water to cover the lentils by at least 1 inch. Bring to a boil and cook until the lentils are just soft, about 20 minutes. Drain the lentils, transfer to a plate, and set aside to cool.

2. While the lentils are cooking, warm the butter in a large sauté pan over medium heat. Add the parsnip, carrot, onion, and celery; sprinkle with salt and pepper to taste. Sauté, stirring, until all the vegetables are just soft, about 15 minutes. Transfer the vegetables to a plate and set aside to cool.

3. When the vegetables and lentils are cooled, combine them in a bowl. Mix in the egg, flour, and herbs. The mixture should hold together when formed into a cake or ball. If too dry, add another egg; if too wet, add a little more flour. The mixture will keep covered in the refrigerator for up to 1 day.

4. Preheat the oven to 375 degrees F. Line a baking sheet with parchment paper and lightly brush the paper with the olive oil.

5. Form the mixture into 6 cakes, each about ½ inch high, and transfer to the baking sheet. Bake until the cakes are firm and lightly browned, 15 to 20 minutes. Remove with a spatula and serve.

Butternut Squash and Potato Gratin

At Arrows we like our Thanksgiving menu quite traditional, and we always have a gratin. With the exception of the turkey (page 323), nothing gets more rave reviews than our gratin.

Makes 6 servings

4 large Yukon Gold or white potatoes, peeled and thinly sliced
Kosher salt
Freshly ground black pepper
1 large butternut squash, peeled, halved, seeded, and thinly sliced
1 teaspoon ground nutmeg
1½ cups heavy cream

1. Preheat the oven to 350 degrees F.

2. Put a layer of potatoes in the bottom of an 8-inch-square baking dish, overlapping the slices. Sprinkle the potatoes with a little salt and pepper. Top with a layer of squash seasoned with salt and pepper. Repeat this process until you have used all the squash and potatoes.

3. Stir the nutmeg into the cream. Gently pour the cream into the baking dish. Cover the dish with foil and bake for 45 minutes. Remove the foil and cook for another 20 minutes until the top is golden brown and the potatoes and squash have absorbed almost all the liquid.

4. Remove the dish from the oven and let cool slightly. Cut the gratin into 6 squares, remove each piece with a metal spatula, and serve. Alternatively, the gratin can be cooled, covered, and refrigerated for up to 1 day. Warm, covered, for 30 to 40 minutes in an oven that has been preheated to 350 degrees F.

SAVING SQUASH

Winter squash can be stored for months as long as you harvest them properly. The key is cutting the squash off the vines before a hard frost, then leaving them in the field for about a week to "cure," which lets the skins dry out and harden in the sun. Don't let them freeze or the skin will soften and the vegetable will rot. (Bring squash inside if a hard frost or several consecutive light frosts are predicted.) After the squash have been field cured, store them in a dark and cool place; around 55 degrees F is best. A garage works great. (A refrigerator is really too cold, but you won't have enough room in there anyway.) One storage trick used by commercial growers is to dip the squash in a weak bleach solution (1 part bleach to 10 parts water) before storage. That kills any bacteria on the surface. Of course, that assumes you can lift them! Some squash, like the huge Blue Hubbard, resemble beached whales in the garden. ❧

Sauternes-Braised Apples with Currants

Apple trees can live for one hundred years, but it always seems amazing that our ancient trees still produce delicious fruit. After a brisk autumn morning working in the orchard, we love to fill our kitchen with the sweet aroma of braising apples. This dish is a perfect fall accompaniment to roasted meat, but it could also be served as a dessert with vanilla ice cream. You can substitute a late-harvest Riesling or Gewürztraminer for the expensive Sauternes.

Makes 6 servings

6 small apples, such as Cortland or Northern Spy
½ cup currants
½ cup Sauternes wine
½ cup brown sugar
4 sprigs thyme
3 sprigs rosemary

1. Preheat the oven to 350 degrees F.
2. Peel and core the apples. (We like to dig out the core from the bottom, leaving the stem at the top for a nice appearance.) Stuff the apples with the currants.
3. Put the apples, stem side up, in an 11 x 9-inch baking dish. Pour over the Sauternes and sprinkle with the brown sugar and the herbs. Cover the dish with foil and bake until the apples are just soft, about 30 minutes.
4. Transfer each apple to a plate and spoon over some of the pan juice. Serve immediately or keep warm for up to 1 hour. Alternatively, the apples can be cooled, covered, and refrigerated overnight. Warm before serving.

Ginger-Roasted Parsnips

Parsnips have a mild, buttery flavor that works well with many other ingredients. When roasted slowly, parsnips caramelize and develop an even richer flavor. You can purée them with mashed potatoes (page 175), add them to a gratin (page 340), make root-vegetable pancakes (page 260), or even fry up crunchy, thinly sliced parsnip chips for a salad. This dish goes well with almost any main course in this chapter and is easy to prepare.

Makes 6 servings

12 medium parsnips, peeled
¼ cup olive oil
2 tablespoons finely chopped gingerroot
Kosher salt
Freshly ground black pepper

1. Preheat the oven to 325 degrees F.
2. Toss the parsnips with the oil and ginger in a medium baking dish; sprinkle with salt and pepper. Cover with foil.
3. Roast the parsnips, shaking the casserole occasionally to turn them, until they are golden and soft, 30 to 40 minutes. Serve at once or keep warm for up to 1 hour.

Roasted Yam Purée

Unlike potatoes, to which they are related, yams don't grow well in Maine. They are tropical plants and need more frost-free days than we can provide. But if you live in the South, yams are easy to grow provided you have a lot of room—the vines can trail sixteen feet or longer! You don't have to wait until Thanksgiving to enjoy this substantial root crop. This purée is great with Roast Pork Loin with Rosemary and Garlic (page 242) and Braised Lamb Shanks (page 246).

Makes 6 servings

3 large yams
1 tablespoon vegetable oil
Kosher salt
Freshly ground black pepper
2 teaspoons finely chopped rosemary leaves
1 teaspoon finely chopped thyme leaves
4 tablespoons (½ stick) unsalted butter, at room temperature

1. Preheat the oven to 400 degrees F.

2. Rub the yams with the oil. Transfer to a rimmed baking sheet, sprinkle with salt and pepper, and place in the oven. Roast until the yams are very soft, about 45 minutes. Remove from the oven and allow to cool slightly.

3. Cut the yams lengthwise in half. Scoop out the flesh with a large metal spoon and transfer it to a food processor fitted with the metal blade. Add the herbs. With the motor running, add the butter 1 tablespoon at a time through the feed tube. Season with salt and pepper to taste. (Alternatively, you can pass the yams through a food mill or potato ricer into a bowl, then mix in the other ingredients.)

4. Serve immediately or keep warm in a double boiler for up to 1 hour. You can also cool the purée, cover, and refrigerate for up to 1 day. Warm it in a covered casserole for 30 minutes in an oven that has been preheated to 350 degrees F.

Pumpkin Dinner Rolls

Pumpkin makes bread fluffy and light, but these rolls aren't sweet like a pumpkin dessert. They are great at Thanksgiving dinner; make some extra for turkey sandwiches the next day.

Makes 18 dinner rolls, or 8 sandwich rolls

3½ cups bread or all-purpose flour
1½ tablespoons sugar
1½ teaspoons salt
1 (¼-ounce) envelope active dry yeast
1 cup cooked pumpkin purée, fresh (page 216) or canned
½ cup milk, warmed
4 tablespoons (½ stick) unsalted butter, at room temperature
Cornmeal for dusting pans

1. In the bowl of a standing mixer fitted with the dough hook, combine the flour, sugar, salt, and yeast. Add the pumpkin purée and warm milk. Mix on low speed until the ingredients come together, scraping down the sides of the bowl as necessary.

2. With the machine on medium speed, add the butter in small pieces, allowing the dough to absorb it between additions. Once all the butter has been added, mix the dough for about 5 minutes until silky. If the dough is too wet, add more flour 1 tablespoon at a time. (Alternatively, combine the ingredients in a large bowl, then turn it out onto a lightly floured board and knead by hand for about 6 minutes until smooth and elastic.) Transfer the dough to a lightly greased bowl, cover with plastic wrap, and let rise until almost doubled in size, about 1 hour.

3. Line 2 baking sheets with parchment paper and sprinkle lightly with cornmeal.

4. Transfer the dough to a lightly floured worktable and divide it into 18 pieces. (If making sandwich rolls, divide into 8 pieces.) Roll each piece of dough between your hands into a ball (for sandwich rolls too) and transfer to the prepared baking sheets, leaving 2 inches between the rolls. Cover with clean kitchen towels and let rise in a warm place until almost doubled in size.

5. Preheat the oven to 350 degrees F.

6. Bake the rolls for 15 to 20 minutes until golden brown. (Add another 5 to 10 min-

utes if making sandwich rolls.) The rolls should sound hollow when tapped. Remove from the oven and serve. The rolls can be stored, tightly wrapped in plastic wrap, at room temperature for up to 2 days. You can also freeze them for up to 1 month. Thaw, then warm for about 10 minutes in an oven that has been preheated to 350 degrees F.

Edible flowers (pages 191–92); top row from left: lavender, rose; second row: calendula, sage, citrus marigold (lemon gem and orange gem); third row: lemon thyme, lavender, chive; fourth row: johnny jump-up, nasturtium, borage; fifth row: calendula, nasturtium, basil; sixth row: calendula, nasturtium, viola

A bouquet of mixed herbs

Heirloom tomatoes (page 126); clockwise from top:
Yellow Brandywine, Orange Strawberry, Black Krim,
Arkansas Traveler, Red Currant, Sungold, Green
Zebra, and Cherokee Purple

*10 Veggies That Let You Have a Life (page 85):
beans, beets, carrots, garlic, lettuce, onions,
parsnips, peas, radishes, and spinach are
easy to care for and grow.*

Planting herbs alongside flowers creates a beautiful—yet practical—garden.

Steamed Lobster, Southeast Asian Style (page 18)

*Different varieties of mint;
clockwise from left: peppermint,
chocolate, orange-pineapple,
and spearmint*

Planting crops such as bok choy in a cold frame (page 80) lets gardeners extend the growing season in chilly climates.

Chefs Mark Gaier and Clark Frasier walk through their garden each day to plan the evening's menu.

A handful of chopped fresh herbs transforms sauces, vegetables, salads, and even desserts.

The Arrows garden is both functional and ornamental, mingling fruits and vegetables with herbs and flowers.

Using your hands to toss greens with vinaigrette keeps tender lettuce leaves from bruising while coating them evenly (page 40).

Stuffing trout with herbs and aromatics for Crispy Trout with Ginger and Lemongrass (page 47)

Salute to Salads (page 35); Arrows cultivates some twenty-eight varieties of lettuce, mixing and matching them in everything from stand-alone salads to main courses.

Orchard trees provide shade for part of the garden, while the greenhouse protects seedlings from the cold.

AFTER THE FALL

Fall cleanup prevents more garden problems than anything you can do in the growing season. The reason is that plant debris left rotting in the beds is a breeding ground for pests, weeds, and diseases that will come back next year, stronger than ever. So when the harvest is over, don't leave anything behind.

Fall is also the best time to prepare beds for spring, when the ground will be too wet to work (at least in Maine). We pay special attention to beds that will hold our early-season crops like peas and spinach, which can be planted as soon as the snow melts, provided the beds are ready. Rototill the beds in fall, add compost and soil balancers like lime, and come spring, you're ready to plant. (Fall is a good time to perform soil tests on spring planting beds; see Digging the Dirt, page 74, for more on soil testing.)

Many home gardeners now recognize the benefits of winter cover crops, sometimes called green manure, which have long been used by organic farmers to prevent soil erosion and increase organic matter. Cover crops include grains like winter rye, and nitrogen boosters like field peas, hairy vetch, and clover. (All are available from good seed catalogs like Johnny's or Fedco.) Rototill them into the garden come spring, and they'll add lots of nutrients and organic matter to your soil.

Fall is also the time to mulch perennial beds with compost or salt marsh hay, which has no seeds. To save the leaves on our rhododendrons and azaleas, we give them a late fall spray of Wiltpruf (available at any nursery), a natural anti-desiccant, followed by two more applications in the winter.

Greens in Your Garden (page 38); top row from left: mustard,
edible chrysanthemum, tatsoi, broadleaf cress; second row: tatsoi, bok choy,
swiss chard (neon, white and red); third row: Red Giant mustard,
amaranth, mizuna; fourth row: orach, arugula, dandelion

Black Walnut Bread

Black walnuts, which come from Mark's home state of Ohio, have a more intense flavor than the regular nut, so this bread is not like traditional French walnut bread. Besides being a delicious starter, it's also great with an after-dinner cheese course. Health-food stores often carry black walnuts or can order them for you.

Makes two 8- to 10-inch loaves

2 teaspoons active dry yeast
1¾ cups warm water
1¾ cups bread flour
1¾ cups whole-wheat flour
1 tablespoon vital wheat gluten (found in health-food stores
   and in some grocery stores)
2 teaspoons kosher salt
1 tablespoon honey
½ cup toasted black walnuts (page 272)
Cornmeal for dusting pans

1. In a small bowl dissolve the yeast in ¼ cup of the warm water.

2. Combine both flours, the wheat gluten, and salt in the bowl of a standing mixer fitted with the dough hook. Add the yeast mixture, honey, and remaining 1½ cups water and mix on low speed for 2 minutes. Increase the speed to medium and mix for 6 to 8 minutes until the dough is elastic and pulls away from the sides of the bowl. (Alternatively, combine the dissolved yeast with the other dough ingredients in a large bowl, turn out onto a lightly floured board, and knead by hand for about 6 minutes until smooth and elastic.)

3. Turn the dough onto a lightly floured worktable, add the walnuts, and knead for 3 to 5 minutes until the dough is soft and elastic. Transfer the dough to a lightly oiled large bowl and cover with plastic wrap. Let the dough rise in a warm place (80 to 85 degrees F) until it is doubled in size and light to the touch, 45 to 60 minutes.

4. Turn the dough out onto the table again and divide it in half. Using your hands, shape each piece into an oval loaf by folding the dough in toward the center and pinching the seam together. Sprinkle cornmeal on 2 baking sheets and set the loaves seam side

down on them. Cover the loaves with clean kitchen towels and let them rise until almost doubled in size, 35 to 45 minutes.

5. Preheat the oven to 400 degrees F.

6. Uncover the loaves and make several $\frac{1}{4}$-inch-deep diagonal slashes across the tops with a very sharp knife or razor blade. Use a spray bottle to mist the loaves with water (which keeps the crusts from setting too quickly and makes them crisper) and transfer them to the oven. After 5 minutes, mist the loaves again with water. Bake for 20 minutes until the loaves sound hollow when lightly tapped. Remove the loaves from the oven, take them off the baking sheets, and cool on racks. The loaves can be stored, tightly wrapped in plastic wrap, at room temperature for up to 2 days. You can also freeze them for up to 1 month.

Toasting and Grinding Nuts

Nut-bearing trees are among the oldest plants on Earth, thriving on every continent except Antarctica. New England's Native Americans enjoyed hazelnuts, hickory nuts, and even acorns, which were boiled to extract their bitterness, then sun-dried and pounded into pastes. (In his classic book *Stalking the Wild Asparagus,* the late Euell Gibbons gives instructions for making acorn glacé, a caramelized acorn candy!) We use nuts in bread (Black Walnut Bread, page 270), salads (Rocket with Lemon-Hazelnut Vinaigrette, page 41), sauces (Deep-Fried Squid with Parsley and Almond Sauce, page 28), and, of course, desserts (Orchard Apple Crisp, page 274).

Toasting brings out the flavor of nuts, which are usually rather bland when raw. It's easy to do, as long as you use very low heat and watch them carefully. Nuts take their time getting to the stage when they begin to brown—and then they can turn black in seconds if you're not careful.

To toast nuts, preheat the oven to 250 degrees F. Spread the shelled nuts evenly on a cookie sheet and bake until golden brown and slightly glossy, about 10 minutes for pine nuts and peanuts, 15 minutes for pistachios and almonds, and 20 minutes for walnuts and hazelnuts. Keep your eye on them!

When the nuts are toasted, remove the cookie sheet from the oven, and if using in a savory dish, sprinkle the nuts with salt while they are still hot. Allow the nuts to cool to room temperature, then store in an airtight container in the refrigerator for up to 1 week.

Ground nuts are used to thicken and flavor sauces and in baking. The basic way to grind nuts is with a knife on a cutting board. But it's fairly slow going, and the nuts tend to scoot away from the knife. That's why someone invented the old-fashioned hand-cranked nut grinder; you put the nuts in the little feeder chute on top, turn the crank, and the ground nuts drop into a glass jar. It works great. The contemporary solution is to put nuts in the bowl of a food processor fitted with the metal blade and pulse briefly—not too long or they'll turn into a paste.

DESSERTS

HERBAL TEAS

Health-food stores and even mainstream supermarkets these days devote whole shelves to soothing and healthful herbal teas. But teas and infusions made from your own garden have much more flavor than store-bought varieties. All you have to do is gather some herbs and other flavorings in a piece of cheesecloth, tie it with kitchen string, set it in a cup or pot, and pour in boiling water. Alternatively, you can just pour boiling water over loose herbs and strain them out after they steep. Try experimenting with ginger, blackberries, mint, apple blossoms, rhubarb, marigolds, tarragon, and rose hips. Here are some of our time-tested herbal teas for two from the garden:

- Strawberry-Lavender: Put 15 strawberries, 6 flowering lavender sprigs, and 2 tablespoons black tea in a cheesecloth bag. Put the bag in a teapot and pour in 2 cups boiling water. Steep for at least 6 minutes or to taste.
- Rose-Honey: Combine the petals of 6 large old roses (page 191) with 2 tablespoons honey in a teapot. Pour in 2 cups boiling water and steep for at least 6 minutes or to taste.
- Green Thumb: Put 2 sprigs tarragon, 1 sprig rosemary, 1 sprig lemon thyme, and 2 tablespoons green tea in a cheesecloth bag. Put the bag in a teapot and pour in 2 cups boiling water. Steep for 10 minutes or to taste.
- Arrows' Wellness Blend: This highly aromatic tea really soothes a cold. Combine 2 cups water, 1 cup freshly squeezed orange juice, 1 stalk lemongrass (cut up and smashed flat with the side of a knife), 1 fresh serrano chile (halved lengthwise), and 2 tablespoons honey in a small saucepan. Bring to a boil, remove from the heat, and steep for at least 6 minutes or to taste. Strain and serve warm. ✑

Orchard Apple Crisp

Apple picking is a fall ritual in New England, where many growers train their trees to allow ground-level picking by letting the lower branches grow out so you don't need a ladder to reach the apples. (Doing so exposes more of the apples to powdery mildew and other soil-borne ailments, however, so most growers keep at least some of their trees pruned high off the ground.) When the fruit ripens, the growers set up a stand in the field, and families come and pick whole bushels of apples to make pies and cider. Many of the varieties are obscure heirlooms that you never see in supermarkets, like Canadian Strawberry, which is a very juicy apple best eaten raw, or Black Oxford, a dark purple baking variety that ripens in late fall and keeps well in the refrigerator (or the root cellar) until spring. This dish is also delicious with Blueberry Ice Cream (page 198), which we make in the fall with blueberries we have frozen.

Makes 8 to 10 servings

1½ cups all-purpose flour
1½ cups firmly packed brown sugar
1 cup old-fashioned rolled oats
1 cup sliced almonds or chopped walnuts or pecans
3 teaspoons ground cinnamon
½ teaspoon ground nutmeg
12 tablespoons (1½ sticks) unsalted butter, melted
1 cup sugar
6 large baking apples, such as Cortland or Macintosh, peeled, halved, cored, and cut into ¼-inch slices
1 teaspoon pure vanilla extract
Juice of ½ lemon

1. Preheat the oven to 375 degrees F. Butter a 9-inch-square baking pan and set it aside.

2. Mix the flour, brown sugar, oats, nuts, 2 teaspoons of the cinnamon, and the nutmeg in a large bowl. Add the melted butter and toss until the mixture resembles coarse crumbs. Set aside at room temperature.

3. In a large bowl mix the sugar and remaining 1 teaspoon cinnamon. Add the apple slices, vanilla, and lemon juice and toss to coat. Pour the apple mixture into the buttered pan and sprinkle the topping over the apples. Press the topping down lightly.

4. Bake the crisp for 35 to 45 minutes until the apple juices thicken and the topping is deep golden brown. Remove the pan from the oven and let it cool for 15 minutes. Serve at room temperature.

NOTE: The crisp is best served the day it is made.

Zucchini Bread with Lemon Verbena Curd

This lovely brunch dessert is a great way to use up the last of the zucchini before the frost. Lemon verbena tastes like a combination of lemon and lime zest. The leaves wilt and turn color quickly, so don't pick them until you're ready to cook. You could also serve the curd with Pecan Pound Cake (page 94) or Blueberry Ice Cream (page 198).

Makes two 8 x 4-inch loaves and about 2 cups curd, or 8 servings

FOR THE ZUCCHINI BREAD
1 pound zucchini
1$\frac{1}{3}$ cups vegetable oil
2$\frac{1}{3}$ cups sugar
3 large eggs
3 cups all-purpose flour
2 teaspoons ground cinnamon
$\frac{1}{2}$ teaspoon ground allspice
1$\frac{3}{4}$ teaspoons baking soda
1 teaspoon baking powder
1 cup toasted walnut pieces (page 272)

1. Preheat the oven to 350 degrees F. Butter and flour two 8 x 4-inch loaf pans and set aside.

2. Grate the zucchini on the large holes of a box grater or in a food processor fitted with the coarsest shredding blade. Measure 3 cups zucchini and set aside.

3. In a large mixer bowl beat the oil and sugar on medium speed until light in color, 3 to 5 minutes. Beat in the eggs one at a time, scraping the bowl between additions.

4. Sift together the flour, cinnamon, allspice, baking soda, and baking powder and add them to the egg mixture. Mix slowly until combined.

5. Fold the zucchini and walnut pieces into the batter with a rubber spatula, then pour the batter into the prepared loaf pans. Bake for 45 to 55 minutes until a toothpick inserted into the center of each loaf comes out clean.

6. Remove the pans from the oven, transfer to a rack, and let cool for 30 minutes. Take the loaves out of the pans and let them cool completely. The bread can be stored, well wrapped, in the refrigerator for up to 3 days or frozen for up to 1 month.

FOR THE CURD

1 cup sugar

⅔ cup freshly squeezed lemon juice, at room temperature

½ cup packed lemon verbena leaves, plus additional for garnish

¼ teaspoon salt

8 tablespoons (1 stick) unsalted butter, at room temperature

4 large eggs, at room temperature

3 large egg yolks, at room temperature

1. In the bowl of a food processor fitted with the metal blade or in the jar of a blender, combine the sugar, lemon juice, lemon verbena leaves, and salt; process to make a paste. Add the butter and pulse until the mixture comes together, then add the eggs and egg yolks and continue to process until smooth.

2. Transfer the mixture to a medium stainless-steel saucepan; set over low heat. Whisk continuously until the mixture thickens and the temperature reaches 190 degrees F on a kitchen thermometer. Do not let it boil.

3. Immediately strain the curd into a heatproof nonreactive container and press plastic wrap on the surface. Refrigerate until cool or for up to 3 days.

TO SERVE

Cut the zucchini bread into 1-inch slices and arrange 2 slices on each of 8 dessert plates. Spoon some lemon verbena curd on top. Garnish with lemon verbena leaves.

Super-Moist Apple Cake

What makes this cake moist is the cream, which is poured over the top just before it bakes. This is a great coffeecake on its own or served warm with Vanilla Ice Cream (page 198).

For different textures within the same cake, try baking with a combination of apples, such as Granny Smith (which is quite tart), Macintosh (which is firm), and Cortland (which gets very soft with cooking).

Makes one 10-inch cake, or 10 servings

2 cups sugar
12 tablespoons (1½ sticks) unsalted butter, at room temperature
3 large eggs
1 cup plus 1 tablespoon cake flour (not self-rising)
1 cup plus 1 tablespoon all-purpose flour
2 teaspoons baking powder
Pinch of kosher salt
¾ cup whole milk
¾ teaspoon pure vanilla extract
3 medium baking apples, peeled, cored, halved, and thinly sliced
¾ cup heavy cream
1½ teaspoons ground cinnamon

1. Preheat the oven to 350 degrees F. Grease a 10-inch round, 2-inch-deep cake pan and line the bottom with parchment paper.

2. In a large bowl beat 1½ cups of the sugar and the butter for 3 to 5 minutes until light in color. Scrape the bowl as needed with a rubber spatula and continue to beat the mixture until it is very light in texture and color, several minutes more.

3. Beat in the eggs one at a time, scraping the bowl between additions.

4. Sift together both flours, the baking powder, and salt. Mix the milk and dry ingredients alternately into the butter mixture, stopping to scrape the bowl as necessary. Add the vanilla and mix the batter just until smooth; do not overbeat it.

5. Pour the batter into the prepared pan and spread it evenly with a rubber spatula.

Arrange the apple slices overlapping in concentric circles on top of the cake batter to completely cover it. Pour the cream evenly over the apples.

6. Stir together the remaining $1/2$ cup sugar and the cinnamon and sprinkle the mixture over the top of the cake. Bake for 45 minutes until a toothpick inserted in the center comes out clean. Remove the pan from the oven, transfer it to a rack, and let cool completely.

7. Invert the cake onto the rack, remove the parchment paper, and invert it once more onto a serving platter. Serve warm or at room temperature. Once cool, the cake can be stored tightly covered in the refrigerator for up to 3 days.

Apple Fritters with Cajeta Sauce

Cajeta is a Mexican caramel sauce that is traditionally made with goat's milk, which gives it quite an earthy taste. There cajeta is sold in jars at supermarkets, sometimes with brandy added. In Maine we make it with cow's milk and cream. The cold sauce drizzled over warm fritters is similar to the contrast of ice cream and hot apple pie—but even more luxurious.

Makes 6 servings

FOR THE SAUCE
3 cups whole milk
1 cup heavy cream
1 1/2 cups sugar
1/2 teaspoon baking soda
1/4 cup water

1. Fill a large bowl halfway with ice water. Have ready a smaller bowl that will sit in the ice bath.

2. In a large saucepan combine the milk, cream, and sugar. Stir to dissolve the sugar over medium-low heat, then simmer the mixture, stirring occasionally, until it is reduced by one-third.

3. Dissolve the baking soda in the water and stir it into the hot milk. The mixture will foam and rise; keep stirring and if needed reduce the heat. Simmer, stirring occasionally, until the mixture is reduced to about 1 1/2 cups and is amber in color.

4. Pour the sauce into the smaller bowl and chill in the ice bath; it will thicken some as it chills. The sauce can be made in advance; cover and refrigerate for up to 1 week.

FOR THE FRITTERS
Vegetable oil for frying
3/4 cup all-purpose flour
3/4 cup cornstarch
1/2 cup sugar
1/4 cup brown sugar
2 tablespoons baking powder

Scant 1 teaspoon ground cinnamon
4 medium tart apples, such as Granny Smith, peeled, halved, cored,
    and cut into ½-inch cubes
1 large egg
¾ cup beer, preferably lager

1. In a heavy pot add enough vegetable oil to come about 3 inches up the side. Warm the oil to 350 degrees F as measured on a kitchen thermometer or until a drop of the flour mixture placed in the oil immediately starts to sizzle. Line a large plate with several layers of paper towels.

2. While the oil is heating, combine the flour, cornstarch, both sugars, baking powder, and cinnamon in a large bowl. Add the apple cubes to the dry ingredients and toss to coat.

3. Whisk the egg and beer together in a small bowl, add it to the dry ingredients, and stir to combine. With a teaspoon, drop spoonfuls of the batter-coated apples into the hot oil, being very careful not to splash yourself with the oil. Cook the fritters in batches to avoid overcrowding. As the fritters float in the oil, turn them over to cook them evenly. Fry until golden brown, about 2 minutes.

4. Scoop the fritters out with a slotted spoon and transfer to the paper-towel-lined plate. Keep in a warm place while you cook the remaining fritters.

TO SERVE
Powdered sugar for dusting
1 apple, halved, cored, and thinly sliced

1. With a spoon drizzle the sauce onto each of 6 plates, arrange some fritters in the centers, and drizzle them with a bit more sauce.

2. Lightly dust the fritters with powdered sugar. Arrange the thin apple slices around the plates.

Peppermint Crème Brûlée

There are dozens of mint varieties. Peppermint is one of the most intense. Chocolate mint, which has a brownish stem, is sweeter than peppermint and truly has a chocolate undertone when it is fresh.

Makes 6 servings

½ cup sugar
½ cup peppermint or chocolate mint leaves
2 cups heavy cream
4 large egg yolks

1. Preheat the oven to 200 degrees F. Arrange six 6-ounce ceramic ramekins on a rimmed baking sheet.
2. Add the sugar and the mint leaves to the bowl of a food processor fitted with the metal blade. Process to make a smooth paste. (Alternatively, use a knife to finely chop the mint with the sugar by hand.) Combine the mint mixture and cream in a medium stainless-steel saucepan and bring to a simmer, stirring occasionally.
3. Whisk the egg yolks in a medium bowl. Pour the warm cream mixture very slowly into the yolks while whisking. Set the mixture aside for 10 minutes, then strain it through a very fine sieve into a large heatproof measure or pitcher.
4. Skim off any foam that may be on top, then gently pour the liquid into the ramekins, being careful not to splash. Wipe the edges of the ramekins clean and place them in the oven. Bake for 40 to 50 minutes until the custards are almost firm. The centers should still jiggle slightly when the ramekins are shaken. Remove the ramekins from the oven and let them cool at room temperature for 1 hour. Refrigerate until completely cold, at least 3 hours, or up to 1 day.

TO SERVE
6 tablespoons sugar

1. Preheat the broiler.
2. Sprinkle the surface of each custard evenly with 1 tablespoon of the sugar. Put the

ramekins on a baking sheet and brown the sugar under the broiler, about 1 minute. Watch carefully so that the sugar does not burn. Let sit for a few minutes to let the caramel top harden. Serve at once.

CREATING LARGE FLORAL ARRANGEMENTS

At Arrows we love cut flowers—they're a great way to bring our gardens into the dining room—but we don't let them clutter up our tables, where the focus is on the food. Instead we create large arrangements for side tables and buffets. At home you can create your own spectacular arrangements for occasions like Thanksgiving, important anniversaries, or milestone birthdays. There is no simpler way to create a festive atmosphere than with a mass of seasonal flowers.

Our arrangements vary according to season, but they always include a skeletal framework of large branches, which support many smaller groupings of cut flowers. The secret is hiding plastic drink cups throughout the branches; filled with water, they become miniature vases for the cut flowers. Start with some basic tools and equipment:

- Good-quality pruning shears (Cheap pruning shears are a waste of money; they won't hold an edge and will soon break. It's better to invest in a more expensive pair that will last a lifetime. Swiss-made Felco shears are good.)
- A folding pruning saw, for cutting saplings
- A pair of long-handled loppers (like pruning shears but capable of cutting much larger branches), for reaching high branches in trees (The 26-inch model made by Corona is what the pros use.)
- A large, heavy vase (Leaded glass is a good choice, but anything substantial and stable will do, even a metal bucket. Avoid styles that flare out at the lip, for branches flop sideways in them.)
- Heavy-duty clear packing tape
- Sharp scissors
- Several 6-inch-deep clear or green plastic drink cups, for making small vases within the branches of the arrangement
- Green floral wire to secure large branches to walls
- Picture hooks to anchor the wire
- Chlorine bleach
- A stepladder
- One or two large plastic buckets, to hold flowers and branches while you work

Begin by selecting the branches that will form the skeleton of the arrangement. In the spring we use cuttings from flowering trees like forsythia, pussy willow, lilac, or apple. All will bloom spectacularly in water if you cut them when the buds are just popping. Smash flat an inch or two of the stem at the bottom (use a hammer and do it in your driveway or walkway) to allow the branch to draw more water.

If you don't have access to any flowering trees (not a problem for anyone who lives in Maine!), use regular tree branches, which is what we do in the summer. Oak branches work well because they last the longest of any leaf tree. (Even in Maine, oak leaves never seem to fall until winter.) Beech and ash leaves also last a long time. In the autumn we love bright gold and red sugar maple leaves that have just turned, but the spectacular color only lasts a couple of days. In winter we use pine, hemlock, and other evergreens. That classic evergreen smell is most pronounced on Douglas fir branches; spruce also looks nice, but the needlelike leaves are painfully sharp and smell more like turpentine.

Whatever the season, keep in mind that ideally your framework will last for a few weeks (you can change the cut flowers more frequently), so don't choose branches with leaves or flowers that fade after a few days. (Fall leaves are the unavoidable exception.) In general stay away from tuberous greens like bamboo; they fade quickly. If you're unsure of a tree's cut life, gather a few branches several days in advance and test them in a bucket of water.

To gather branches, head outside with your saw and loppers—and think BIG—we're talking branches at least 4 feet long. Most people wimp out and cut tiny sprigs, but you're going for a massive effect here, so start sawing. Don't worry about cutting branches that are too big; you can trim them down later.

Back inside lay out the branches so you can study them and start thinking about ways to combine the shapes. Fill your vase about three-quarters full with water, then stir in some bleach—about $\frac{1}{4}$ cup for each gallon. This helps keep the water clear for a few days, and it won't hurt the branches. Then start adding branches to the vase, trimming them as necessary. You're going for a natural shape, not a ball! Always keep the weight of the branches balanced as you progress. Intermittently secure the branches with floral wire to a nearby wall or door frame. (Heavy-duty picture hooks work well. Don't fret about putting a nail hole in your wall;

you can fill it in seconds with lightweight patching compound, like Red Devil One Time, which doesn't require sanding. If your walls are white, you won't even need to touch up the paint.)

Once the branches are in place, start positioning the cups throughout the arrangement (a foot or so below the tops of the branches), using the packing tape to secure them. Use lots of tape; the cups will be holding water and flowers, so they need to be firmly in place. Fill each cup about three-quarters full with water, then hide them with smaller leftover sprigs from the branches, which can be wired in place.

Now you're ready to start adding cut flowers. First trim the flower stems to the desired length, then strip off excess leaves before adding them to the cups. Begin with "filler" flowers like mums, daisies, and carnations, which tend to be more prolific in the garden or less expensive to buy. Distribute them evenly around the whole arrangement. Finally add accents of more eye-catching flowers like roses, lilies, and irises. When finished, top off the water in the main vase and the cups. Check the water levels every day. ◦⌣

Rose Petal Granita

Roses add an unexpected delicacy to granita, the traditional Italian ice more rustic than sorbet. The most fragrant roses are the so-called old roses (as opposed to hybrid tea roses), which do well in cold climates. We have many of these low-growing shrub types at Arrows, and we love to include their flowers in desserts. You can use any type of sweet-scented rose here, but be absolutely certain it has not been sprayed or dusted with chemicals.

Makes 6 servings

2 cups loosely packed, organically grown, fragrant pink or red rose petals,
    plus additional for garnish
1 cup sugar
1 teaspoon rose water, optional
2 cups water
3 tablespoons freshly squeezed lemon juice

1. Gently rinse the rose petals under cold water and dry them in a salad spinner.

2. Combine the rose petals, sugar, and rose water if using in the bowl of a food processor fitted with the metal blade, or in the jar of a blender. Process to make a paste, scraping the bowl as needed.

3. Combine the water and lemon juice in a medium bowl. Add the rose-sugar paste and stir until the sugar is completely dissolved. There should be bits of rose petals in the mixture. Pour the mixture into a nonreactive 9-inch-square baking pan and put the container in the freezer.

4. Freeze, stirring the mixture with a fork every 20 minutes and scraping the sides and the bottom of the pan, for 1½ to 3 hours, depending on the temperature of your freezer. Once large crystals have formed, press plastic wrap on the surface and leave in the freezer for up to 1 week.

5. Scoop the granita into 6 chilled bowls. Sprinkle with rose petals and serve at once.

WINTER

FAREWELL AGAIN

Here's where we're supposed to complain about the harsh Maine winters, right? Well, the truth is, thanks to the moderating effect of the ocean, coastal Maine stays much warmer than inland spots like upstate New York or the Midwest. Ogunquit doesn't often get below zero. Still, we are very far north, which means our winters are dark and long, long, long. Maybe that's why Mainers are so adept at enjoying the summer.

Here in Maine, we tend to ring in winter at Thanksgiving, which is always gray and barren—and frequently blanketed in snow. It's the most inward-looking holiday of the year, nowhere more so than in New England where, of course, it all began.

Thanksgiving is always special at Arrows. Our old farmhouse, with its warm wood floors and frosty windowpanes, seems to beg for a traditional feast. We serve Roast Turkey (page 323), naturally, but also Plank-Roasted Salmon with Rosemary-Mustard Vinaigrette (page 317). The garden gives us Warm Red Cabbage Slaw with Creamy Herbed Goat Cheese (page 314), Fire-Roasted Onion and Rosemary Sauce (page 332), and Celery Root Pancakes (page 338).

Hardy herbs like sage, rosemary, and thyme are still thriving in our garden beds at Thanksgiving (most stay green under deep snow for at least a month), as are root vegetables. Parsnips, in particular, benefit from a frost or two, which enhances their sweetness. The trick is to dig them up before the ground freezes totally. If you forget and find that you can't get them out, just leave them until spring; they'll taste great. Meanwhile storage crops like cabbage and leeks, which we generally pull out in October, are piled high in our old stone cellar. (Leeks will keep for months in a cool basement or garage, especially if you bury the light parts in a bucket of sand.) We welcome these "cellar crops" around the holidays, when they still taste as fresh as the day they were harvested.

Our Thanksgiving guests are a great group. Many have been coming for years and are virtually family. When we finish serving our "extended family" that evening, the whole Arrows staff sits down for dinner with spouses, girlfriends, boyfriends, and kids (our "immediate family"), and we toast our friendships long into the night.

After Thanksgiving darkness seems to envelop Maine. The shortest days aren't until the week of Christmas, but the earliest sunsets take place during the first week of December—at around 4:00. No wonder Mainers are obsessed with Christmas lights. During the holiday season we love to walk down country roads in the gathering chill of early evening to see stately farmhouses glowing from candles in the windows and Christmas trees shimmering behind lace curtains. At Arrows we wrap trees in thousands of white lights, under which we pile hay bale "presents" tied with brightly colored ribbons.

In the dining room Big Bertha is trimmed with fir branches, filling the house with a woodsy aroma. Glossy sprays of holly, with their long-lasting red berries, add texture and color.

We enjoy bringing the winter woods indoors, but like most Mainers we don't let a little cold stop us from communing with nature. Winter is perhaps the best time of year to walk in the Maine woods. With no bugs to swat and no rustling leaves to mask the sound of wildlife, the mind can truly focus. The first thing you notice is that the woods are anything but "dead" in winter. Listen carefully, and you can hear a pileated woodpecker, the largest in North America, drilling for carpenter ants in a tree stump. You'll see tooth scrapings on the bark of red maple trees, where moose have enjoyed a tasty winter meal. You might see a white snowshoe hare bound across the trail. And if you head out to the woods after a fresh snowfall, you can follow dozens of tracks, from coyotes to bobcats to porcupines.

The winter woods are also alive with people, and not just hunters. Many Mainers still supplement their income by cutting fir boughs for Christmas wreaths, a significant cottage industry here. (Made-in-Maine holiday wreaths are shipped around the world.) And loggers are hard at work in winter, when the frozen ground makes it easier to haul out trees.

Many fishermen also brave the cold to bring in Maine shrimp, which are caught from around December to March. Maine shrimp are a distinct species from the Gulf and Asian shrimp that are sold frozen in supermarkets, and they are strange creatures indeed. The males turn into females at the age of three and a half, when they move to within ten miles of shore to hatch their eggs during winter. That's a godsend to Maine fishermen, who don't like being far out at sea in winter. Using special nets that allow larger fish to escape, they cruise just off the coast and haul in tons of Maine shrimp every day; most are consumed eagerly by locals, who buy them fresh at roadside stands.

Because Maine shrimp have a complicated and tenuous life cycle, their harvest is strictly regulated by the Atlantic State Marine Fisheries Commission. In years when the shrimp population is deemed low, fishermen must wait until after the females have hatched their eggs; in that case the entire season might be just a few weeks. But in plentiful years the fishermen are allowed to net for several months, and the Maine shrimp we buy are brimming with delicious, briny eggs, which add extra flavor to the shrimp as they cook.

Shrimp season tells us that soon it will be time to close up the house for our late-winter break. The last event is making our prosciutto hams (page 306), which will hang from the dining-room beams and air-cure until next spring. Air-curing meat is another ancient way to preserve food (and transform its taste) over the winter; removing moisture makes the meat inhospitable to bacteria.

Once the hams are hung, there's just one piece of unfinished business: the farewell dinner for our staff. After dessert, we wrap ourselves in warm coats and walk the dark and deserted beach, bracing each other against the northeast wind and snapping flash photos that could probably be used as blackmail. It's great fun and really just a way to put off saying goodbye—the hardest part. But winter's farewell is just one more season. Like summer's first tomato, it will come around again.

APPETIZERS

Escarole and White Bean Soup

In the garden escarole grows much like lettuce. It thrives in cool weather and bolts in high summer, sending up a tall flower stalk that signals the plant is maturing, which turns the leaves bitter. That's when you pull up lettuce, but because escarole stands up to cooking (which mellows the flavor), you can keep it going well into fall and early winter. It's also a great greenhouse performer.

Contrary to conventional wisdom, we salt our beans during the cooking process, which allows them to absorb the flavor of the salt. Some cookbooks tell you that salt makes beans tough; others say it makes them fall apart. We have never found it to have any effect one way or the other. We also don't bother soaking beans overnight; the process does not make them cook all that much faster but does prevent people from enjoying beans as often as they could.

Makes 6 servings

1 tablespoon olive oil
1 medium yellow onion, peeled and finely chopped
1 pound (2 cups) white beans, rinsed and picked clean of small stones
Kosher salt
18 large cloves garlic, peeled
2 tablespoons freshly squeezed lemon juice
Freshly ground black pepper
8 ounces escarole (about 1 large head), leaves separated, washed and dried

1. Warm the olive oil in a medium saucepan over medium heat. Add the onion and sauté, stirring occasionally, until translucent, about 5 minutes. Add the beans, 2 tea-

spoons salt, and enough cold water to cover them by 2 inches. Cook the beans at a brisk simmer over medium heat, adding more water if the level falls below that of the beans, until they are very soft, about 45 minutes.

2. Put the garlic cloves in a small saucepan and add enough water to cover them by 2 inches. Gently simmer the garlic over medium heat until very soft when pierced with a knife, 6 to 8 minutes. Drain and reserve the garlic.

3. When the beans are very soft, purée the beans with some of their cooking liquid in small batches in the jar of a blender to the consistency of thick cream. Combine the batches in a large saucepan and bring to a boil over medium heat.

4. Add the lemon juice to the bean purée and season with salt and pepper. Add the escarole and poached garlic to the soup and cook until the escarole is wilted, about 1 minute.

5. Divide the soup among 6 warm bowls and serve at once. Alternatively, the soup can be cooled, covered, and refrigerated overnight. Warm it before serving.

Oysters with Spicy Jícama Salad

Jícama, a big tuber that looks a little like celery root, is a staple in both Asian and Latin American cuisine. It has a clean, refreshing taste. More and more grocery stores are carrying jícama, even if few people seem to know what to do with it. It makes a delicious hors d'oeuvre simply peeled and sliced, then drizzled with lime juice and dusted with paprika and salt. This spicy preparation is a wonderful accompaniment to oysters. If you like a sauce with your oysters, try mixing ½ cup sweet red chile sauce (available in Asian and specialty markets) with 3 tablespoons rice vinegar.

Makes 6 servings

½ cup chopped mint leaves
½ cup chopped cilantro leaves
¼ cup rice vinegar
¼ cup sugar
1 serrano chile, stemmed, seeded, and finely chopped
2 tablespoons finely chopped gingerroot
2 teaspoons kosher salt
2 medium jícama
24 fresh oysters, washed and shucked (page 298)

1. In a medium bowl make a dressing by stirring together the mint, cilantro, vinegar, sugar, chile, ginger, and salt.

2. Peel the jícama and slice into ⅛-inch-thick rounds. Cut the jícama rounds into ¼-inch matchsticks. Toss with the dressing.

3. Make 4 little nests of jícama salad on each of 6 chilled plates. Set an oyster on top of each nest. Serve at once.

How to Shuck an Oyster

Maine is almost as famous for its oysters as its lobster. Dedicated oystermen along the Damariscotta and other Maine rivers provide us with some of the best oysters in the world—icy cold, deliciously briny, and not too plump, so you can eat the whole thing in one heavenly bite.

It's easy to open, or shuck, an oyster, once you have the right tool: a sturdy hand-held implement called, amazingly enough, an oyster shucker. In New England you can buy them at any housewares store, or you can find them in kitchen supply catalogs. Nothing else works quite as well (especially not a clam shucker, which is a totally different tool), although a medium-sized screwdriver will do in a pinch.

The first step is to wash the oyster under cold running water, scrubbing it with a kitchen brush, preferably one made of brass, which is sturdier than plastic. (Unlike clams, oysters never have any grit inside the shell, but mud on the outside can sometimes find its way in during the shucking process, so try to get the shells clean.) Then lay the oyster on a clean kitchen towel that's been folded lengthwise in half, with the flatter side of the oyster facing up and the pointed hinged end of the shell facing to the right (if you're right-handed). Fold some of the kitchen towel over the left side and top of the oyster and press down firmly on the shell, through the towel, with your left hand. (The towel gives you a better grip and protects your left hand should you slip with the shucker.) Holding the shucker in your right hand, stick the tool into the little crevice at the point of the oyster. Then twist the handle of the tool as if you were revving a motorcycle until the joint is pried apart. Once you break the seal, it's easy to pull the top shell off the bottom. Use the shucker to scrape the oyster free of both shells where it's attached with a muscle on each side.

If you're using oysters in a recipe, scrape them out of the shells into a bowl along with the delicious liquid, which is actually called liqueur. If you're planning to eat them on the half shell, leave the shucked oysters and their liqueur in the rounder bottom shell. To keep the liqueur

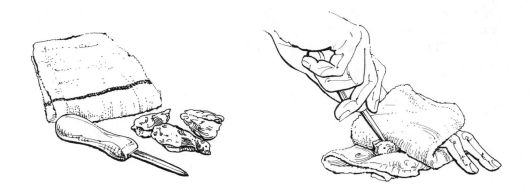

from spilling, nestle the oysters on a platter heaped with crushed ice, rock salt, or, in authentic Maine style, a bed of seaweed gathered from the rocks at low tide.

Fresh briny oysters on the half shell require no embellishment, although lemon is traditional. For something a little different, try them with Vietnamese Clear Dipping Sauce (page 161). ᴄ᷒

Colby Cheese Fritters with Chicory Salad

A couple of years ago we decided to have a special "Heartland" dinner at Arrows. Many of our diehard New England customers were skeptical, wondering out loud what sort of cuisine the Midwest could offer, until they sat down to dinner. Much of the inspiration for the menu came from Mark's mother's cooking. He had several long phone conversations with her about the menu, during which she reminded him of the many tastes of his childhood. One of those is mild Colby cheese, a Midwestern specialty.

Makes 24 to 30 fritters, enough for 6 servings

FOR THE FRITTERS
Vegetable oil for frying
1 cup water
8 tablespoons (1 stick) unsalted butter
½ teaspoon kosher salt
1 cup all-purpose flour
4 large eggs
2¾ cups shredded Colby cheese

1. In a large heavy pot add enough vegetable oil to come about 3 inches up the side. Warm the oil to 350 degrees F as measured on a kitchen thermometer or until a drop of the flour mixture placed in the oil immediately starts to sizzle. Line a large plate with several layers of paper towels.

2. While the oil is heating combine the water, butter, and salt in a large saucepan over medium heat and bring to a boil. Add the flour and cook, stirring constantly, until the mixture begins to pull away from the sides of the pan and form a ball, about 5 minutes.

3. Reduce the heat to low and add the eggs one at a time, beating well after each addition. Once all of the eggs have been added, continue to stir until the mixture turns shiny, about 1 minute; remove from the heat. Stir in the cheese.

4. Scoop heaping tablespoons of the dough and carefully drop them into the oil, being very careful not to splash yourself. Cook the fritters in batches to avoid overcrowding. As the fritters float in the oil, turn them to cook evenly. Fry until golden brown, 2 to 3 minutes.

5. Scoop the fritters out with a slotted spoon and transfer to the paper-towel-lined plate. Cover loosely with foil and keep warm on the back of the stove while cooking the remaining fritters.

FOR THE SALAD

¼ cup red wine vinegar
1 tablespoon Dijon mustard
1 teaspoon kosher salt
¼ teaspoon freshly ground black pepper
½ cup extra-virgin olive oil
6 ounces chicory (about 1 medium head), leaves separated,
    washed and dried

While the fritters are frying, combine the vinegar, mustard, salt, and pepper in a large bowl. Slowly whisk in the oil in a fine stream to create an emulsion. Toss the chicory with the vinaigrette and divide among 6 room-temperature plates.

TO SERVE

Divide the fritters among the plates and serve at once.

Maine Shrimp Dumplings with Cilantro

The winter in Maine may be long and dark, but at least we have fresh Maine shrimp (page 292)! Delicate and small (cooked, they're the size of a nickel), these sweet pink morsels are perfect in dumplings. You can substitute store-bought shrimp, which are always frozen although the store may have thawed them for you. Fortunately shrimp freezes quite well—one reason it has become so popular. Serve these dumplings with Vietnamese Clear Dipping Sauce (page 161).

Makes about 30 dumplings, enough for 6 servings

10 ounces (about 1 cup) raw Maine or other small shrimp, shelled
½ cup finely chopped cabbage
¼ cup cilantro leaves
2 tablespoons sugar
1 tablespoon finely chopped gingerroot
1 tablespoon sweet chile paste (available at Asian and specialty markets)
2 teaspoons soy sauce
1 teaspoon sesame oil
30 to 40 (3-inch-square) wonton wrappers, fresh or frozen and thawed
2 large eggs, lightly beaten
1 tablespoon kosher salt
1 tablespoon vegetable oil

1. In a medium bowl combine the shrimp, cabbage, cilantro, sugar, ginger, chile paste, soy sauce, and sesame oil. Mix well with a wooden spoon.

2. Spoon ½ tablespoon of the mixture onto the center of a wrapper. (Keep the remaining wrappers covered with a clean kitchen towel or plastic wrap, so they don't dry out.) With a pastry brush, coat 2 adjacent edges of the wrapper with beaten egg. Fold the wrapper over to form a triangle and seal the edges, pushing out any air. Join the 2 opposite points to form a "bishop's hat," sealing the joint with a dot of beaten egg. Transfer to a cookie sheet lined with parchment paper and cover with a clean kitchen towel. Repeat this process until you have used all of the filling. The dumplings will keep covered in plastic wrap in the refrigerator for up to 3 hours.

3. Bring 6 quarts water with the salt and vegetable oil to a boil in a large pot. Taking

care not to overcrowd the pot and working in batches if necessary, put the dumplings in the boiling water and cook until soft and the filling is cooked through, 1 to 2 minutes. Remove with a slotted spoon and transfer to a cookie sheet. Cover with foil to keep warm while you cook the remaining dumplings. Serve at once.

New Zealand Cockles with Chinese Dark Wine and Ham Sauce

This recipe is not a direct translation of any dish but more an impression of the spicy and intense flavors of northern China. It's also a good way to use up the small ends of prosciutto hams. (You can substitute good Virginia ham.) It bears a resemblance to clam chowder, which traditionally includes bacon, but the black beans, dark wine, and soy sauce give this dish a more hearty flavor.

The world can't seem to agree on what constitutes a cockle. In New England they are tiny sea snails picked from the rockweed at low tide, but in New Zealand cockles are buttery-tasting clams with very little sand and no neck. (They are one of the so-called Venus shells, a group of clams that includes the larger and more familiar quahog.) If you can't find New Zealand cockles, littlenecks or other small clams work well.

Makes 6 servings

3 tablespoons vegetable oil
4 ounces prosciutto (page 306) or Virginia ham, finely chopped
2 tablespoons finely chopped garlic
1 tablespoon finely chopped Chinese fermented black beans
   (available at Asian and specialty markets)
2 teaspoons chile paste (available at Asian and specialty markets)
4 cups Chicken Stock (page 23)
½ cup Xiao Xing wine (available at Asian markets) or dark beer
2 tablespoons soy sauce
2 tablespoons rice vinegar
1 tablespoon finely chopped gingerroot
3 pounds cockles or small clams (about 15 per person), scrubbed clean
4 tablespoons (½ stick) unsalted butter, at room temperature
1 cup Tomato Concassé (page 179)
1 tablespoon sesame oil
4 scallions, light and dark part, thinly sliced

1. In a large stainless-steel pot warm the vegetable oil over medium heat. Add the prosciutto, garlic, beans, and chile paste and cook, stirring, for about 5 minutes. Add the chicken stock, wine, soy sauce, vinegar, and ginger and bring to a boil. Reduce the heat to low and simmer for 15 minutes.

2. Increase the heat to high and return to a boil. Add the cockles, cover, and cook, shaking the pot, until the cockles open, about 2 minutes. Reduce the heat to medium. Using a slotted spoon, remove the cockles and divide them among 6 warm soup plates or bowls.

3. Whisk the butter into the sauce a tablespoon at a time. Stir in the tomato concassé and turn off the heat. Whisk in the sesame oil. Ladle the sauce on top of the cockles. Sprinkle with the scallions and serve at once.

NOTE: This dish is best served with a good ale, but on a really cold night you could try warm Xiao Xing wine, which is Chinese rice wine. It's a bit of an acquired taste, but you can always keep beer on hand as a backup.

Homemade Prosciutto

For the last fourteen years we have made our own prosciutto at Arrows. It's a winter project because the hams need to be hung in a cool place, like a garage or porch, for several months. Gradually we've refined the process; here is our time-tested method for home-curing ham.

Commercial prosciutto makers use temperature- and humidity-controlled rooms to ensure consistency with every batch. You won't have that advantage at home, but we've found a way to approximate the perfect environment with an electric fan and a common light timer, available at any hardware or discount store. It's not strictly necessary, but it dries the ham faster and requires little attention once you've set it up.

1 fresh ham, about 15 pounds
1 cup brandy
1 (3-pound) box kosher salt
$\frac{1}{2}$ cup sugar
1 head garlic, cut crosswise in half
$\frac{1}{4}$ cup freshly ground black pepper

SPECIAL EQUIPMENT NEEDED
A plastic tub larger than the ham, such as a restaurant bus tub
     or a large dish basin. (Most buckets aren't wide enough.)
A clean stainless-steel oven rack that fits over the tub and will support
     the ham.
3 square feet of cheesecloth
Kitchen string
An electric fan, optional
An inexpensive light timer, optional

1. Set the fresh ham on a large cutting board. At the widest part of the ham, where the meat is exposed, there is a small flat pelvic bone protruding. Using a sturdy boning knife, cut around this bone and remove it from the ball joint of the femur, directly underneath. Carefully sprinkle $\frac{1}{2}$ cup of the brandy over the exposed meat, including the top pointy part of the ham, and massage it in thoroughly.

2. In a large bowl combine the salt and sugar. Position the rack on the tub and set the ham skin side down on the rack. Pack the salt mixture onto every place the meat is exposed, as opposed to the fat, completely covering the meat with salt. If some of the salt mixture is left, save it for later. Put the tub with the ham in a very cold, dry room, 38 to 42 degrees F; an unheated garage, porch, or attic in winter works well, as long as the ham is protected from animals.

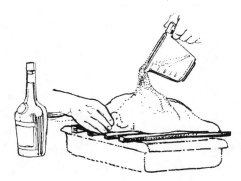

3. Check the ham each day for 3 days, repacking with the salt mixture that has fallen away or with new salt. During this time, a fair amount of liquid will be coming from the ham, which is a normal part of the drying process. After the first 3 days, the ham should be checked and repacked every third day, for 6 weeks.

4. After 6 weeks, clean the salt from the ham by scraping it off with the back of a knife. Dry the ham with paper towels. Sprinkle the remaining ½ cup brandy all over the ham and rub the garlic over it. Cover the exposed meat with the pepper. Wrap a double layer of cheesecloth around the ham, then secure the cheesecloth with string, wrapping it around the wide part of the ham twice, then wrapping twice from top to bottom. Make a loop at the top of the ham with the string and hang it from a hook or nail in the cold room. (At this point, the ham should have stopped dripping, but you can put a tray or rimmed cookie sheet underneath just to be safe.)

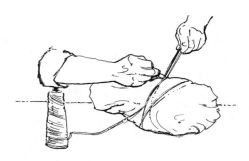

5. Position a household fan if using in front of the ham and plug the fan into a timer. Set the timer so that the fan blows on the ham for about 6 hours a day. Check the ham once a week or so. If the ham becomes covered with mold, unwrap it, clean it off with a knife, and cover with clean cheesecloth. The ham inside will not be affected by the exterior mold. As the ham gets drier, it's okay for the room temperature to start climbing a little. (The lack of moisture in the ham slows bacterial growth.) But if springtime is approaching and the room starts climbing above 50 degrees, clear space for the ham in the refrigerator, trying to maintain air circulation around it. After 6 months, the ham should have lost about half its original weight and be ready to eat. (A year or two of drying will make the ham even better, because as it gets drier it becomes firmer and easier to slice.)

6. Remove the cheesecloth and set the ham on a cutting board. Use a sturdy boning knife to locate the femur, which is visible at the top of the ham and runs to the ball joint. Cut along the top of the bone to expose it, then gradually cut it away from the meat. Using a chef's knife, cut the wide end of the ham flat. Cut off the outside skin but leave some of the remaining fat, then scrape off any mold and pepper. The whole ham can now be wrapped in plastic wrap and kept refrigerated for up to 2 months. Thinly slice the prosciutto for serving.

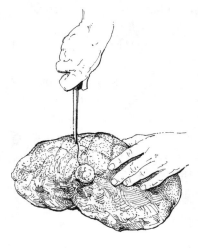

NOTE: Sliced prosciutto can be wrapped carefully, first in parchment paper and then in plastic wrap, and kept refrigerated for up to 3 days; any longer and the thin slices start to dry out, so don't slice more than you need at one time.

SALADS

Winter Greens with Pink Grapefruit and Red Onion

Walking into our greenhouse on a cold day is a pleasure, as the air is moist and filled with life. Under the protective cover, all sorts of delicate salad greens continue to thrive in winter. We also enjoy citrus during winter, because it is at its peak. Mellow pink grapefruit is especially good with tender lettuces.

Makes 6 servings

2 large pink grapefruits
1 small red onion, peeled and thinly sliced
¼ cup red wine vinegar
1 medium shallot, peeled and finely chopped
2 teaspoons finely chopped thyme leaves
1 teaspoon kosher salt
¼ teaspoon freshly ground black pepper
¼ cup extra-virgin olive oil
¼ cup olive oil
6 ounces mixed greens, such as romaine, red leaf lettuce, arugula, and mizuna (about 6 handfuls), washed and dried
4 ounces crumbled blue cheese, optional

1. Section the grapefruits (page 310) and set the sections aside. Squeeze the juice from the membranes into a sieve set over a small bowl. Measure 3 tablespoons of the juice into a large bowl.

2. Add the onion to the juice remaining in the small bowl and set aside.

3. Add the vinegar, shallot, thyme, salt, and pepper to the grapefruit juice in the large bowl. Whisk in both olive oils. The vinaigrette will keep covered in the refrigerator for up to 1 day.

4. Toss the greens with the vinaigrette and arrange on 6 chilled plates. Garnish with the grapefruit sections, marinated red onion (discard the juice), and blue cheese if using. Serve.

SECTIONING CITRUS

We use citrus sections in salads and in sauces and dressings such as Citrus and Parsley Gremolata Vinaigrette (page 59). To section citrus, first cut off the top and bottom of the fruit, removing a thin layer of flesh along with the peel and pith. Put the fruit on a cutting board on one of its now flat ends, and with a small knife cut down the sides of the fruit, following the curve of the fruit and again slicing away a bit of flesh. Working over a bowl to catch the juice, hold the peeled fruit in your hand and cut down along the membranes to release the citrus sections. Once you've removed all the sections, squeeze the membrane in your hand to release any extra juice; discard the membrane. Use the juice in recipes and drinks; cover and refrigerate for up to 2 days. Citrus sections can be refrigerated in an airtight container for up to 2 days.

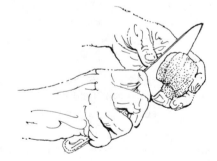

Radicchio Chiffonade Salad
with Creamy Blue Cheese Vinaigrette

Chiffonade is just a fancy word for finely sliced or "julienned" lettuce. Radicchio prepared this way not only looks beautiful but also is easier to eat. Pair this salad with one of the others in this chapter; the Reine de Glace with Roasted Shallot Vinaigrette (page 312) is especially good.

Makes 6 servings

4 ounces blue cheese, crumbled
¼ cup sour cream
¼ cup champagne vinegar
2 teaspoons kosher salt
½ teaspoon freshly ground black pepper
¼ cup buttermilk
¼ cup olive oil
3 large heads radicchio, cut lengthwise in half, cored, washed, and dried

1. In a large bowl combine the cheese, sour cream, vinegar, salt, and pepper. Whisk in the buttermilk, followed by the oil. The vinaigrette will keep covered in the refrigerator for up to 1 day.

2. Separate the leaves of the radicchio and gather them in stacks of 6 or 7 leaves of about the same size. Using a sharp chef's knife, cut each stack crosswise into thin strips.

3. Toss the radicchio with the vinaigrette and serve, dividing the salad among six chilled plates.

Reine de Glace Lettuce Salad
with Roasted Shallot Vinaigrette

Reine de Glace (Ice Queen) is a beautiful lettuce with some of the textural qualities of iceberg lettuce. It has great flavor, and grows well in harsh conditions. (Iceberg makes a good substitute.) The roasted shallot vinaigrette is rich and full bodied, perfect for a winter salad.

Makes 6 servings

6 large shallots, peeled
4 tablespoons olive oil
Kosher salt
Freshly ground black pepper
¼ cup extra-virgin olive oil
¼ cup red wine vinegar
1 tablespoon Dijon mustard
1 tablespoon whole-grain mustard
½ cup flat-leaf parsley
1 tablespoon tarragon leaves
1 teaspoon finely chopped thyme leaves
12 whole black peppercorns
6 ounces Reine de Glace lettuce (about 1 medium head), leaves separated, washed and dried

1. Preheat the oven to 375 degrees F.
2. Toss the shallots with 2 tablespoons of the olive oil in a small baking dish. Sprinkle with salt and pepper. Cover the dish with foil or a lid and roast until the shallots are soft and starting to caramelize, about 30 minutes.
3. Transfer the shallots to the jar of a blender. Add the remaining 2 tablespoons olive oil, the extra-virgin olive oil, vinegar, both mustards, the herbs, 1 teaspoon salt, and the peppercorns. Blend until all the ingredients are puréed. The vinaigrette will keep covered in the refrigerator for up to 3 days.
4. Toss the lettuce in a bowl with the vinaigrette. Divide the salad among 6 chilled plates and serve at once.

Winter Lettuce Salad
with Sherry–Walnut Vinaigrette

When there is snow on the ground in Maine, our raised beds and cold frames keep our winter lettuce thriving. This rich vinaigrette will cut the bitterness of hearty late-season lettuces such as frisée, chicory, and radicchio. Field greens and more tender lettuces work in this mix as well.

Makes 6 servings

12 thin slices Black Walnut Bread (page 270), or honey whole wheat
½ cup olive oil
¼ cup sherry vinegar
1 tablespoon finely chopped shallot
2 teaspoons Dijon mustard
1 teaspoon finely chopped thyme leaves
1 teaspoon kosher salt
¼ teaspoon freshly ground black pepper
½ cup walnut oil
6 ounces mixed greens, such as romaine, Red Oakleaf lettuce, arugula,
    and mizuna (about 6 handfuls), washed and dried
½ cup toasted walnuts (page 272)

1. Preheat the oven to 325 degrees F.

2. Arrange the walnut bread slices in a single layer on a cookie sheet and drizzle with ¼ cup of the olive oil. Bake until golden brown, about 10 minutes. Remove from the oven and set aside to cool.

3. In a large bowl combine the vinegar, shallot, mustard, thyme, salt, and pepper. Gradually whisk in the walnut oil and remaining ¼ cup olive oil. The vinaigrette will keep covered in the refrigerator for up to 3 days.

4. Toss the greens with the vinaigrette and divide among 6 chilled plates. Garnish with the toasts and walnuts and serve.

Warm Red Cabbage Slaw
with Creamy Herbed Goat Cheese

One of Mark's favorite dishes growing up was his mother's pork roast, which she served with his uncle's homemade sauerkraut or with braised red cabbage. When we cooked at Stars for Jeremiah Tower, we made several different red cabbage salads. Gradually we changed this recipe to be more like Mark's mom's, but the cooking technique that we learned from Jeremiah is still the best. Serve with Roast Pork Loin with Rosemary and Garlic (page 242).

Makes 6 servings

4 ounces soft, fresh goat cheese
1 tablespoon freshly squeezed lemon juice
2 teaspoons finely chopped flat-leaf parsley
1 teaspoon finely chopped thyme leaves
Kosher salt
Freshly ground black pepper
$\frac{1}{2}$ cup heavy cream
12 thin slices pancetta
$\frac{1}{2}$ cup olive oil
1 small head red cabbage, halved, cored, and thinly sliced
$\frac{1}{2}$ cup red wine vinegar

1. In a medium bowl combine the goat cheese, lemon juice, parsley, thyme, 1 teaspoon salt, and $\frac{1}{4}$ teaspoon pepper. Stir in the cream. Cover and refrigerate until needed or for up to 1 day.

2. Preheat the oven to 350 degrees F.

3. Line a cookie sheet with parchment paper. Spread the pancetta slices on the cookie sheet and bake until the pancetta is crisp, about 10 minutes. Remove from the oven and set in a warm place.

4. Warm the olive oil in a large sauté pan over medium-high heat. Toss the cabbage with the vinegar in a large bowl and sprinkle with 1 teaspoon salt and $\frac{1}{4}$ teaspoon pep-

per. Add the cabbage to the pan and cook, stirring constantly, until the cabbage is hot and slightly wilted, about 5 minutes.

5. Divide the cabbage among 6 warm plates, arrange a dollop of goat cheese and 2 slices of pancetta on top, and serve at once.

Cole Slaw with Creamy Mustard–Ginger Vinaigrette

Cole slaw is not just for summer picnics. If you save your fall harvest of cabbages in a cool, dry place, you can enjoy slaw throughout the winter.

Makes 6 servings

1/4 cup sour cream
1/4 cup cider vinegar
2 tablespoons sugar
2 tablespoons finely chopped gingerroot
1 tablespoon Dijon mustard
1 tablespoon whole-grain mustard
2 teaspoons Mayonnaise (page 158)
2 teaspoons soy sauce
1 teaspoon Worcestershire sauce
1 teaspoon kosher salt
1/2 teaspoon freshly ground white pepper
1/4 cup olive oil
1/4 head green cabbage, cored and thinly sliced
1/4 head red cabbage, cored and thinly sliced
1 bunch scallions, light and dark parts, thinly sliced

1. In a large bowl combine the sour cream, vinegar, sugar, ginger, both mustards, the mayonnaise, soy sauce, Worcestershire, salt, and pepper. Whisk together well, then whisk in the oil.

2. Toss the cabbage and scallions with the dressing. Serve immediately or cover and refrigerate for up to 2 days. Serve chilled or at room temperature.

&MAIN COURSES

Plank-Roasted Salmon with Rosemary-Mustard Vinaigrette

Plank-roasting is an ancient method of cooking among the Indians of the Pacific Northwest. For important feasts known as potlatches, whole salmon fillets were suspended on cedar planks and placed around a fire to cook.

Plank-roasting in your home oven is simple and infuses the salmon with a complex woody flavor, similar to the way oak barrels add flavor to wine. At your local lumberyard or home center, select a piece of 1 x 8-inch or 1 x 6-inch cedar just long enough to fit inside your oven. (The salmon fillets will be laid out in a row on this board.) About 20 inches long should work, but measure your oven to be sure. Pine or fir can be substituted, with a little less aromatic flavor; it's better to spend a few dollars more for the real thing. Make sure that the wood has not been primed or treated with any chemicals.

At Arrows we often use fresh herbs or dry seasonings to add another level of flavor to the plank-roasted fish. Rosemary, with its robust character, is a perfect match for salmon.

Makes 6 servings

FOR THE VINAIGRETTE
¼ cup Worcestershire sauce
3 tablespoons balsamic vinegar
3 tablespoons soy sauce
3 tablespoons whole-grain mustard
2 tablespoons brown sugar
1 teaspoon finely chopped rosemary leaves

1 teaspoon kosher salt
1 teaspoon freshly ground black pepper
¼ cup olive oil

In a medium bowl mix together the Worcestershire, vinegar, soy sauce, mustard, sugar, rosemary, salt, and pepper. Gradually whisk in the olive oil. The vinaigrette will keep covered in the refrigerator for up to 3 days.

FOR THE SALMON
1 cedar board large enough to hold 6 salmon fillets (see above)
4 tablespoons olive oil
6 skinless salmon fillets, 6 to 7 ounces each
6 sprigs rosemary
Kosher salt
Freshly ground black pepper

1. Brush one side of the board with 2 tablespoons of the olive oil and let it sit overnight.

2. Arrange a rack in the center of the oven and preheat the oven to 450 degrees F. Place a large rimmed baking sheet underneath the center rack to catch the salmon drippings.

3. Lay the salmon fillets skinned side down on the plank. Tuck a sprig of rosemary under each fillet. Lightly brush the salmon with the remaining 2 tablespoons olive oil and sprinkle with salt and pepper.

4. Place the board in the oven for 10 minutes. To make sure the fish is cooked properly, lightly squeeze the fillet with your finger; it should feel firm and just start to give way. Carefully remove the board from the oven. With a metal spatula, transfer the salmon fillets to warm plates.

5. Whisk the vinaigrette briefly to recombine and spoon some of it over each fillet. Serve at once.

SAVING SEEDS

Some heirloom seeds like beans are easy to save. Just leave some of the pods to dry on the vine (the pods will become brown and brittle), then remove the hard, dried beans and save them in a tightly sealed jar in a cool, dry place for next year's planting. Make sure they are completely dry or they'll rot; they should shatter when smashed with a hammer. And freeze overnight any beans that you plan on saving for seed; that kills a tiny worm that can live inside and prevent them from sprouting.

Peas are just as easy; leave some pods on the vines until they dry out, then shuck the hardened peas into a jar for storage in a cool, dry place.

Saving biennials like carrots and parsley is less convenient because you have to let the plant grow two years to get seeds. During that time they get massive and take up valuable garden space; like us, you'll probably find it easier just to buy new seeds every year.

Other plants, particularly members of the cucurbit family (squash, cucumbers, and melons), are tricky because they tend to cross-pollinate. That means if you grow zucchinis and yellow crookneck squash next to each other, the seeds could produce a crop of "zucchnecks" the following year. The rule with cucurbits is that only members of the same *species* can cross-pollinate; thus buttercup squash (*Cucurbita maxima*) can't cross with zucchini (*Cucurbita pepo*), but it will cross with Blue Hubbard, which is another *maxima*. Once you know the scientific names of your squash plants (seed catalogs always list them), you can plan accordingly. Incidentally the reason cucurbits cross-pollinate is because they depend on insects like bees to spread their pollen. Bees are more crucial to our food supply than many people realize, but pesticides are wiping them out. It's another reason to grow, and buy, organic.

Fortunately seeds from tomatoes—by far the most popular heirloom vegetable—are easy to save. They're self-pollinating and rarely cross-pollinate, so you can grow all sorts of varieties side by side. To save tomato seeds, always gather from several fully ripe tomatoes—the best-looking ones you have of the same variety—and from the most vigorous plants. Squeeze the seeds into a glass of water and let them ferment indoors for three days; this breaks down the jellylike sack around each seed, which cleverly prevents germination within the tomato itself. When the surface is covered with mold and begins to bubble and smell bad, add some more water and stir; the good seeds will settle to the bottom. Everything on top can then be poured or skimmed off. Wash the remaining seeds with a little more water, then strain and dry on a glass or ceramic plate—not on a paper towel, to which they will stick. Store dried seeds in a cool, dark place, but it's okay to gaze longingly at them in January.

The bible on seed saving is a book called *Seed to Seed* by Suzanne Ashworth.

Sautéed Maine Cod with Burnt Tangerine
and Star Anise Sauce

Cod is a sweet, delicate fish that in New England is often overpowered by butter, bread crumbs, and stuffing. We like to pair this northeastern classic with Far Eastern spices. Serve with Baby Bok Choy with Chives and Smoked Ham (page 69), omitting the ham.

Makes 6 servings

FOR THE SAUCE
12 tangerines
2 tablespoons clarified butter (page 44)
6 whole star anise
1 tablespoon rice vinegar
2 teaspoons finely chopped gingerroot
8 tablespoons (1 stick) unsalted butter
Kosher salt
Freshly ground black pepper

1. Using a vegetable peeler, remove the zest from the tangerines, taking care to avoid the white pith. Set the zest aside. Juice the tangerines.

2. In a medium stainless-steel saucepan warm the clarified butter over high heat until smoking. Add the tangerine peels and stir continuously until the peels are nicely browned all over, almost burnt around the edges, 4 to 5 minutes. Add the tangerine juice, star anise, vinegar, and ginger. Boil until the liquid is reduced by three-quarters and the sauce is thick and syrupy. Strain through a fine sieve into another stainless-steel saucepan, discarding the solids.

3. No more than 30 minutes before serving, warm the syrup over medium-low heat; do not boil. Whisk in the butter, 1 tablespoon at a time, and season to taste with salt and pepper. Cover and keep warm while you cook the fish.

FOR THE FISH
2 tablespoons clarified butter or vegetable oil
6 skinless cod, haddock, or halibut fillets, about 6 ounces each

Kosher salt
Freshly ground black pepper

1. Preheat the oven to 450 degrees F.
2. Warm the butter in a large sauté pan over medium-high heat. Sprinkle the cod fillets with salt and pepper. Brown the cod for 1 minute on each side. (Depending on the size of your pan, you may have to brown the cod in 2 batches.) Transfer the pan to the oven. (If you browned the cod in 2 batches, arrange them on a baking sheet large enough to hold them all.) Bake for 4 minutes until the cod is just translucent; do not overcook the cod, as it will fall apart.

TO SERVE
3 scallions, light and dark parts, thinly sliced

Remove the pan from the oven and transfer the cod fillets to 6 warm plates. Ladle some of the sauce over each fish, sprinkle with the scallions, and serve at once.

Roast Duck with Paprika, Garlic, and Herbs

By turning a duck during roasting, the breast cooks in its own rendered fat (and a little water), yielding a tender and flavorful bird. Both the process and the taste bear some resemblance to confit—without the days of marinating, hours of slow cooking, and extra fat required for genuine confit. This technique comes from Clark's mother, who learned it from a Hungarian friend. (That explains the paprika.) We have simply added fresh herbs. Serve with Green and Yellow Beans with Toasted Pine Nuts (page 257), Lentil, Root Vegetable, and Herb Cakes (page 260), or Yam and Leek Gratin (page 177).

Makes 6 servings

2 ducks, 3 to 4 pounds each, rinsed and patted dry
4 large cloves garlic, peeled and cut into slivers
4 sprigs rosemary
2 sprigs thyme
Sweet paprika
Kosher salt
Freshly ground black pepper

1. Preheat the oven to 450 degrees F.
2. With a paring knife, make incisions 1 inch deep all over the ducks. Insert a sliver of garlic into each incision. Stuff each duck cavity with 2 sprigs rosemary and 1 sprig thyme. Cover the ducks with a heavy dusting of paprika and sprinkle with salt and pepper.
3. Pour 1 inch cold water into a large roasting pan. Arrange the ducks breast side up in the water and roast for 5 minutes. Reduce the heat to 400 degrees F and roast for another 20 minutes until the ducks start to turn golden. Turn the ducks breast side down and roast for another 20 minutes. Continue to turn the ducks about every 20 minutes, finishing with the breast side up. The total cooking time should be about 2 hours, at which point the meat should be tender and the skin glossy brown.
4. Remove the ducks from the oven. Cover with foil and allow the ducks to rest for 10 minutes before carving and serving.

Roast Turkey

Over the years we have developed a foolproof method for roasting the perfect Thanksgiving bird. The three-day (mostly untended) process involves brining, which keeps the bird moist and adds flavor, and marinating in olive oil and herbs. In fact, this turkey is so good you'll want to serve it more than just once a year. Make sure to buy a fresh, organic turkey, which usually can be ordered from your supermarket or specialty market.

Makes 10 to 20 servings

FOR THE TURKEY
1 fresh turkey, 15 to 20 pounds
1 to 2 (3-pound) boxes kosher salt
1 cup olive oil
1 cup chopped herb leaves, such as tarragon, thyme, and sage
16 tablespoons (2 sticks) butter, at room temperature
Freshly ground black pepper
3 cups Chicken Stock (page 23)

1. Two days before serving, remove the giblets and neck from the cavities of the turkey and cut off the wing tips; reserve for stock or gravy. Put the turkey into a 5-gallon or larger bucket and add enough cold water (about 3 gallons) to cover the bird. Remove the turkey and set it aside. (This tells you how much water you need to cover the bird.) To the bucket add 1 pound salt (roughly 2 cups) for every gallon or so of water and stir to dissolve it well. Return the turkey to the bucket, put it in a cool place, and let sit for at least 8 hours. An unheated garage or porch overnight works fine in cool climates; otherwise remove a shelf from the refrigerator to clear enough space.

2. The next day remove the turkey from the brine. Dry it thoroughly with paper towels. Discard the brine. Transfer the turkey to a large bowl. Pour the olive oil over the turkey and rub the herbs over the outside and inside of the turkey. Cover with plastic wrap and marinate overnight in the refrigerator.

3. The day of serving, preheat the oven to 450 degrees F.

4. Scrape off the marinade. Transfer the turkey to a large roasting pan fitted with a rack. Rub the outside of the turkey with 1 stick of the butter to coat the entire bird. Sprinkle salt and pepper liberally over the outside and inside of the turkey. Tie the legs together

with kitchen twine. Put the turkey into the oven and immediately reduce the heat to 325 degrees F.

5. In a large saucepan melt the remaining 1 stick butter over medium heat. Remove the pan from the heat and let the butter cool. Put a quadruple layer of cheesecloth, about a foot square, into the pan and coat it with the butter. In another saucepan, warm the chicken stock over medium-low heat.

6. After the turkey has roasted for about 1 to 1½ hours and the skin is turning golden brown, lay the butter-soaked cheesecloth over the turkey breast to keep it moist. Ladle about 1 cup of the chicken stock over the breast. Continue to baste the turkey with the warm stock every hour. Roast the turkey for about 3 hours total until a kitchen thermometer inserted into the thigh registers 175 degrees F. Remove the turkey from the oven and discard the cheesecloth. Transfer the turkey to a platter, cover with foil, and allow it to rest for 1 hour before carving.

FOR THE GRAVY
Fat and drippings from the roasted turkey
4 tablespoons (½ stick) unsalted butter
½ cup all-purpose flour
4 cups Enriched Stock (page 325) or Chicken Stock (page 23), hot
Kosher salt
Freshly ground black pepper

1. While the roast turkey is resting, pour the drippings from the roasting pan through a fine sieve into a small bowl. Wait about 5 minutes while the fat rises to the surface, then use a spoon or ladle to remove the fat. Reserve separately ¼ cup of the fat and all the pan juices; discard the remaining fat.

2. Combine the ¼ cup fat and the butter in a medium saucepan and warm over low heat until the butter is melted. Whisk in the flour and increase the heat to medium. Cook over medium heat, stirring constantly, until the mixture is slightly brown and has a nutty smell, about 3 minutes.

3. Slowly pour the stock into the flour mixture, whisking until smooth. Stir in the reserved pan juices and bring the gravy to a boil over medium heat. Reduce the heat to very low and simmer for 10 minutes, whisking frequently so as not to scorch the gravy. Season with salt and pepper.

4. Pour the gravy through a fine sieve into another pot. Serve at once or cover and keep warm on the back of the stove for up to 2 hours.

TO SERVE
Carve the turkey and serve with the gravy on top, passing extra gravy in a sauceboat.

Enriched Stock

Enriched stock is often called "double stock" because it starts with chicken or vegetable stock as its liquid base instead of water. In addition, we brown the poultry and vegetables first for added rich color and taste. We encourage you to take the extra step to make enriched stock for certain sauces, especially the gravy for Thanksgiving turkey; it's not much additional effort to have the stock simmering away on the back of the stove as you prepare the other dishes for your holiday table, and the depth of flavor is truly extraordinary.

Makes 4 cups

1 tablespoon olive oil
Neck and wingtips from 1 turkey or 2 chickens
1 yellow onion, peeled and coarsely chopped
1 stalk celery, coarsely chopped
1 large carrot, peeled and coarsely chopped
2 quarts Chicken Stock (page 23)

1. Warm the olive oil in a pot or large saucepan over medium-high heat. Using a heavy knife or cleaver, cut the turkey neck into 4 pieces. Add the neck, wingtips, onion, celery, and carrot to the pan and cook, stirring frequently, until the meat and vegetables are browned, about 10 minutes.

2. Add the chicken stock to the pot, reduce the heat to low, and bring slowly to a simmer; do not boil. Cook the stock, skimming the surface occasionally with a ladle to remove any fat and foam, for about 2 hours until reduced by half; you should have about 4 cups liquid left.

3. Strain the stock through a fine sieve into a large bowl or pan. If you are not ready to use it right away, cool the stock, then cover and refrigerate for up to 3 days or freeze for up to 2 months.

Boiled Dinner, Our Way

Classic boiled beef dinner is New England home cooking at its best, which is why you won't find it on the menu at Arrows or many other restaurants. This easy, crowd-pleasing meal was made for the hearth, not dining out, and we savor it at home on snowy nights with family and friends. It dates to the time when homesteaders cooked over the unregulated heat of woodstoves, which required dishes that were flexible about temperature and timing.

Simplicity is just one virtue of the boiled dinner; the other is taste. Something almost transcendent occurs when you combine lowly root vegetables and that most prosaic of meat cuts, corned beef. Both meat and vegetable gain by the association; the sweetness of the vegetables gilds the meat, which in turn lends assertion to the vegetables.

The only meat to use is corned brisket of beef, which is a piece of the foreleg that has been cured in a spiced brine. Like chuck, it's one of those flavorful but chewy cuts that benefits from long, slow cooking. Sliced thin, it rivals sirloin.

If boiled dinner is practically a religious experience in New England, we confess to one sacrilege: We prefer to roast the vegetables separately, which makes them richer and less watery. The exception is cabbage, which takes on a pleasant, meaty taste when cooked with the brisket.

Makes 8 to 10 servings

1 corned brisket of beef, 4 to 5 pounds
6 bay leaves
1 teaspoon whole black peppercorns
1 teaspoon whole mustard seeds
½ teaspoon whole celery seeds
18 small potatoes
6 small onions, peeled
3 small carrots, peeled and quartered
3 parsnips, peeled and quartered
3 small turnips, washed and quartered
¼ cup olive oil
Kosher salt
Freshly ground black pepper

2 sprigs thyme

2 sprigs rosemary

1 large head green cabbage, outer leaves removed and cut
　　into 8 to 12 wedges (do not remove the core, or the
　　cabbage will fall apart when cooking)

1. Rinse the brisket under cold running water. Put the brisket in a large pot along with the bay leaves, peppercorns, and mustard and celery seeds. Add cold water to cover the meat by 2 inches. Bring to a boil over medium-high heat, then reduce the heat to low. Simmer for about 30 minutes per 1 pound meat, 2 to 2½ hours.

2. After the brisket has been cooking for 1½ hours, preheat the oven to 325 degrees F.

3. Toss the potatoes, onions, carrots, parsnips, and turnips in a large roasting pan with the olive oil. Season with salt and pepper and sprinkle with the thyme and rosemary sprigs. Bake uncovered for about 45 minutes, turning the vegetables with a large spoon every 15 minutes, until lightly browned and tender when pierced with the tip of a knife.

4. Once the brisket is tender, after about 2 hours, add the cabbage to the pot and cook until it is tender, about 15 minutes. Remove the pot from the heat and transfer the cabbage to a warm large serving platter. Transfer the brisket to a cutting board and thinly slice across the grain, arranging the slices in the center of the platter. Arrange the roasted root vegetables around the brisket and cabbage. Serve at once.

NOTE: Mustard is the traditional condiment for boiled dinner, but we like to serve it with Horseradish Crème Fraîche (page 251).

SAUCES

Carrot and Ginger Sauce

This brightly colored, fresh-tasting sauce goes perfectly with roasted white fish like cod or halibut. You could substitute it for the sauce in Sautéed Maine Cod with Burnt Tangerine and Star Anise Sauce (page 320).

Makes about 1½ cups

3 medium carrots, peeled and cut into ½-inch pieces
1 tablespoon vegetable oil
1 teaspoon kosher salt
½ teaspoon freshly ground black pepper
1 cup Chicken or Vegetable Stock (page 23 or 24)
1 tablespoon finely chopped gingerroot

1. Preheat the oven to 375 degrees F.
2. Toss the carrots with the oil, salt, and pepper in a baking dish. Cover and roast for about 1 hour until the carrots are soft when poked with a knife.
3. Transfer the carrots to the jar of a blender and purée, slowly adding the stock, until the mixture is very smooth. Add the ginger. If not using immediately, cool, cover, and refrigerate for up to 1 day. Warm before serving.

Citrus and Lemongrass Vinaigrette

Use this sweet-and-sour vinaigrette as a marinade for scallops, shrimp, or chicken, or as a salad dressing.

Makes about 2 cups

1 cup vegetable oil
3 shallots, peeled and finely chopped
1 stalk lemongrass, yellow part only, finely chopped
¼ teaspoon chile paste (available at Asian and specialty markets)
Finely grated zest and juice of 2 lemons
Finely grated zest and juice of 2 limes
Finely grated zest and juice of 1 orange
¼ cup sugar
1 teaspoon fish sauce (available at Asian and specialty markets)
Kosher salt
Freshly grated black pepper

1. Warm 2 tablespoons of the oil in a medium stainless-steel saucepan over medium-low heat. Add the shallots, lemongrass, and chile paste and cook, stirring, until the shallots are translucent, about 5 minutes; do not brown.

2. Add the citrus zest and juice, sugar, and fish sauce and simmer over low heat until the liquid is reduced by roughly one-third, about 10 minutes.

3. Whisk in the remaining ¾ cup plus 2 tablespoons oil and season with salt and pepper. Use at once or cool, cover, and refrigerate for up to 3 days.

GROWING LEMONGRASS

Lemongrass has become popular enough in America that we now see it in grocery stores, albeit sporadically. You can grow your own quite easily just about anywhere in North America. It really is a type of grass—an attractive perennial, in fact, although it won't overwinter in cold climates. To grow lemongrass, start the tiny seeds (available by mail from Johnny's and other catalogs) indoors in late winter (mid-March in Maine, earlier farther south). Transplant in early summer after there is no longer any danger of frost and grow it dry—it doesn't like really damp soil. Lemongrass grows slowly and will take all summer to mature. In the fall, cut off and discard the top leaves, so about eight inches remain.

Lemongrass has a big, tenacious root system (common to most grasses) and can be hard to pry loose; before harvesting, water well to loosen the soil. If necessary, use a pitchfork to dig it out. It's important to harvest all the crop before the ground freezes, or you won't be able to pull it out.

If you buy or harvest a lot of lemongrass at once, it will freeze nicely and be there when you need it. The most convenient way to freeze it is to mince the light parts in a food processor fitted with the metal blade until it resembles horseradish (or finely chop by hand), then transfer the minced stalks to a small container. When you need a little lemongrass, use a spoon or knife to scrape some out; the frozen pulp thaws in minutes. ◦⌒

Fire-Roasted Onion and Rosemary Sauce

This recipe calls for wrapping onions in foil and roasting them right in a fire, such as your fireplace, your grill, or even the oven. The balsamic vinegar and the natural sugar in the onions will caramelize, creating a smoky, savory flavor. Eat them whole as a side dish or purée them to make this sauce. We like to serve it with Roast Pork Loin with Rosemary and Garlic (page 242) and Braised Lamb Shanks (page 246).

Makes about 1½ cups

2 large red onions, peeled
2 tablespoons olive oil
1 tablespoon balsamic vinegar
1 teaspoon kosher salt
½ teaspoon freshly ground black pepper
2 slices bacon
1 cup Chicken or Vegetable Stock (page 23 or 24), hot
2 tablespoons unsalted butter, at room temperature, optional
1 teaspoon red wine vinegar
1 tablespoon finely chopped rosemary leaves

1. If not using the hot coals of a fireplace or grill, preheat the oven to 375 degrees F. Cut two 6-inch squares of foil.

2. Toss together the onions, olive oil, balsamic vinegar, salt, and pepper in a medium bowl. Wrap each onion in a slice of bacon and put the onion on a foil square. Pour the remaining balsamic mixture over the onions and wrap them tightly in the foil. Bake for 1½ hours until very soft, turning once.

3. Remove the onions from the coals or the oven. Unwrap the foil and serve at once if using as a side dish. Otherwise allow the onions to cool slightly. Remove and discard the bacon. Transfer the onions to the jar of a blender and pour in the stock. Purée until very smooth, about 1 minute.

4. Transfer the purée to a medium stainless-steel saucepan and whisk in the butter if using over low heat; do not boil. Stir in the red wine vinegar and the rosemary. Serve at once or cover and keep warm for up to 1 hour. Alternatively, the sauce can be cooled, covered, and refrigerated for up to 1 day.

# SIDE DISHES

Pickled Daikon

Daikon is the Japanese name for a long white radish that is used all over Asia. It grows well in any cool climate, but unless your soil is deeply tilled, it won't grow as perfectly straight as those in the supermarket. No matter: The shapes can be amusing, and the fresh, hot flavor of just-picked daikon is superb. Serve with virtually any Asian-inspired dish, especially Crispy Trout with Ginger and Lemongrass (page 47) and Oysters with Spicy Jícama Salad (page 297).

Makes 6 servings

1 medium daikon, peeled
2 cups rice vinegar
1 cup sugar
1 serrano chile, stemmed, seeded, and finely chopped
3 tablespoons thinly sliced gingerroot

1. Cut the daikon lengthwise in half and lay it flat on a cutting board. Using a sharp chef's knife, slice the root paper thin. (A mandoline works well for this.)

2. In a medium stainless-steel saucepan combine the vinegar, sugar, chile, and ginger. Stir over medium-high heat until the sugar is dissolved. Bring the mixture to a boil, add the daikon, and reduce the heat; simmer for 1 minute. Transfer the mixture to a bowl and refrigerate until chilled or for up to 1 week.

Red Beet Mousse

This bright pink mousse is an unusual way to serve beets. Try it with Bourbon and Brown Sugar Gravlax (page 219).

Makes 6 servings

Kosher salt
1 pound medium-size red beets, trimmed
About ¾ cup cold water
2 teaspoons powdered gelatin
1 teaspoon grated fresh horseradish, optional
½ cup heavy cream

1. In a large pot bring 2 quarts water and 1 tablespoon salt to a boil. Add the beets and cook until tender, about 30 minutes.

2. Drain the beets. When cool enough to handle, peel them and cut into chunks. Put the beet chunks in the jar of a blender, add ½ cup of the water, and purée until smooth. The purée should be the consistency of sour cream; if it is too thick, add more water. Reserve 1 cup of the purée. (Any extra can be used for a beet vinaigrette or mixed with mashed potatoes, page 175.)

3. Sprinkle the gelatin over the remaining ¼ cup water either in a microwave-safe bowl or small saucepan, and let sit for 2 minutes. Warm just to melt the gelatin; transfer to a medium serving bowl. Stir in the 1 cup beet purée. Add 1 teaspoon salt and the horseradish if using. Refrigerate or set aside until cool, but do not let the mixture set.

4. With an electric mixer (or by hand using a wire whisk), whip the cream until it holds soft peaks. Fold the cream into the beet mixture. Cover and refrigerate until set, about 8 hours.

5. To serve, scoop dollops of the mousse onto plates or simply pass the bowl at the table.

Beijing Cabbage

All over the world, cabbage is preserved and fermented, then stored for winter. This recipe is inspired by the flavors Clark remembers when he spent a winter in Beijing. Serve with white fish or as a condiment with almost any Chinese-inspired dish.

Makes 6 servings

1 large head Napa cabbage, halved, cored, and thinly sliced
¼ cup sugar
2 tablespoons kosher salt
1 bunch scallions, light and dark part, finely chopped
½ cup rice vinegar
1 tablespoon finely chopped gingerroot
1 tablespoon finely chopped garlic
1 teaspoon chile paste (available at Asian and specialty markets)
1 tablespoon black bean paste (available at Asian and specialty markets)

1. Put the cabbage in a large bowl and mix it with the sugar and salt. Transfer the mixture to a nonreactive colander. Set a bowl under the colander and another on top of the cabbage. Put a weight in the top bowl (such as several cans of food) and leave in a cool place for at least 2 hours or overnight. The salt will draw moisture out of the cabbage, helping to preserve it and allowing the flavors of the added ingredients to permeate the cabbage. The sugar activates the fermenting process.

2. Transfer the cabbage to a large bowl and toss with the scallions, vinegar, ginger, garlic, chile paste, and black bean paste. Serve immediately or cover and refrigerate for up to 1 day.

Braised Red Cabbage

Braised red cabbage is a classic German side dish with roasts. At Arrows we serve it with Roast Pork Loin with Rosemary and Garlic (page 242) but also with grilled tuna or salmon, and even more delicate seafood such as grilled scallops.

Makes 6 servings

1 tablespoon olive oil
4 slices bacon, cut into ¼-inch pieces
1 yellow onion, peeled and finely chopped
1 head red cabbage, halved, cored, and thinly sliced
½ cup red wine vinegar
¼ cup red wine
1 tablespoon kosher salt
1 teaspoon freshly ground black pepper

1. Warm the oil in a large stainless-steel pot over medium heat. Add the bacon and onion and cook, stirring, until the onion is translucent, 5 minutes. Add the cabbage and sauté for 5 minutes, stirring often.

2. Pour in the vinegar and red wine and add the salt and pepper. Cover and reduce the heat to low. Cook, stirring occasionally, until tender, about 30 minutes. Serve at once or keep covered in a warm place for no more than 30 minutes. Alternatively, the cabbage can be cooled, covered, and refrigerated for up to 1 day. Warm before serving.

Kale, Swiss Cheese, and Bacon Casserole

In early winter one of the last garden survivors is hardy kale, which seems to enjoy the first snowfall as much as children do. Like parsnips, kale gets sweeter after a frost. Combined with cheese and bacon, it makes a filling, custardlike casserole that can be served as a side dish or even a main course.

Makes 6 side-dish or 4 main-course servings

4 slices bacon, cut into $\frac{1}{2}$-inch pieces
1 pound kale, stems removed, leaves washed and drained
1 cup heavy cream
2 large eggs
1 teaspoon kosher salt
$\frac{1}{4}$ teaspoon freshly ground black pepper
4 ounces Swiss cheese, cut into 4 slices

1. Preheat the oven to 350 degrees F.
2. In a large sauté pan cook the bacon over medium heat until crisp, about 5 minutes. Remove from the heat and transfer the bacon to a paper-towel-lined plate.
3. Prepare the kale leaves by rolling them up lengthwise and slicing them crosswise into thin strips about $\frac{1}{8}$ inch wide. Transfer the kale to an 8-inch-square baking dish, and toss in the bacon.
4. In a medium bowl mix together the cream, eggs, salt, and pepper. Pour the cream mixture over the kale and lay the Swiss cheese on top. Bake for 35 to 45 minutes until the cheese is golden and the kale mixture is set.
5. Remove the baking dish from the oven and let rest for 10 minutes. Cut into 6 pieces and serve. The casserole can be made up to 1 day ahead, cooled, and kept covered in the refrigerator. Before serving, warm the covered casserole for about 30 minutes in an oven that has been preheated to 325 degrees F.

Celery Root Pancakes

We store our celery root as did the original owners of our farmhouse—in the root cellar. Before refrigeration, root cellars kept apples and vegetables crisp through the winter, as well as protected next year's seed crop. Many heirloom varieties of vegetables had the word "long" in their names, which told seed buyers that these vegetables would last until spring. One better-known example that we still grow is Long Fall leek. Root cellars usually had dirt floors and stone walls with tightly fitting wooden doors to keep out animals. Some root cellars were freestanding, but many, like the one at Arrows, were part of the farmhouse cellar and located conveniently below the kitchen. When people started putting furnaces in cellars, the temperature got too warm to store vegetables. Fortunately our heating system is located above ground, so we can still use our root cellar.

These celery root pancakes are easy and go well with Plank-Roasted Salmon with Rosemary-Mustard Vinaigrette (page 317) and Sautéed Turbot with Lemon-Parsley Butter (page 237).

Makes 6 servings

1 large celery root, peeled
4 large Yukon Gold or white potatoes, peeled
½ small yellow onion, peeled and finely chopped
½ cup all-purpose flour
Kosher salt
Freshly ground black pepper
3 large eggs, lightly beaten
6 tablespoons clarified butter (page 44)

1. Using the large holes of a box grater or the shredding disk in a food processor, shred the celery root and potatoes and put them into a bowl. Add the onion and flour. Stir the mixture and sprinkle with salt and pepper to taste. Mix in the eggs. The celery root mixture will be quite wet.

2. Preheat the oven to 350 degrees F.

3. Warm 1 tablespoon of the clarified butter in a 6-inch nonstick sauté pan over medium-high heat. Divide the celery root mixture into 6 equal portions. When the oil is hot, put 1 portion in the pan and spread it out evenly to form a pancake. Cook until

golden brown on each side, 1 to 2 minutes per side. Remove the pancake with a spatula and transfer to a nonstick cookie sheet. Cover with foil and keep in a warm place. Wipe out the pan with a paper towel and repeat the process until all the pancakes are browned.

4. Bake the 6 pancakes on the cookie sheet for 10 minutes until the potatoes are cooked through. Serve at once.

Root Vegetable Gratin

This dish grew out of our love for classic New England root vegetables, which are often boiled or roasted. Here we use them in a rich, creamy gratin, which makes them even more substantial.

Makes 6 servings

4 medium Yukon Gold or white potatoes, peeled
6 medium parsnips, peeled
3 large golden beets, peeled
1 large turnip, peeled
Kosher salt
Freshly ground black pepper
2 cups heavy cream
2 teaspoons ground nutmeg

1. Preheat the oven to 375 degrees F.

2. Slice all the vegetables ⅛ inch thick either by hand or using a mandoline. Cover the bottom of an 8-inch-square baking dish with the potatoes, carefully overlapping them by about ½ inch. Sprinkle with salt and pepper. Arrange the parsnips in a layer on top, followed by the beets, and finally the turnip, sprinkling each layer with salt and pepper.

3. Mix together the cream and nutmeg and pour over the vegetables. Cover the dish with foil and bake for 1 hour. Remove the foil and continue baking for another 30 minutes, until the top is golden brown and the vegetables have soaked up nearly all the liquid.

4. Remove the gratin from the oven and allow it to set up for 15 minutes. Cut into 6 portions and serve.

Sage and Cheddar Bread Pudding

This is a great accompaniment to Roast Duck with Paprika, Garlic, and Herbs (page 322) and Roast Pork Loin with Rosemary and Garlic (page 242), as well as a good way to use up scraps of sourdough or white bread.

Makes 6 servings

2 cups heavy cream
2 large eggs
2 large egg yolks
1/2 cup grated sharp Cheddar cheese
1 tablespoon unsalted butter, melted
2 teaspoons kosher salt
1 teaspoon freshly ground black pepper
1 teaspoon finely chopped sage leaves
6 cups 1/2-inch cubes white or sourdough bread

1. Preheat the oven to 350 degrees F. Butter a deep 8-inch-square baking dish or 2-quart soufflé dish.

2. In a large bowl whisk together the cream, eggs, yolks, cheese, butter, salt, pepper, and sage. Add the bread and toss to combine. Let sit for 10 minutes to let the bread soak up some of the batter.

3. Transfer the mixture to the buttered baking dish. Bake for 30 minutes until golden brown on top and a knife inserted into the center comes out clean. Remove the baking dish from the oven and let cool for 5 to 10 minutes.

4. Cut the pudding into 6 pieces and serve. Alternatively, the pudding can be cooled and kept covered in the refrigerator for up to 1 day. Warm for 30 minutes in an oven that has been preheated to 350 degrees F.

DESSERTS

Rosemary Poached Pears
with Chocolate Crème Anglaise

Pears thrive in cool climates because the trees require chilly nights to set fruit. (Commercial varieties are grown in northern California and Oregon.) Still, Maine is a little *too* cold for pears, so up here the pear trees tend to fruit only every other year. Whether you're buying pears in the supermarket (when they are at their peak in late fall and early winter) or harvesting your own, pick pears that are not quite ripe and store them in a cool, dark place until soft and sweet.

The flowery pinelike flavor of rosemary is subtle when combined with pears; you don't quite know what it is—you just know it is good.

Makes 6 servings

FOR THE POACHED PEARS
6 cups water
4 cups sugar
6 sprigs rosemary, each 3 inches long
6 Bartlett or Anjou pears, ripe but firm
Juice of 1 lemon

1. In a large saucepan bring the water and sugar to a boil. Stir to dissolve the sugar. Remove from the heat, add the rosemary sprigs, cover the pan, and set aside for 30 to 45 minutes.

2. Peel, halve, and core the pears. Place them in a bowl of cold water, add the lemon juice, and set aside for the moment.

3. Remove and discard the rosemary from the poaching liquid. Drain the pears and add them to the pan. Cut a circle of parchment paper to fit inside the pan, poke a hole in the center, and lay the parchment on top of the pears to keep them under the liquid. Bring the liquid to a gentle simmer and cook the pears for 20 to 30 minutes until tender when pierced with a knife.

4. Remove the pan from the heat. Line a large plate with several layers of paper towels. Remove the pears from the liquid with a slotted spoon and transfer to the plate. Refrigerate until cool or for up to 1 day.

5. Measure 1 cup of the poaching liquid, put it in a small saucepan, and bring to a boil over medium heat. Cook until the liquid is thick and syrupy, about 10 minutes. Cool, cover, and refrigerate for up to 1 day.

FOR THE CHOCOLATE CRÈME ANGLAISE
2 cups whole milk
³/₄ cup sugar
2 ounces bittersweet chocolate, chopped
4 large egg yolks

1. Fill a large bowl halfway with ice water; have ready a smaller bowl or container that will fit inside of it.

2. In a medium saucepan combine the milk, sugar, and chocolate and stir to dissolve the sugar. Put the saucepan on the stove and bring to a boil over medium heat.

3. Whisk the egg yolks in a medium bowl until light in color. Slowly pour the hot milk over the yolks, whisking until the mixture is combined. Return the liquid to the saucepan and cook, stirring constantly with a wooden spoon, over medium heat until it reaches a temperature of 180 degrees F on a kitchen thermometer or it coats the back of the spoon.

4. Strain the mixture through a fine sieve into the smaller bowl, place it in the ice bath to chill, and stir from time to time until cold. Cover the sauce and refrigerate until needed, up to 2 days.

TO SERVE
Ladle some of the crème anglaise onto each of 6 plates. Thinly slice the pears, stopping ½ inch from the stem end so that the slices stay together. Place 2 pear halves on each plate and fan them out. Drizzle some of the reduced syrup over the pears.

Chocolate Pound Cake with Frozen Berries

This cake stays moist for several days, is simple to make, and is full of chocolate flavor. It's an excellent winter dessert if you use frozen berries. (For more on freezing berries, see page 195.)

Makes one 10-inch tube cake, or 12 servings

16 tablespoons (2 sticks) unsalted butter, at room temperature
2½ cups sugar
6 large eggs, at room temperature
2 cups cake flour (not self-rising)
1 cup unsweetened cocoa powder
½ teaspoon kosher salt
¼ teaspoon baking soda
1 cup sour cream
1 teaspoon pure vanilla extract
Powdered sugar for dusting
2 cups mixed frozen berries (page 195), such as blackberries, strawberries, and raspberries, thawed

1. Preheat the oven to 350 degrees F. Butter a 10-inch tube pan and dust with sugar.
2. In a large mixer bowl beat the butter until smooth, 3 to 5 minutes. Add the sugar and beat for 5 minutes until light and fluffy. Add the eggs one at a time, beating well after each addition and scraping the inside of the bowl as needed with a rubber spatula.
3. Sift together the flour, cocoa powder, salt, and baking soda. Stir together the sour cream and vanilla and add them to the butter mixture alternately with the dry ingredients, beating after each addition until the mixture is just combined.
4. Pour the cake batter into the prepared pan, smooth the top, and bake for 50 to 65 minutes until a toothpick inserted in the center comes out clean.
5. Cool the cake in the pan on a rack for 15 minutes. Remove the cake from the pan and let it cool completely. Well wrapped, the cake will keep at room temperature for up to 2 days.
6. To serve, dust the cake with powdered sugar, slice, and serve with the mixed berries.

Chocolate Carrot Cake
with Chocolate–Sour Cream Frosting

This dessert combines two classic cakes—chocolate and carrot—into one. It's not as rich or heavy as a pure chocolate cake, although the buttery frosting is a nod to chocoholics. In olden days carrots were a staple during winter because they store well in a root cellar.

Makes one 9-inch layer cake, or 12 servings

FOR THE CAKE
1 pound carrots, peeled
$\frac{1}{2}$ cup packed shredded sweetened coconut
Finely grated zest of 1 orange
16 tablespoons (2 sticks) unsalted butter, at room temperature
2 cups packed brown sugar
4 large eggs
$2\frac{1}{4}$ cups all-purpose flour
$\frac{3}{4}$ cup unsweetened cocoa powder
2 teaspoons baking soda
$\frac{1}{2}$ teaspoon ground cinnamon
$\frac{1}{4}$ teaspoon kosher salt
$\frac{1}{2}$ cup sour cream

1. Preheat the oven to 350 degrees F. Grease two 9-inch round cake pans. Line the bottom of each one with a circle of parchment paper and grease the parchment.

2. Using the large holes of a box grater or the shredding disk in a food processor, shred the carrots. Measure 4 cups loosely packed and transfer to a large bowl. Mix in the coconut and orange zest and set aside.

3. With an electric mixer (or by hand using a wire whisk), beat the butter and sugar on medium speed until light and fluffy, 3 to 5 minutes. Beat in the eggs one at a time, scraping the bowl with a rubber spatula as necessary, and mix until again light and fluffy.

4. Sift together the flour, cocoa powder, baking soda, cinnamon, and salt. With the mixer on the lowest speed, alternately add the dry ingredients and sour cream to the but-

ter mixture in the bowl. Combine the mixture well, scraping the bowl between additions, but do not overmix. With a rubber spatula, fold the carrot mixture into the cake batter.

5. Divide the batter between the prepared pans, smooth the tops, and tap the pans on the counter a couple of times to release any air bubbles. Bake the cakes for 25 to 30 minutes until a toothpick inserted in the center of the cakes comes out clean.

6. Cool the cakes in the pans on racks for 20 minutes. Remove the cakes from the pans by inverting each cake onto another rack or cookie sheet. Peel off the parchment and cool right side up. Well wrapped, the cakes will keep at room temperature for up to 1 day.

FOR THE FROSTING

9 ounces bittersweet chocolate, finely chopped,
    or 1½ cups semisweet chocolate chips
4 tablespoons (½ stick) unsalted butter, at room temperature
¾ cup sour cream
2 teaspoons pure vanilla extract
2 cups powdered sugar, sifted

Bring 1 inch water to a simmer in the bottom part of a double boiler. In the top part, melt the chocolate and butter, stirring occasionally, until smooth. Remove from the heat and whisk in the sour cream, vanilla, and powdered sugar until completely smooth. Let the mixture cool until it is of spreading consistency.

TO ASSEMBLE

Set 1 cake layer on a cardboard cake round or plate. Spread one-third of the frosting on top of the cake. Set the other cake layer on top, and frost the top and sides of the cake. Refrigerate until the frosting is set, at least 1 hour, or for up to 1 day. Cut into 12 slices and serve at room temperature.

Ginger–Pear Upside-Down Cake
with Lemongrass Caramel Sauce

This recipe calls for cooking lemongrass in a syrup, which is then caramelized and strained. The flavor remains but not the actual pieces of lemongrass. We learned this infusion technique from Jerry Traunfeld of the Herbfarm Restaurant near Seattle. It also works with herbs like basil and mint. The tangy sauce and spicy ginger are delicious with sweet, delicate pears.

Makes one 10-inch cake, or 12 servings

FOR THE CAKE

16 tablespoons (2 sticks) unsalted butter, at room temperature
1 cup packed brown sugar
4 Anjou, Bartlett, or Bosc pears, peeled, cored, and cut into ¼-inch slices
½ cup sugar
5 large eggs
2¼ cups all-purpose flour
1 teaspoon ground cinnamon
1 teaspoon baking soda
½ teaspoon baking powder
1 cup buttermilk
2 teaspoons finely grated gingerroot
¼ cup chopped candied ginger, plus additional for garnish

1. Preheat the oven to 350 degrees F. Butter a 10-inch round, 2-inch-deep cake pan and line the bottom with a circle of parchment paper. Butter the parchment.
2. Melt 4 tablespoons of the butter and pour it into the cake pan. Sprinkle ½ cup of the brown sugar evenly on top. Starting at the outside edge, arrange the pear slices slightly overlapping in concentric circles to cover the bottom of the pan.
3. In a large mixer bowl beat the remaining 12 tablespoons butter until smooth, 3 to 5 minutes. Add the sugar and the remaining ½ cup brown sugar and beat until light and fluffy. Beat in the eggs one at a time, scraping the bowl with a rubber spatula as needed.
4. Sift together the flour, cinnamon, baking soda, and baking powder. Alternately

add the dry ingredients and the buttermilk to the butter mixture, mixing each addition until combined. Do not overmix. Fold in the grated and candied gingers by hand. Gently spread the batter over the pears.

5. Bake the cake for about 45 minutes until a toothpick inserted in the center comes out clean. Cool the cake in the pan on a rack for 10 minutes. Loosen the cake from the pan by running a thin knife around the edge and invert it onto the cooling rack. Peel off the parchment and let the cake cool completely. It will keep covered at room temperature for up to 1 day.

FOR THE SAUCE

1½ cups sugar
1 stalk lemongrass, coarsely chopped
½ cup water
2 tablespoons freshly squeezed lemon juice
1 tablespoon light corn syrup
1 cup heavy cream

1. In the bowl of a food processor fitted with the metal blade, process the sugar and the lemongrass to make a paste, or finely chop them together by hand. Scrape into a medium, heavy-bottomed, stainless-steel saucepan. Stir in the water, lemon juice, and corn syrup and bring to a boil over medium heat. Cook, stirring with a wooden spoon, until the sugar dissolves. Stop stirring and brush the inside of the saucepan with a pastry brush soaked in cold water to keep sugar crystals from forming on the sides of the pan. Cook without stirring until the syrup is amber in color.

2. While the syrup is caramelizing, warm the cream in a small saucepan. When the syrup is ready, remove it from the heat and carefully—the hot mixture will splatter—whisk the warm cream into the caramel. Return the saucepan to the heat and, whisking constantly, cook over medium heat just until the sauce is smooth. Remove from the heat and strain the sauce through a fine sieve into a heatproof container. Cool the sauce to room temperature, stirring occasionally. If not using immediately, cover and refrigerate for up to 2 days. Bring to room temperature before serving.

TO SERVE

Cut the cake into 12 slices. Spoon a pool of the lemongrass sauce onto each plate and set a piece of cake on top. Garnish with candied ginger if desired.

SHOULD YOU INVEST IN A GREENHOUSE?

A greenhouse takes gardening into another dimension by dramatically extending the growing season. It accommodates many more plants than a cold frame, and if heated allows you to start tender seedlings in the coldest months of winter. That's not possible indoors because seedlings get weak and leggy with long spells under artificial light. And, in the fall, you can keep on growing greens and even potted tomatoes long past the first frost. If you heat your greenhouse, you can use it right on through the winter, nurturing potted herbs, peppers, Asian cucumbers, and greens, as well as orchids, fuchsias, and flats full of geraniums for the first window boxes on your block. For gardeners who enjoy starting their own heirloom seeds (page 319), a greenhouse is a great tool.

The Arrows greenhouse measures 400 square feet and is set up for serious commercial use with an overhead-mounted propane heater, electric backup heat, and thermostatically controlled cooling fans. So-called hobby greenhouses for homeowners are usually about one-quarter that size and outfitted more simply, but there are still many options to consider.

Home greenhouses fall into two basic categories: freestanding and those that are attached to the house. Attached greenhouses (sometimes called conservatories) have several advantages. In the daytime during winter they contribute free heat to your living space, and at night they receive warmth from your home's heating system. They are convenient to use, and household electric and water supplies are within reach. But in summer they can make your house hot unless you ventilate and install sunscreening material. By definition, no attached greenhouse gets as much sun as a freestanding model because at some point in the day, the home itself will shade it. (Attached greenhouses on the south side obviously receive the most sun.)

Freestanding greenhouses are more serious affairs, designed for maximum sun exposure. But unless you heat them, they will get as cold as the outdoors once the sun sets. In fact, unheated greenhouses are called cold greenhouses. (They are also known as three-season greenhouses—a misnomer because, unless you're growing cacti, you're not likely to use one much in the summer.) They still give you a big jump on the season as long as you remember to bring your seedlings indoors on chilly nights. (Small pepper seedlings, for example, suffer below 55 degrees F.)

You can build your own greenhouse from scratch, but most people buy prefab kits, usually featuring a framework of lightweight aluminum. Wood frames look nice but cost more and require maintenance to prevent rot. Painted steel frames are strong and have a classic European look, but they are also expensive. Their rigid structure makes them the best choice if you plan to use real glass, which also looks nice but is tricky (even dangerous) to install and can be a disaster in a hailstorm. More popular than glass these days are polycarbonate panels, which insulate quite effectively (much better than glass) by trapping air inside tiny ribbed channels. They are virtually unbreakable, easy to install, and relatively attractive. The cheapest form of greenhouse glazing is plastic sheeting. It doesn't look very romantic and needs frequent replacing, but commercial growers value its economy.

When it comes to size, our advice is to buy the biggest greenhouse you can afford or accommodate; you'll still wish it were bigger. But note that the cost of a greenhouse kit (around $2,000 for a 100-square-foot aluminum model with polycarbonate panels) will not be your only expense. You'll need to build a simple foundation, typically a frame of 6 x 4-inch pressure-treated timbers (sold at home centers) containing a 6-inch-deep layer of gravel. For a 100-square-foot greenhouse that comes to about 2 cubic yards of gravel, which can be delivered by a local building supplier. If the dump truck can't maneuver right to the foundation site, you'll need to transfer the gravel by wheelbarrow; eat your Wheaties that morning. Be sure to lay down a weed-barrier fabric (available at nurseries and home centers) under the gravel; otherwise your greenhouse floor will quickly sprout a forest.

Then you'll need shelving to keep your plants off the ground and make it easier to work. Position shelves along the sides and maybe down the center, leaving room enough to walk. They can be as high or low as you find convenient, but most people put them at table height (30 inches or so off the ground). They needn't be fancy, but they must be sturdy, as pots full of wet soil are quite heavy. We make our own: The frames are pressure-treated lumber and the shelves are simply metal mesh, which allows water to drain through.

Greenhouse suppliers can sell you all manner of accessories like min-max thermometers (useful for determining how cold it got in there last night) and plant hangers. One neat gadget costing about $50 is a solar-powered device that automatically opens a vent when the temperature rises above a set point. (A greenhouse with no ventilation becomes a furnace on sunny days.)

If you decide to heat your freestanding greenhouse, the two most popular options are propane and electric. Propane is cheaper but usually requires professional installation, including vent pipes to release fumes harmful to both humans and plants. And you'll have to schedule propane deliveries. Electric heaters are much simpler but costlier to run and, of course, they require a power supply; the best heaters run on 240 volts. (Extension cords should not substitute for a permanent power source; sooner or later the cord will become damaged and potentially dangerous.) Electric heaters are much smaller than gas models, which can make a difference in a cramped hobby greenhouse.

Another consideration is water supply. For three-season greenhouse gardening, a hose works fine. But if you plan to use your greenhouse year-round, you'll need to run a proper cold-water line beneath the frost line (four feet in Maine!) and install a special frost-proof hydrant.

One final thought: Assembling a greenhouse requires a sense of humor, not to mention several helpers. The pieces never seem to come together quite like the instructions suggest. Pick a nice wind-free day, and enlist one helper to make a picnic lunch. ✍

Steamed Pumpkin Puddings
with Vanilla Crème Anglaise

We like the moist texture of this dessert and prefer it to pumpkin pie, which has a similar flavor. In fact, we serve this at Arrows every Thanksgiving. You can certainly use canned pumpkin, but we make it with small Baby Bear pumpkins we grow. Don't use jack-o-lantern pumpkins, which aren't sweet enough.

Makes 6 servings

FOR THE STEAMED PUDDINGS
8 tablespoons (1 stick) unsalted butter, at room temperature
1½ cups packed brown sugar
½ cup sugar
3 large eggs, at room temperature
1 cup fresh (page 216) or canned pumpkin purée
1 teaspoon finely grated gingerroot or ground ginger
2 cups all-purpose flour
2 teaspoons baking powder
1½ teaspoons ground cinnamon
½ teaspoon kosher salt

1. Preheat the oven to 350 degrees F. Butter and dust with sugar six 8-ounce ramekins, heatproof ceramic coffee cups, or disposable aluminum cups.

2. In a large mixer bowl, beat the butter until smooth. Add both of the sugars and mix for 3 to 5 minutes until light in color. Beat in the eggs one at a time, scraping down the sides of the bowl as needed with a rubber spatula; continue to beat until the mixture is light and fluffy.

3. Add the pumpkin and fresh ginger if using. Mix well, scraping the sides and bottom of the bowl with a rubber spatula. Mix until well combined. The mixture may look curdled, but it will become smooth again once the flour is added.

4. Sift together the flour, baking powder, cinnamon, salt, and ground ginger if using. With the mixer on the lowest speed, add the dry ingredients to the bowl and mix until just combined.

5. Fill the ramekins two-thirds full with the batter and place them, evenly spaced, in a deep roasting pan. Fill the roasting pan with hot water to come halfway up the sides of the ramekins. Cover the pan tightly with lightly buttered foil, placing the buttered side down. Bake for 25 to 35 minutes until a toothpick inserted in the center of each pudding comes out clean.

6. Remove the pan from the oven and immediately take the puddings out of the water bath. Place them on a rack to cool for 15 minutes. Remove the puddings from the molds by running a knife around the edge and inverting them onto a rack. If not serving immediately, cool the puddings in the ramekins and wrap each one in plastic wrap. Refrigerate for up to 1 day. Before serving, unwrap the puddings and arrange the ramekins on a cookie sheet. Warm for about 15 minutes in an oven that has been preheated to 350 degrees F. Invert onto a rack.

FOR THE CRÈME ANGLAISE
$\frac{1}{2}$ vanilla bean, or $1\frac{1}{2}$ teaspoons pure vanilla extract
2 cups whole milk
$\frac{2}{3}$ cup sugar
4 large egg yolks

1. Fill a large bowl halfway with ice water; have ready a smaller bowl or container that will fit inside of it.

2. Split the vanilla bean lengthwise in half and scrape the seeds into a medium saucepan. Toss the scraped pod into the pan as well. (If using vanilla extract, do not add it yet.) Add the milk and sugar and stir to dissolve the sugar. Put the saucepan on the stove and bring to a boil over medium heat.

3. Whisk the egg yolks in a medium bowl until light in color. Slowly pour the hot milk over the yolks, whisking until the mixture is combined. Return the liquid to the saucepan and cook, stirring constantly with a wooden spoon, over medium heat until it reaches a temperature of 180 degrees F on a kitchen thermometer or it coats the back of the spoon.

4. Strain the mixture through a fine sieve into the smaller bowl and place it in the ice bath to chill, stirring from time to time until cold. Stir in the vanilla extract if using. Cover it and refrigerate until needed, up to 2 days.

TO SERVE
Ladle some of the crème anglaise onto each of 6 plates. Place the warm puddings in the center of the plates and serve at once.

Blood Orange Sorbet with Butter Cookies Dipped in Mint Chocolate

Blood oranges arrive in Maine during the winter from Italy and California, reminding us that warm weather is on the way! You could serve the sorbet or the cookies separately, but we like the combined textures and flavors of soft and crunchy, chocolate and orange.

Makes about 1 quart sorbet and 12 cookies, or 6 servings

FOR THE SORBET
2 cups sugar
1½ cups cold water
Finely grated zest of 1 blood orange
2 cups strained blood-orange juice (about 12 blood oranges)

1. Fill a large bowl halfway with ice water; have ready a smaller bowl or container that will fit inside of it.

2. In a medium stainless-steel saucepan mix the sugar, ½ cup of the water, and the orange zest over medium heat. Boil the mixture for 1 minute, then pour it into the smaller bowl. Set the bowl into the ice bath.

3. When the mixture is very cold, add the juice and remaining 1 cup water. Pour the liquid into an ice cream machine and freeze according to the manufacturer's instructions.

4. Transfer the sorbet to a nonreactive container. Cover the surface of the sorbet with plastic wrap, then top with a lid. Freeze for at least 3 hours, or for up to 1 week. If the sorbet gets too hard to scoop, break it up, transfer to a food processor fitted with the metal blade, and pulse it a few times to soften it. Or if you have time, let it sit in the refrigerator for 30 minutes before serving.

FOR THE COOKIES
4 ounces bittersweet chocolate, chopped
1½ teaspoons unsalted butter
12 large mint leaves, finely chopped, plus additional mint leaves for garnish
12 Butter Cookies (page 196)

1. Line a cookie sheet with waxed paper.

2. Bring 1 inch water to a simmer in the bottom part of a double boiler. In the top combine the chocolate, butter, and mint. Melt the chocolate, stirring, until the mixture is smooth. Remove it from the heat and strain the chocolate through a fine sieve set over a bowl.

3. Carefully dip each cookie halfway into the melted chocolate. Shake off the excess chocolate and place the cookie on the cookie sheet to cool. Refrigerate the cookies for 15 minutes. Tightly covered, they will keep at room temperature for up to 1 week.

TO SERVE

Place 2 scoops of the sorbet in each of 6 dessert bowls or stemmed glasses. Arrange 2 cookies on either side of the sorbet and garnish with mint leaves.

RESOURCES

GARDEN BOOKLIST

From Seed to Bloom
Eileen Powell
Storey Books
Pownal, VT

The Self-Sufficient Gardener
John Seymour
Dolphin Books
Doubleday and Company
Garden City, NY

Greenhouse Gardener's Companion
Shane Smith
Fulcrum Publishing
Golden, CO

The Vegetable Gardener's Bible
Edward C. Smith
Storey Books
Pownal, VT

The New Seed-Starters Handbook
Nancy Bubel
Rodale Press
Emmaus, PA

Four-Season Harvest
Eliot Coleman
Chelsea Green Publishing
White River Junction, VT

Great Garden Formulas
Joan Benjamin
Rodale Press
Emmaus, PA

*Rodale's Color Handbook of
    Garden Insects*
Ann Carr
Rodale Press
Emmaus, PA

The Flower Farmer
Lynn Byczynski
Chelsea Green Publishing
White River Junction, VT

The Gardener's Bug Book
Barbara Pleasant
Storey Books
Pownal, VT

Building Soil for Better Crops
Fred Magdoff
Sustainable Agriculture Publications
University of Vermont
Burlington, VT

The Backyard Orchardist
Stella Ott
Ottographics
Maple City, MI

Seed Sowing and Saving
Carole B. Turner
Storey Books
Pownal, VT

The New Victory Garden
Bob Thomson
Little Brown and Company
Boston, MA

Oriental Vegetables: The Complete Guide for the Gardening Cook
Joy Larkcom
Kodansha International
New York, NY

Organic Pest and Disease Control
Barbara Ellis
Houghton Mifflin
New York, NY

Gardening with Herbs
Emelie Tolley
Clarkson Potter Publishing
New York, NY

The Encyclopedia of Herbs and Herbalism
Malcom Stuart
Crescent Books
New York, NY

Great Garden Companions
Sally Jean Cunningham
Rodale Press
Emmaus, PA

The New Organic Grower
Eliot Coleman
Chelsea Green Publishing
White River Junction, VT

The Heirloom Gardener
Carolyn Jabs
Sierra Book Club
San Francisco, CA

Seed to Seed
Suzanne Ashworth
Seed Savers Exchange
Decorah, IA

HELPFUL ASSOCIATIONS

Agricultural Extension Services
Maine: Agricultural Extension Service
University of Maine
Orono, ME 04478
(All states have them, affiliated with land-grant universities)

Organic Farmers Associations (varies
from state to state; ask an organic farmer
at your local greenmarket)
Maine: Maine Organic Farmers and
Gardeners Association (MOFGA)
Common Ground Country Fair
PO Box 170
Unity, ME 04988

GARDEN SUPPLIERS

Johnny's Selected Seeds
1 Foss Hill Rd
Albion, ME 04910-9731
(207) 437-4301

The Cooks Garden
PO Box 520
Hodges, SC 29653-5010
(800) 457-9703

Fedco Seeds
PO Box 520
Waterville, ME 04903-0520
(207) 873-7333

Gardener's Supply Co.
128 Intervale Rd
Burlington, VT 05401-2850
(800) 660-3501

Gardens Alive
5100 Schenley Place
Lawrenceburg, IN 47025
(812) 537-8650

Harris Seeds
PO Box 22960
Rochester, NY 14692-2960
(585) 295-3600

Heirloom Seeds
PO Box 245
West Elizabeth, PA 15088-0245
(412) 384-0852

J.W. Jung Seed Co.
335 S. High St.
Randolf, WI 53957-0001
(800) 247-5864

Park Seed
1 Parkton Ave.
Greenwood, SC 29647-0099
(800) 845-3369

Pinetree Garden Seeds
PO Box 300
New Gloucester, ME 04260
(207) 926-3400

Seeds of Change
PO Box 15700
Santa Fe, NM 87506-5700
(888) 762-7333

Shepherd's Garden Seeds
30 Irene St.
Torrington, CT 06790-6658
(860) 482-3638

Smith and Hawken
PO Box 6900
Florence, KY 41022-6900
(800) 776-3336

Vesey's Seeds
PO Box 9000
Calais, ME 04619-6102
(800) 363-7333

Tomato Growers Supply Company
PO Box 2237
Fort Meyers, FL 33902
(888) 478-7333

SPECIALTY FOOD SUPPLIERS
(These companies sell primarily to restaurants but will take retail orders.)

Dominic's
62 Jensen Rd
Moss Landing, CA 95039
(831) 722-0181
Specialty produce

Earthy Delights
1161 E. Clark Rd, Ste. 260
DeWitt, MI 48820
(800) 367-4709
www.earthydelights.com
Morel mushrooms and other specialty produce and dry goods

Browne Trading Company
Merrill's Wharf
260 Commercial St.
Portland, ME 04101
(207) 766-2402
www.browne.trading.com
Finest seafood and caviars

ACKNOWLEDGMENTS

Very shortly after the opening of Arrows in 1988, Mark's brother Mike Gaier brought his friend and colleague Gene Burns to dinner. From the first, Gene understood Arrows and what it was all about. Gene was instrumental in making urban critics and food writers aware that there was something other than delicious lobster rolls to come up here for; there was something new and exciting starting to happen in Maine. His steadfast support and friendship throughout the years have been crucial in making Arrows—and hence this book—possible.

Writing a cookbook is a bit like creating a restaurant: It's an incremental process that requires many creative people working together. Stacey Glick, our agent, must be thanked for having the vision to see what a unique book this could be—and for introducing us to Max Alexander, our co-author. With Max we have spent countless hours huddled around stoves, grills, and laptop computers in both California and Maine. With Max's knowledge and discipline, this book became reality. And through all the hard work, we had lots of laughs.

Our former pastry chef, Lucia Velasco-Evans, created the dessert recipes for this book. Her constant devotion and friendship has been a great joy in our lives. Sarah Patch and Justin Walker, our sous-chefs, have been our right and left hands for many years at Arrows. The unstinting dedication and loyalty of these three friends has not only helped make Arrows what it is but also made our book much better. We would like to thank the three talented women for tending our garden at one point or another over the years—Robin Barnard, Marcia MacDonald, and Patti Parrott—and for sharing their knowledge in this book.

Without the right editor, no book is possible. Therefore, we thank Beth Wareham and Rica Allannic for fine-tuning our vision.

Clark Frasier and Mark Gaier

From many years working in restaurants, I learned that the most successful restaurant owners are like those jolly innkeepers in Shakespeare plays: They have a natural talent for putting people at ease. By that standard, Mark and Clark are ready for the Old Vic. Collaborating on this book for over a year was like becoming a member of a new family. Mark and Clark made me feel instantly at home, whether at Arrows or working from their own homes in Maine and California. I can't imagine a more pleasant partnership.

Their generosity has also infected their staff. I owe special thanks to Arrows former pastry chef, Lucia Velasco-Evans, who was always happy to share her insights and time. The same goes for master gardener Patti Parrot, who took time out from a busy greenhouse season to impart earthly wisdom. From the looks of my own giant tomatoes this year, her advice is sage. And sous-chefs Justin Walker and Sarah Patch were always accommodating of my kitchen intrusions.

This book could not have happened without the work of my agent, Stacey Glick, who masterminded this partnership, and our editors at Scribner, Beth Wareham and Rica Allannic, who "got it" from the get-go.

Thanks to Taylor Pohlman for pushing the right buttons.

Finally I thank Sarah—my wife, my inspiration, and my Arrows dining partner. Luckily enough for me, my debt to her can never be fully repaid.

Max Alexander

INDEX

butter:
    brown, 26
    brown, fiddlehead ferns
        with bundnerfleisch
        and, 27
    clarified, 44
    lemon-parsley, sautéed
        turbot with, 237
    sage, roasted eggplant
        and lentil soup with,
        210–11
butter cookies:
    cantaloupe sorbet with,
        196–97
    dipped in mint chocolate,
        blood orange sorbet
        with, 354–55
butterhead lettuce, 36, 37
butternut squash and potato
    gratin, 262

cabbage:
    Beijing, 335
    in boiled dinner, our way,
        326–27
    braised red, 336
    Napa, and apple cole slaw,
        229
    salad, seared orange and,
        174
    warm red, slaw with
        creamy herbed goat
        cheese, 314–15
cajeta sauce, apple fritters
    with, 280–81
cake(s):
    chocolate carrot, with
        chocolate–sour cream
        frosting, 346–47
    chocolate pound, with
        frozen berries, 345
    ginger-pear upside-down,
        with lemongrass
        caramel sauce, 348–49
    pecan pound, with bal-
        samic sabayon and
        strawberries, 94–95
    super-moist apple,
        278–79
calendula, 191

California, 2, 4, 6
Canadian Strawberry apples,
    274
cantaloupe sorbet with butter
    cookies, 196–97
Carmel, Calif., 2
carrot(s), 63, 85
    cake, chocolate, with
        chocolate–sour cream
        frosting, 346–47
    and ginger sauce, 329
Carson, Rachel, 103
casserole, kale, Swiss cheese,
    and bacon, 337
celery root:
    pancakes, 338–39
    and sour cream sauce,
        253
champagne vinegar, 40
chanterelles, 139
chard, 63, 176
    Swiss, smoked duck breast
        with pearl onions and,
        54–55
cheese:
    Cheddar and sage bread
        pudding, 341
    Colby, fritters with chicory
        salad, 300–301
    creamy blue, dressing with
        bacon lardons, 127
    creamy blue, vinaigrette for
        radicchio chiffonade
        salad, 311
    creamy goat, toasts, 82
    creamy herbed goat, warm
        red cabbage slaw with,
        314–15
    Dry Jack, custard,
        asparagus and, 76–77
    Dry Jack, in warm beet
        greens and beets, 230
    feta or farmer's, in red and
        golden beet salad with
        sherry-shallot
        vinaigrette, 225–26
    Gruyère, in gratin of ramps
        and morels, 72–73
    Gruyère, radicchio gratin
        with bacon and, 218

cheese (cont.)
    Parmesan and basil
        sauce, slow-roasted
        tomato, 168
    Reggiano Parmesan,
        grilled asparagus with
        shaved, 68–69
    Swiss, kale, and bacon
        casserole, 337
    toasts, creamy goat, 82
Cherokee Purple tomatoes,
    126
cherry clafouti with mint,
    92
chervil, asparagus soup with
    lobster, morels, and,
    15–16
chicken:
    lemongrass and lemon
        roasted, 152
    stock, 22, 23
chicory, 38, 42
    salad, Colby cheese fritters
        with, 300–301
    salad with creamy mustard
        vinaigrette, 228
Child, Julia, 89
chile pastes, 149
Chinese dark wine and ham
    sauce, New Zealand
    cockles with, 304–5
Chioggia beets, 56
chips, eggplant, 119
chive(s):
    baby bok choy with
        smoked ham and, 69
    mashed potatoes, 175
    mayonnaise, spicy, Maine
        Peekytoe crab cakes
        with, 30–31
    -potato bread, 86–87
chocolate:
    carrot cake with
        chocolate–sour cream
        frosting, 346–47
    crème anglaise, rosemary
        poached pears with,
        343–44
    mint, butter cookies
        dipped in, 354–55

ABOUT THE AUTHORS

Clark Frasier grew up in Carmel, California, where fresh vegetables and fruit were available year-round. Before becoming a chef, he studied Chinese in Beijing and ran an import-export business in San Francisco. In 1988 he and Mark Gaier formed a business partnership and bought Arrows Restaurant in Ogunquit, Maine. Today they split their time between southern Maine and northern California.

Mark Gaier grew up in a big family near Dayton, Ohio. After working in magazine publishing in Maine, he studied culinary arts under Jean Wallach in Boston. He later became chef at Maine's landmark restaurant The Whistling Oyster, before moving to San Francisco. There, along with Clark Frasier, he was a *chef tournant* at Stars Restaurant.

Max Alexander is a former senior editor of *People* magazine in New York, and, before that, was the executive editor of *Variety* and *Daily Variety* in Los Angeles. He lives with his wife and two children on a 150-acre farm in Maine, where he cooks from his garden and tends a large field of wild blueberries.

Anybody's Guide to

TOTAL FITNESS

Ninth Edition

Len Kravitz
University of New Mexico

KENDALL/HUNT PUBLISHING COMPANY
4050 Westmark Drive   Dubuque, Iowa 52002

Book Team
Chairman and Chief Executive Officer   Mark C. Falb
President and Chief Operating Officer   Chad M. Chandlee
Vice President, Higher Education   David L. Tart
Director of National Book Program   Paul B. Carty
Editorial Development Manager   Georgia Botsford
Developmental Editor   Denise LaBudda
Assistant Vice President, Production Services   Christine E. O'Brien
Senior Production Editor   Carrie Maro
Permissions Editor   Colleen Zelinsky
Cover Designer   Heather Richman

Cover images:

Yoga Woman Image © ZM Photography, 2008
Used under license from Shutterstock, Inc.

Woman on Exercise Ball Image © Andresr, 2008
Used under license from Shutterstock, Inc.

Swimmer Image © Factoria Singular fotografia, 2008
Used under license from Shutterstock, Inc.

Man Stretching Image © Stephen Coburn, 2008
Used under license from Shutterstock, Inc.

Fruit Image © Ledo, 2008
Used under license from Shutterstock, Inc.

Woman Walking Image © Claudio Rossol, 2008
Used under license from Shutterstock, Inc.